The Work of the Imagination

B

...standing Children's Worlds
Series Editor: Judy Dunn

...al research on children's development can have a profound influ-
...n how children are brought up, cared for, educated and studied. Even if
...ur knowledge is incomplete, many psychologists argue, we have a responsi-
bility to share information with all those concerned in the care, education and
study of children.

The central aim of this series is to encourage developmental psychologists
to set out the findings and implications of their research for others – teachers,
doctors, social workers, students and fellow researchers – whose work involves the care, education and study of young children and their families.
Ideas are presented in an interesting and accessible way, and potential consequences for those working with children are discussed. By making available
recent innovative research to other professionals and other disciplines, the
series provides a vital resource.

Published

Children doing Mathematics
Terezhina Nunes and Peter Bryant

Children and Emotion
Paul L. Harris

Bullying at School
Dan Olweus

How Children Think and Learn
David Wood

Making Decisions about Children, 2nd edition
H. Rudolph Schaffer

Children's Talk in Communities and Classrooms
Lynne Vernon-Feagans

Children and Political Violence
Ed Cairns

The Work of the Imagination
Paul L. Harris

Forthcoming

Children and Family Transitions
Jan Pryor and Bryan Rodgers

The Work of the Imagination

Paul L. Harris

Copyright © Paul L. Harris 2000

The right of Paul L. Harris to be identified as author of this work has been asserted in accordance with the Copyright, Designs and Patents Act 1988.

First published 2000

2 4 6 8 10 9 7 5 3 1

Blackwell Publishers Ltd
108 Cowley Road
Oxford OX4 1JF
UK

Blackwell Publishers Inc.
350 Main Street
Malden, Massachusetts 02148
USA

British Library Cataloguing in Publication Data

A CIP catalogue record for this book is available from the British Library.

Library of Congress Cataloging-in-Publication Data

Harris, Paul L.
    Children and imagination / Paul Harris
        p.   cm. — (Understanding children's worlds)
    Includes bibliographical references and index.
    ISBN 0-631-21885-8 (alk. paper) — ISBN 0-631-21886-6 (pb. : alk. paper)
    1. Imagination in children.   I. Title.   II. Series.

  BF723.I5 H37 2000
  155.4′133– dc21

                                                                    00 036054

Typeset in 10.5 on 12.5 pt Sabon
by Ace Filmsetting Ltd, Frome, Somerset
Printed in Great Britain by TJ International, Padstow, Cornwall

This book is printed on acid-free paper.

Contents

Acknowledgements

I started to write this book during a year's leave at the Center for Advanced Study in the Behavioral Sciences in 1992–3. I am grateful to the Center for its support, and particularly to John Flavell, Alison Gopnik, Angeline Lillard and a large group of graduate students at Stanford University who discussed some of the ideas that I was developing in that early period.

Both before and after, I have been fortunate in having many students and colleagues who have made a sustained contribution to the various empirical studies and to my interpretation of them. I should especially like to thank Maria Dias, Tim German, Robert Kavanaugh, Carl Johnson, Hilary Leevers and Maria Núñez. Their influence on particular chapters will be evident in the course of the book.

Much of the experimental testing was carried out by Gill Surman. I am very grateful to her for the dedication, patience and enormous skill that she displayed in working with the young children. None of that testing would have been possible without the cooperation of many schools and preschools, most of them in and around Oxford. I thank all of them for their help.

Several people have commented in detail on chapters of the book. I thank Michael Cole, Greg Currie, Carl Johnson, Robert Kavanaugh, Maria Núñez, Francisco Pons, Karl Rosengren, Arietta Slade, Eugene Subbotsky and Arlene Walker-Andrews. I should also like to thank a patient group of graduate students in Oxford who read through the final draft of the book.

Peter Carruthers and Judy Dunn kindly read the entire manuscript. Their constructive and wide-ranging comments alerted me to numerous important omissions and alternative lines of speculation. I sincerely thank them both.

Various institutions have provided stimulus and hospitality. Fernando Vidal and the staff at the Piaget Archives in Geneva assisted my research on the early writings of Piaget. Stein Bråten and the hospitality of the Norwegian Academy of Sciences provided me with an opportunity to think more about fictional absorption. A conference at the MacDonald Archaeological Institute in Cambridge introduced me to the fascination of prehistory.

Finally, I thank my wife Pascale for all her support and encouragement. This book is dedicated to her and to our three sons, Simon, Rémi and Louis.

Introduction

In the Upper Palaeolithic, a period that began approximately 40,000 years ago, a revolution in human culture occurred. This revolution is frequently attributed either to the onset, or to the sudden acceleration, of a new and distinctive human cognitive capacity. One line of interpretation has emphasised a change in the depth of temporal organisation. Tools were increasingly produced well in advance of their actual use; dwelling sites were created with a lengthy period of occupation in mind. However, alongside this shift in the organisation of food and shelter, another set of activities emerged that can be less easily linked to the pragmatics of survival: cave painting, the diversification and stylisation of tools, the manufacture of bodily ornaments and new burial practices.[1]

The significance of these new activities is underlined by the fact that they are typically associated only with anatomically modern humans – *homo sapiens*. Neanderthals co-existed in Europe with humans for thousands of years before their extinction approximately 30,000 years ago. Neanderthal material culture is usually characterised in terms of its stability over time and its uniformity across different geographical areas. While local adaptations are acknowledged in the record, most investigators believe that the human cultural revolution found no equivalent among Neanderthals. Occasional innovations in the artefacts produced are tentatively attributed to imitation by the Neanderthals of human practices – or to trade between the two groups. Such similarities are not generally regarded as the first sign of a comparable, but abortive, revolution among Neanderthals.[2]

The proposition that human culture moved onto a new plane in the course of the Upper Palaeolithic, and the absence of that shift among the genetically similar, albeit anatomically distinct Neanderthals, raises the possibility that it was underpinned by some change in brain capacity. Yet the most obvious and measurable index of brain capacity, namely brain size, offers no clues. There was no apparent change in brain size associated with the Upper Palaeolithic – although there had been a spurt that tailed off more than 150,000 years earlier. Moreover, Neanderthal brains were as large as those of their human contemporaries, and indeed as large as those of modern humans.[3] However, if we look carefully not at the bones of our ancestors but at what they made with their hands, we can begin to characterise the cognitive change more precisely, even if we are far from understanding the conditions that had set it in motion.

In a nutshell, the material record testifies to a new power of the imagination. Some of the newly emerging artefacts have much the same function as props in children's games of make-believe.[4] They help to transport participants out of reality and into some imagined setting. These artefacts have three characteristic features: (i) they are collectively produced and socially recognisable; (ii) there is a discrepancy or mismatch between the imagined world that they help to instantiate and the actual situation in which the props themselves are constructed and displayed; (iii) their manufacture calls for a capacity to move back and forth between those two contexts – to take account of actual physical constraints, while simultaneously creating a meaningful artefact. Let us take cave art as one example of these claims.

In a vivid account, the palaeontologist Ian Tattersall describes his visit to the cave of Comarelles 1 in southwestern France. One hundred and fifty yards from the entrance, after a tortuous journey along a narrow, cramped passageway the visitor is eventually confronted by a magnificent display of cave art: "Horses, mammoths, reindeer, bison, mountain goats, lions and a host of other mammals cascade in image along the cave walls over a distance of almost a hundred yards."[5] The archaeological evidence from the caves of the Upper Palaeolithic suggests that such paintings were social as opposed to individual works in two important senses. They were produced by several artists working in collaboration or in succession. In addition, they were visited by people who were probably just spectators rather than artists. In one cave, for example, the footprints of three children can be identified, alongside those of two adults.[6] It is also obvious that the scenes depicted do not match anything that actually happened at the underground site of their creation or contemplation. The paintings were executed at some considerable distance from the entrance to the cave in a space that was often cramped and poorly illuminated. Whether for the artists themselves or for those who simply looked at them, the paintings served to overlay the dank, physical surroundings with an alternative, imagined world. Nevertheless, the artists would have needed to acknowledge the properties of the physical setting in which they worked as they transformed those surfaces into paintings. Indeed, they incorporated features of the rock surfaces into the images depicted upon them.[7]

A similar analysis can be applied to the emergence of ritualised burial. Again, the archaeological record indicates that such symbolic acts were an organised, social activity. In the case of certain elaborate burials, thousands of ornamental beads have been recovered, implying a major investment of time by several individuals. In addition, the arrangement of the bodies and the inclusion of burial goods such as ivory lances indicate that the interment was far from being a straightforward act of disposal. Rather it was carried out in anticipation – or instantiation – of an after-life, where the adornments and weapons would be needed or appropriate. Third, that presumed after-life obviously does not correspond to the actual situation in which the burial was planned and executed. Effectively, these new burial practices involved treating the dead person – concurrently but distinctly – as a corpse on the one hand, and as a candidate for the after-life on the other.[8]

In short, cave art and ritualised burial provide clear examples of the trio of properties mentioned about: the artefacts and props were collectively produced and understood; they served to conjure up an imagined world distinct from the physical context in which they were manufactured or displayed. Yet, in each case that physical context needed to be acknowledged and re-worked if the artefacts were to serve their function.

Whatever the ultimate explanation for the shift of cognitive gear that lead to the cultural transformation of the Upper Palaeolithic some 40,000 years ago, we can be sure that it was a long time in the making. The evolutionary line that gave rise to anatomically modern humans branched off from the higher primates some 6 million years earlier. When seen in relation to that colossal time frame, the new power of the imagination was just a last-minute pulsation in the evolution of our species. Yet, its consequences for human history and culture were immense.

In the following chapters, I set out an ontogenetic description of the human imagination. I argue that the capacity to imagine alternative possibilities and to work out their implications emerges early in the course of children's development and lasts a lifetime. This capacity is especially obvious in children's games of pretend play, but it invades and transforms their developing conception of reality itself. Before making that case, it will be helpful to examine a very different analysis of the imagination – one that has dominated developmental research for much of the last century.

Notes

1 Various dimensions of the cultural transformation that took place during the Upper Palaeolithic are reviewed in Mellars and Stringer (1989) and Mithen (1996). Evidence for a change in temporal organisation and planning is discussed by Binford (1989).

2 Stringer and Gamble (1993) and Mellars (1996) set out the standard view concerning the restrictions on Neanderthal culture. For discussion of local adaptation and flexibility in Neanderthal tool-making, notwithstanding an overall paucity of innovation, see Kuhn and Stiner (1998). The more controversial proposal that Neanderthals show signs of genuine creativity that cannot be explained in terms of the emulation of co-existing anatomically modern humans has been set out by D'Errico, Zilhão, Julien, Baffier and Pelegrain (1998) and contested by Mellars (1999).

3 Stringer and Gamble (1993) review evidence on the evolution of the human and Neanderthal brain. It should be emphasised that an overall similarity in cranial capacity (when Neanderthals and humans are compared) might mask critical variation in brain organisation. Another possibility is that the two types of brain differed, not in size or organisation at maturity, but in their respective patterns of growth during early childhood – with Neanderthal brains reaching adult size more rapidly than those of humans. Evidence pointing in that direction has been reported by Stringer (Stringer, 1990; Stringer and Gamble, 1993) but was not consistently obtained by Zollikofer, Ponce de Leon, Martin and Stucki (1995). The difficulty of inferring organisation and development from cranial capacity should also be kept in mind when considering the evolution of the human brain itself. Constancy of mature cranial capacity over evolutionary time might mask critical changes in overall brain organisation, in brain development from conception to maturity, or in both.

4 For a persuasive, conceptual analysis of the links between art and make believe, see Walton (1990).

5 Tattersall (1998, p.1).

6 Clottes (1996, p. 185–186).

7 Dowson (1998).

8 For a description of burial practices, see White (1993). For an analysis of the symbolic function of bodily ornaments, see White (1992).

1

Bleuler in Weimar

At the Weimar Psychoanalytic Congress in 1911, with Freud and Jung among his audience, the Swiss psychiatrist Eugen Bleuler argued for a distinction between two different modes of thinking: logical or realistic thinking on the one hand, and what he called 'autistic' thinking on the other (Bleuler, 1951). Bleuler is generally remembered for his contribution to our understanding of schizophrenia, but he also made an indirect, and inadvertent, contribution to the study of child development. His ideas influenced both Piaget and Vygotsky, albeit in different ways. They transposed his concept of autistic thinking from the study of adult pathology pursued in Zurich and Vienna in the early years of the twentieth century to the study of cognitive development that began to flourish in Geneva and Moscow during the 1920s. As a result, the proposals that Bleuler made in Weimar turn out to be important for the way that developmental psychologists have conceived of pretence, fantasy and wishful thinking – what I shall call the work of the imagination.

Today, we normally associate the term 'autistic' with the developmental pathology first identified by Kanner (1943). Kanner borrowed Bleuler's terminology because the children that he had observed displayed a withdrawal from other people and from the external world into the self that is similar to the withdrawal that Bleuler associated with autistic thinking. However, Bleuler conceived of autism not as a pathology confined to a special group of children but as a normal mode of thinking, found among children and adults alike.

Autistic thinking, Bleuler claimed, is especially evident in dreams, in the pretend play of young children, in the reveries of normal adults, and in the fantasies and delusions of the schizophrenic. It is a mode of thought that is dominated by free association and wishful thinking. In logical or realistic thinking, by contrast, affective and emotional considerations are set aside, or tempered by an acknowledgement of what is rational and what is feasible. Bleuler acknowledged that autistic thinking can sometimes override logical thinking among normal adults. For example, faced with a situation that strains our rational comprehension, wishful thinking in the autistic mode gains the upper hand. In the case of pathology, however, there is a sustained rather than a transient disturbance in the balance between the two modes of thinking: the schizophrenic makes some limited contact with reality, but is primarily absorbed in an unrealistic, fantasy world: 'the patient adapts himself in many ways to the institution, puts up with reality . . . but within he remains the Emperor of Europe around whom the whole world revolves, and in contrast to whose imperial dignity the humiliations of institutional life do not even count' (Bleuler, 1951, p. 415).

Bleuler's distinction between autistic and realistic thinking echoes a distinction that Freud had made earlier between primary processes guided by the Pleasure principle and secondary processes guided by the Reality principle (Freud, 1961a; Freud, 1961b). However, it is important to notice that Bleuler explicitly dissents from one central component of Freud's formulation. According to Freud, it is primary or autistic thinking that is present initially in the mental life of the infant; realistic thinking is secondary in the sense that it emerges later in development. Thus, according to Freud, the infant is dominated by primary processes or autistic thinking and 'hallucinates' the fulfilment of his inner needs.

Bleuler crisply rejects this developmental sequence as biologically implausible: 'I do not see any hallucinatory gratification in the infant, but only a gratification by actual food intake. A chick in the egg grows up on physically and chemically tangible food and not on ideas of eating' (Bleuler, 1951, p. 427). Bleuler proposes a very different account of development. He argues that the ability to conceive of alternatives to reality is not a primitive process but something that is relatively sophisticated. Indeed, the conceptual material that is needed to entertain such alternatives is not likely to be available to the infant mind. The child who pretends to bathe a doll needs to know something about water and about baths. The schizophrenic with delusions of grandeur needs to be able to conceive of an Emperor or a Saviour. Accordingly, Bleuler proposes that: 'at a certain level of development, the autistic function is added to the reality-function and develops with it from there on' (Bleuler, 1951, p. 427). In short, for Bleuler, reality-directed thinking comes first and autistic thinking comes later.

Immediately after the First World War, Piaget came to Zurich where he attended lectures by Jung, Pfister and Bleuler (Piaget, 1952, p. 244). In the course of Bleuler's lectures, he learned about the distinction between autistic thinking on the one hand, and reality-directed thinking on the other. However, ignoring Bleuler's criticisms of Freud, he went on to adopt the assumption that autistic thinking dominates the infant's psyche from the outset, and is only gradually subordinated to rational thought. His early experimental work in Paris in the laboratory that had been set up by Alfred Binet was intended to document this gradual subordination of autism to rationality (Harris, 1997a). In 1922, he presented his findings at the Berlin Psychoanalytic Congress (Piaget, 1923). His paper is a striking attempt to weld together the concept of early autistic thinking and his own empirical observations of children's developing logical abilities. Piaget sets out a three-step sequence. Early childhood is dominated by autistic thinking in which reality is subordinated to the child's affective life. Next, various transitional forms including egocentric thinking are apparent, interposed between early autistic thinking and logical thinking. Finally, with the development of logic, autistic thinking is suppressed, and the child becomes more rational and objective.

More generally, Piaget argues that early thinking has a ludic or playful character; it does not accommodate to reality but instead distorts reality to fit the self and its desires. In making this assertion, Piaget cites with approval the distinction initially made by Freud: 'Everyone knows the distinction that Freud introduced between the Pleasure principle and the Reality principle: thinking, according to Freud and indeed according to Baldwin and many others, is aimed in the first place at immediate, quasi-hallucinatory satisfaction, at pleasure, and only later at adaptation and reality' (Piaget, 1923, p. 303, my translation).

This incorporation of Bleuler's ideas, or more precisely of the Freudian distinction that led to those ideas, had a wide-ranging impact on Piaget's interpretation of development. For example, in his analysis of language, Piaget emphasized that children's early speech springs from their own inner mental world and is not adjusted to the external world, especially the needs of their listener. When they play alongside one another, young children may appear to be communicating but a large proportion of what they say is egocentric – it is not primarily intended as a form of communication with a play partner but constitutes a kind of monologue. Piaget went on to argue that this mode of thinking and communicating is a transitional form, intermediate between the early autistic mode on the one hand, and the later-developing, logical intelligence on the other: 'Now between autism and intelligence there are many degrees, varying in their capacity for being communicated. . . . The chief of these intermediate forms, i.e. the type of thought which like that exhibited by our children seeks to adapt itself to reality, but does not communicate itself as such, we propose to call *egocentric* thought' (Piaget, 1959, p. 45). Thus, starting as he did from the conception of the infant as prone to autistic thinking and therefore poorly adapted to the external world, Piaget concluded that what we initially take to be communication with others is no such thing; it is more appropriately seen as speech-for-the self and not as genuine communication.

While Piaget was developing his ideas about egocentricity, and recording the incidence of egocentric speech, his Russian peer, Lev Vygotsky, had also read and been influenced by Bleuler's ideas.[1] However, in contrast to Piaget, Vygotsky paid careful attention to Bleuler's argument that autistic thinking can scarcely be regarded as a primitive mode of thought (Vygotsky, 1986, p. 21). Accepting this argument, he concluded that Piaget's developmental analysis of egocentric speech was untenable. If the autistic mode is not the starting point for development, then egocentric speech cannot be explained by supposing that it is a transitional form that grows out of the autistic mode. As is well known, Vygotsky went on to develop his own creative analysis of egocentric speech, claiming that it reflects the child's tendency, especially when engaged in planning or the circumvention of an obstacle, to think in words. The fate of such speech, according to Vygotsky, is not to be suppressed by the advent of a more socialized intelligence as Piaget implied, but to go underground – to become inner speech – once the child makes a clean separation between speech for communication and speech in the service of thinking.

Piaget published his findings on the development of pretence – or symbolic play as he called it – several years after his early research on language (Piaget, 1962). By that time, he had made detailed studies of the infant's developing sensory-motor intelligence and his description of the emergence of pretend play takes its place alongside his detailed account of other sensory-motor capacities, especially imitation. Nonetheless, there remain important continuities between his analyses of language and pretend play. He contends that both functions have their roots in early autism. Thus, in his theoretical account of pretend play, Piaget maintained his earlier contention that such play is a retreat from reality: 'Unlike objective thought, which seeks to adapt itself to the requirements of objective reality, imaginative play is a symbolic transposition which subjects things to the child's activity without rules or limitations' (Piaget, 1962, p. 87). Echoing Freud, he proposed that play offers the child an opportunity to secure via fantasy what is not available in reality. For example, he describes how his daughter Jacqueline, having been told that she could not play with the water that was to be used for the washing, took an empty cup, went to the forbidden tub of water, and made pretend movements saying, 'I'm pouring out water' (Piaget, 1962, observation 84). To underline the continuity in his thinking, Piaget refers back to the proposals he had made at the Berlin Congress more than 20 years earlier (Piaget, 1962, p. 166). In short, Piaget's analysis of pretend play has clear parallels with his analysis of egocentric speech. He implies that pretend play, like egocentricity, is a primitive and temporary phase of maladaptation that will be outgrown in the course of development.

Piaget's negative analysis of pretend play continues to be influential. Children who are engaged in pretence are thought to assimilate reality to their own distorting, cognitive schemas. Second, they are alleged to get carried away by their imagination and to blur the distinction between fantasy and reality. Indeed, a pretend episode may arouse many of the emotions associated with a real episode. As a result, children's pretend play is often seen as an important window into their unconscious emotional life, much as dreams are thought to provide a window into the adult unconscious. Finally, children's imagination is thought to be undisciplined – to be dominated by primary process thinking, in which free association and loose analogy link one idea to another. Older children are thought to gradually replace such primary process thinking with a more objective approach.

In this book, I take Piaget's pioneering description of pretend play as an important starting point. However, I take a different stance from Piaget toward its role in the child's mental life. Echoing Bleuler, I argue that it is a mistake to think of pretence as a primitive or primary mode of thinking. Echoing Vygotsky's analysis of the fate of egocentric speech, I argue that pretence is not a psychological function that is gradually suppressed in the course of development. There are three reasons for considering this more positive stance. In the first place, pretend play is not something that we observe in very young infants. It is more or less entirely absent in the first year of life, it starts to emerge in the second year, and it becomes increasingly elaborate thereafter. Thus, the developmental timetable is what Bleuler might expect.

Second, the great apes engage in only limited and sporadic pretending, and even this limited disposition may be confined to those that are reared alongside human beings. By contrast, pretending appears to be a widespread feature of early human childhood. From a biological point of view, it is reasonable to ask what function this early human capacity might serve rather than to assume that it is a maladaptive tendency that will disappear with the advent of maturity.

Finally, the study of early pathology shows that it is the absence of early imagination, and not its presence, that is pathological. One of the major characteristics of the syndrome of early childhood autism is an absence or impoverishment of pretend play. Although children with autism can be prompted to engage in pretence, they rarely do so spontaneously (Harris, 1993; Harris and Leevers, 2000b). This deficit (along with deficits in joint attention and pointing) is one of the earliest markers of the syndrome. The long-term social and cognitive restrictions of people with autism suggest that the capacity for pretence is an important foundation for lifelong normality. It is reasonable to ask, therefore, just what that capacity might contribute to normal cognitive and emotional functioning.[2]

I shall argue that when pretend play does emerge, children draw to a remarkable extent on the causal understanding of the physical and mental world that they have already built up during infancy. Thus, in pretence, young children may step back from current reality, or go beyond it, but that does not necessarily entail any cognitive distortion of the general principles by which reality operates.

Second, if we regard children's disposition to become emotionally involved in an imaginary world as an index of cognitive immaturity, we ought to draw similar conclusions regarding that disposition among adults. Yet most adults become absorbed in novels, films or the theatre. To the extent that absorption in fiction is not a short-lived phenomenon of childhood but a capacity that endures a lifetime, it is appropriate to ask what it is about the cognitive and emotional make-up of human beings that disposes them toward such sustained involvement in other people's lives – including the lives of fictional characters.

Finally, I argue that the consideration of alternatives to reality may be linked with a move toward objectivity rather than away from it. As they think about alternative possibilities, children can consider them in a consequential and orderly fashion. Eventually, the conceptually infused alternatives to reality that children conjure up feed back on their assessments of reality. For example, children's ability to entertain counterfactual alternatives to an actual outcome is critical for making causal and moral judgements about that outcome. Thus, what Bleuler called autistic thinking remains a constant companion to reality-directed thinking in the course of development, and enlarges the scope of children's objectivity.

In the chapters that follow, I lay out this more positive assessment of the work of the imagination.

Notes

1   It is not clear exactly when Vygotsky first encountered Bleuler's ideas. In *Thought and Language*, first published in 1934, he uses them extensively in his critique of Piaget. It is possible, however, that he had encountered them considerably earlier, either by reading Bleuler's original paper published in German, or its translation into Russian published in 1927. It is also interesting to note that Sabina Spielrein, Bleuler's former doctoral student and Piaget's psychoanalyst, returned to Moscow from Geneva in 1923 (Kerr, 1994). Given their joint acquaintance with Luria, their common interest in language (cf. Spielrein, 1923), and their respective contacts with the Institute for Psychoanalysis in Moscow (Miller, 1998), it would be surprising if Vygotsky and Spielrein had not exchanged views – and the topic of autistic thinking might well have been included in that exchange.

2   Bleuler assumed that pathology was mainly characterized by the failure of reality-directed thinking to temper the autistic mode. The developmental pathology of autism (Kanner, 1943) provides an interesting counter-example. One can reasonably argue that in the case of children with autism it is the imagination that fails to inform judgements about reality. In more prosaic ways, for example in conceptualizing physical mechanisms and the organization of space, children with autism are well equipped to think about reality.

2

Pretend Play

One of the earliest and most obvious indices of children's imagination is their pretend play. At first sight, the disposition to engage in pretence is puzzling from an evolutionary point of view. One might suppose that nature would have ensured that children construct and maintain a veridical representation of the world rather than entertain flights of fantasy. An important aim of this chapter is to show that children do depart from the real world in their pretend play but take much of their conceptual knowledge with them. In particular, they still acknowledge the causal powers of the real world. Once this conclusion is accepted, it becomes clear that early pretence is at most a distortion of reality in so far as various objects are put to creative use as props. At a deeper level, it offers a way to imagine, explore and talk about possibilities inherent in reality.

Much of our knowledge of the early development of pretend play comes from Piaget's account published in *Play, Dreams and Imitation* (Piaget, 1962). He describes how, from the second year on, pretending becomes more elaborate and more flexible – elaborate, in that children can produce a more sustained and complex series of pretend actions, and flexible in that they become less dependent on the support and prompting provided by a familiar context and its props. Despite his acknowledgement of this developmental progress, Piaget's overall characterization of pretend play is negative. As I described in the last chapter, he presents it as an early mode of thinking destined to give way eventually to logic and rationality. Pretend or symbolic play, he argues, leads children to twist and rework reality in the light of their own cognitive schemas rather than to adapt their cognitive schemas to reality: 'Symbolic play represents in thought the pole of assimilation, and freely assimilates reality to the ego. . . . But why is there assimilation of reality to the ego instead of immediate assimilation of the universe to experimental and logical thought? It is simply because in early childhood this thought has not yet been constructed' (Piaget, 1962, p. 166). Thus, make-believe play is alleged to be a poor tool for the analysis of reality because it involves its assimilation and deformation; it cannot be otherwise because the child has no objective understanding of reality in the first place.

Piaget's negative stance toward the production of pretend play ignores various interesting features that are especially evident in joint pretence. For example, the following interchange took place between Richard, aged 24 months, and his older sister, who were playing at trains with the help of some cushions and a toy tractor (Dunn and Dale, 1984, p. 141, example 1). Richard's sister pointed out that the train had got stuck and asked him to get some more petrol. Richard pretended to put some petrol in, making a suitable 'Ssss' sound as he did so. His sister then 'noticed' that the petrol was leaking and told him to put it in at a different place. Even in this brief exchange, it is interesting to note that Richard had no difficulty in realizing that his sister was referring to make-believe petrol, not real petrol. He responded to her request with relevant gestures and vocalizations. She, in her turn, understood what he was doing but she spotted a further problem – the leakage of the petrol. This example illustrates how successful collaborative pretend play can scarcely be construed as autistic withdrawal from the external world. Even if mundane reality is set to one side or transformed – the cushions serve as a tunnel and the tractor becomes a train – joint pretence still calls for mutual comprehension and the accommodation of one partner to the other as they construct a make-believe episode. Below, I analyse this constructive process in more detail.

Teddy Gets Wet

Consider the following episode that we might enact in partnership with a 2-year-old. Having made a twiddling gesture at one end of a shoebox, we seat a Teddy Bear in the box. We ask, 'Where's the soap?', pick up a wooden brick and rub Teddy's back with it. The 2-year-old joins in by lifting Teddy out of the box, announcing that, 'He's all wet', and wraps him in a piece of paper.

Viewed as a piece of pretence, this episode is easy to make sense of. We turned on the tap at one end of a bath, put Teddy in the bath, and rubbed his back with a piece of soap. The 2-year-old then lifted Teddy out of the water and dried him with a make-believe towel. To the extent that we arrive at this interpretation of the pretend episode without much effort, it is easy to assume that there are no subtle cognitive processes at work. However, we can glimpse some of the cognitive work that is being done if, for a moment, we adopt an objective or literal point of view toward the episode. From that naive standpoint, the episode is decidedly odd. If Teddy really needs a bath, what's the use of a cardboard box? Why rub him with a wooden brick? Why say that he is wet when he is manifestly dry. Why wrap him in a piece of paper?

Clearly, a child who makes sense of our actions must set aside such naive literalism. In doing so, several key features of joint pretence need to be appreciated. First, either play partner can bring make-believe entities into a temporary, public existence via a simple fiat or stipulation. In the course of Teddy's bath, for example, the make-believe existence of the tap is stipulated by the adult's twiddling gesture at one end of the cardboard box, and the make-believe existence of the soap is stipulated by the adult's query – 'Where's the soap?' – and by the subsequent pretend rubbing with the brick. Second, once instantiated, these make-believe entities have causal powers – a pretend tap can deliver water and pretend soap can be used to clean Teddy. Third, having become engaged in a make-believe world, play partners can, without further ado, suspend objective truth in favour of make-believe truth. When Teddy is lifted from his bath, it is appropriate to say that he is 'all wet', even though he is objectively dry. There is no need to belabour the status of that claim by saying: '*We're pretending that* Teddy is all wet'. From a perspective situated inside the pretend framework, it is evident that he is indeed wet. Finally, a pretend episode includes causal chains with an unfolding structure much like a narrative. Turning on the pretend tap delivers water into the bath; so, if Teddy is seated in that bath, he will get wet; and if he is then rubbed with a towel, he will become dry.

Below, I argue that each of these features of pretence – (1) pretend stipulations, (2) causal powers, (3) the suspension of objective truth and (4) an unfolding, causal chain – are all understood by 2-year-olds. By implication, they engage in the same cognitive work as we do when we interpret a pretend episode in a make-believe rather than a literal mode.

Pretend Stipulations

Once set in motion, a make-believe stipulation has various implications and restrictions for both partners. In particular, when one partner introduces a stipulation, its possibilities can be exploited by the other partner. For example, if one partner stipulates that a cardboard box is to be treated as a bath, the other partner can 'fill' that bath with water, or bathe animals in the bath. At the same time, a make-believe stipulation is temporary – to be retained only for the duration of the pretend episode in question. So, the cardboard box might assume a new pretend identity in some later episode. If young children understand a pretend stipulation, then they should understand these possibilities and restrictions. In a series of experiments, we have tested for that understanding.

We first asked whether 2-year-olds would acknowledge the possibilities implied by a stipulated entity (Harris and Kavanaugh, 1993, experiment 1). Each child was given two different sets of props – a cup and teapot were placed on one side of the table, and a bowl, spoon and cereal box on the other side. All of these various containers were empty. A series of animals was then marched in, one by one. As each animal was introduced, the adult explained whether the animal wanted tea or cereal and asked the child to give the animal what it wanted. Young 2-year-olds proved to be very cooperative. They did not protest that the teapot or the cereal box was empty. Rather, when asked to supply tea, they typically picked up the teapot, 'poured' make-believe tea from it into the cup, and then lifted the cup to the animal's lips. When asked to supply cereal, they typically 'poured' make-believe cereal from the cereal box into the bowl and then lifted the spoon to the animal's lips. Thus, depending on which stipulated entity the adult had designated, children accepted the unstated implication of what was available. In much the same way that Richard accepted his sister's implication that petrol was available and responded with an appropriate delivery, children accepted the adult's implication and offered an appropriate serving.

Once a prop has been assigned an identity, the assignation need not be restricted to that particular prop. Other props in the same category may take on the same identity. In his book on make-believe, Kendall Walton (1990) develops this point in a graphic fashion. He introduces the example of two boys playing in the forest who pretend that a tree-stump is a bear. Once they have made this stipulation, it can generate further make-believe truths. Specifically, there may be other 'bears' elsewhere in the forest. Suppose that there is an unseen tree-stump concealed in a thicket that the two boys are approaching. During their approach, neither of the boys may appreciate the 'danger' that awaits them. Still, it remains true, within the make-believe world that they have invented, that they are approaching a bear, and once they spot it, they should recognize it as such. This hidden danger, and its eventual recognition by the two boys, is a plausible extrapolation from the initial, pretend stipulation. In short, once the make-believe identity of a given type of prop, such as a tree-stump, has been stipulated, that stipulation is fertile or generative: it breeds further make-believe possibilities. These may not be immediately apparent, but children can discover and explore them as they proceed.

We found that young 2-year-olds take the fertility of a pretend stipulation for granted (Harris and Kavanaugh, 1993, experiment 2). The children watched as we introduced two animals, a monkey and a horse. We 'fed' the monkey with a yellow brick, explaining that he wanted some banana, and we 'fed' the horse with a red brick, explaining that he wanted some cake. Next, we introduced more animals, telling children whether the animal wanted banana or cake to eat. The 2-year-olds almost invariably responded in accordance with the generativity principle. In 'feeding' the newly introduced animals, none of them touched either the 'banana' or the 'cake' that had been given to the monkey and the horse. Instead, they spontaneously reached out and appropriately selected either another 'banana' or another 'cake' from two separate piles of yellow and red bricks available on the table. Like the boys in Walton's example, they assumed that an earlier stipulation extended across time and space to include hitherto ignored props from the same category, although there had been no explicit agreement or statement to that effect.

Two-year-olds also appreciate the restricted, episodic nature of a pretend stipulation. To show this, we presented two separate episodes one after the other, and stipulated different identities for the same prop within each distinct episode. We then watched to see if 2-year-olds would appropriately tailor their pretence to the stipulation currently in force (Harris and Kavanaugh, 1993, experiments 3 and 4). For example, we might begin with an episode in which Teddy was said to be having his dinner. Children were handed a brick and asked, 'Show me what Teddy does with his sandwich'. Children engaged appropriately in pretend feeding with the brick. In a second episode, in which Teddy was getting ready for bed, children were handed the same brick once more but asked, 'Show me what Teddy does with his soap'. They now engaged in pretend washing with the brick rather than pretend feeding.

Children's flexibility also highlighted the fact that it was not the prop *per se* that was cueing them about what to do. They did not perceive anything intrinsically sandwich-like or soap-like about the brick. Instead, when they acted on the prop they were guided by the currently valid stipulation. So, although the brick obviously retained the same objective features across the two different episodes, the children pretended that it had different features depending on the episode in which it was embedded.

Summing up the findings of these studies, it is clear that 2-year-olds understand several aspects of a make-believe stipulation. Once a prop has been assigned a make-believe identity or make-believe properties by a play partner, children produce pretend actions toward the prop that exploit the possibilities implied by its make-believe identity or properties. An (empty) teapot is used to pour tea and a brick is used to feed Teddy with a sandwich or to rub him with soap. Moreover, children spontaneously extend such pretend actions to other nearby props in the same category, even if there has been no explicit agreement to do so. Yet they also recognize the transient nature of a make-believe stipulation. In particular, they acknowledge that any new episode opens the way for a new make-believe stipulation, which overwrites any stipulations made in previous episodes.

Causal Powers

Once instantiated, a make-believe entity or property can be incorporated into a causal sequence. Recall Teddy's bath described earlier. When Teddy was lifted out of the cardboard box he was described as 'all wet'. Although he had only been bathed in make-believe water from make-believe taps, the causal powers of make-believe entities are equivalent to those of the real entities that they represent. So, when make-believe taps are turned on they will fill a bathtub with make-believe water; and when something is immersed in that water it gets wet, including Teddy.

Granted that 2-year-olds understand how the identity or properties of a prop can be stipulated, do they also understand the causal powers that emanate from such a stipulation? To start to answer this question, we sat 2-year-olds in between two toy pigs. They watched as a glove puppet, introduced as 'Naughty Teddy', picked up a container and pretended to pour or squeeze out some of its contents. For example, in one episode, Teddy picked up a closed tube of toothpaste and applied it to the tail of one of the two pigs, as if squirting toothpaste onto the tail. The child was handed a tissue and asked to clean 'the pig who's all dirty'. In another episode, Teddy picked up an (empty) carton of milk and 'poured' milk onto the floor in front of one of the pigs. The child was handed a sponge and asked to dry 'the floor where it's all wet'.

Two-year-olds typically directed their pretend action to the correct location – the correct pig or the correct part of the floor (Harris and Kavanaugh, 1993, experiment 5). Admittedly, the adult had encouraged them to engage in pretend cleaning or drying. However, the children needed to work out where they should set to work. Specifically, they had to decide which of the two pigs or which part of the floor to wipe. They could only do that if they had watched Teddy and understood the implied consequence of his make-believe mischief. For example, although the adult talked about drying the floor where it was 'all wet', there were no visual cues to guide children's pretend drying to a particular part of the floor. So, children needed to accept that when the empty milk carton was tipped, it would deliver its usual contents, albeit in a make-believe form. In turn, these make-believe contents would fall to a spot on the floor directly underneath the carton, making it 'wet'. Thus, children had to set aside what they could see objectively, namely that no milk came out of the carton and that the relevant part of the floor was dry. Instead, they had to imagine, guided by familiar causal principles, the make-believe puddle that was brought about by Teddy's actions, and set about wiping it up.

Children were prompted a good deal in this exploratory experiment. In particular, the adult drew their attention to the outcome of Naughty Teddy's intervention by explicitly referring to it in the request she made: she talked about one of the pigs as *dirty* or about part of the floor as *wet*. In follow-up experiments, we used a more demanding procedure. Instead of verbally identifying the make-believe outcome in her request, the adult laid out several pictures and asked children to select a picture illustrating the make-believe outcome. So, they needed to visualize the make-believe outcome for themselves and select the matching picture.

Figure 2.1 Three pictures showing the monkey (a) with stripes, (b) with no change and (c) covered in talcum powder.

Children again watched various, somewhat messy, pretend transformations. For example, the experimenter might pick up a bottle of talcum powder and pretend to shake some powder over a toy monkey. When children were asked to say how the animal looked as a result of this pretend change, their attention was drawn to three pictures laid out in front of them (see figure 2.1). One picture showed the monkey with some irrelevant change, for example with dark stripes on its body. A second picture showed the animal with no change – in its pristine, powder-free state. A third showed the animal with the relevant change – sporting a layer of powder – as it might actually appear following the transformation implied by the adult's pretend action.

As shown in figure 2.2, young 2-year-olds (ranging from 24 to 30 months) very rarely chose the irrelevant change picture, they occasionally chose the no change picture, but they frequently chose the relevant change picture (Kavanaugh and Harris, 1994, experiment 2). Particularly striking was the paucity of 'realist' errors – the error of choosing the no change picture, which showed the animal in its objective, unaltered state. Children rarely made this mistake, even though the toy animal used by the experimenter to enact the episode was, of course, not actually changed by the make-believe transformation, as children could see for themselves by looking at the toy monkey in front of them.

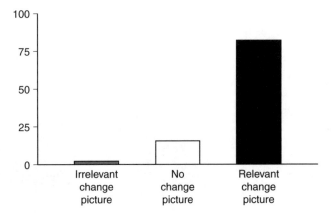

Figure 2.2 Percentage of three types of picture choice.

The same response pattern emerged when the choices following any given episode were made even trickier. The irrelevant change picture was altered to depict another plausible pretend outcome, but one that children saw enacted in a different episode. For example, two episodes involved a toy horse. In one episode of this pair, the pretend intervention involved 'colouring' the horse's muzzle green and in the other it involved squirting his tail with white toothpaste. For both episodes, children were offered the same three pictures, representing the horse unchanged, the horse with a coloured muzzle and the horse with toothpaste on its tail. So, depending on the episode, the horse with a coloured muzzle was the correct choice and the horse with a white tail the irrelevant choice, or vice versa. As in the earlier experiment, young 2-year-olds mostly chose the correct picture, and once again 'realist' errors were comparatively rare (Harris, Kavanaugh and Dowson, 1997, experiments 1 and 2).

In summary, it is clear that 2-year-olds not only understand stipulations, they also understand the causal powers associated with a stipulated entity. In particular, they use that causal knowledge to work out the consequence of a pretend transformation in their imagination. That capacity is reflected both in their pretend actions, such as wiping or drying, and in their ability to select a representation of the imagined outcome, such as a picture.

The Suspension of Objective Truth

In the episodes involving two pigs described earlier, the adult described one of the pigs as 'dirty' or part of the floor as 'wet'. Children appeared to understand these non-literal descriptions because they responded appropriately. We wondered if they were capable of producing such non-literal descriptions themselves. In particular, we wanted to find out how they would respond if they saw an adult partner act out a pretend episode, especially one involving a transformation, and the adult then asked them to say what had happened. Would children opt for an objective description of what had actually occurred? Alternatively, would they suspend objective truth and provide a non-literal description of what had happened within the pretend world? If they opted for a non-literal description – invoking various imaginary outcomes – this would provide converging evidence that children use their imagination to fill in those parts of a pretend episode that are invisible but causally implied. In addition, it would confirm that once they are drawn into a make-believe world, young children suspend objective truth in favour of make-believe truth when offering a description.

The episodes that we used were similar to those used in other experiments in which Naughty Teddy victimized various toy animals with make-believe substances. For example, he squirted make-believe toothpaste from a tube onto the rabbit's ear, or he poured make-believe tea from a teapot onto the monkey's head. The children were then asked a simple, open-ended question: 'What happened – what did Naughty Teddy do?' In principle, children could reply to this question by describing what they had really seen. For example, in reality, they had seen Teddy pick up an empty teapot, lift it above the monkey, tilt it and put it down again. Children almost never gave such literal descriptions. Instead, they offered a description of the make-believe episode, not the movements that were used to enact it. Thus, 2-year-olds, especially older 2-year olds, offered descriptions in which they referred to several elements of the episode that were implied but not objectively visible: the type of action performed by Teddy ('squeezed', 'poured' etc.), the pretend substance that he acted on ('toothpaste', 'tea' etc.) and the way in which that substance was displaced ('on' or 'over' the victim). So, they might say that Teddy 'poured tea on the monkey' (Harris and Kavanaugh, 1993, experiment 6).

When questioned further, they could also describe the consequences of Teddy's intervention for his victim. If the adult said: 'Teddy made the monkey's head all . . . ?' with a rising intonation and an expectant pause, children typically replied by describing the effect of the dousing with a variety of adjectives, both conventional and unconventional, but almost always appropriate: 'dirty', 'black', 'wet', 'soggy', 'grubby', 'soaky' and 'teaey'. Finally, when asked to choose between two possible descriptions, for example: 'Is the monkey's head wet or dry?', the majority correctly said that he was wet. Notice that the experimenter's options included the current, objective state of the monkey's head, namely 'dry'. Just as they had done in the picture-choice experiments, children successfully avoided making 'realist' errors. They selected the option that characterized the imaginary as opposed to the objective outcome – 'wet' as opposed to 'dry' – notwithstanding the visibility of the objective outcome in front of them.

We went on to ask how children would describe episodes involving the substitution of one object for another. Recall Teddy's bath once more. He was actually seated in a cardboard box, but in the pretend world it would be appropriate to say that he was seated in the bath. To produce such a description, however, means that the standard name for the prop ('box') has to be set to one side and replaced by the name of the object that the prop is temporarily standing for ('bath'). In principle, these object substitutions might be more difficult for young children than referring to purely imaginary substances such as make-believe tea or toothpaste where no prop is involved and no alternative literal name is available.

An illustrative episode was as follows: a yellow brick was placed on a paper plate and pushed toward a toy animal. Children were told that the animal liked to eat 'banana'. Based on the findings described earlier, we knew that 2-year-olds would accept this stipulation and regard the brick as a make-believe banana. Naughty Teddy then intervened in his usual roguish fashion, but instead of directing his intervention at the toy animal, he aimed for the 'food' that the animal had just been given. For example, he picked up a tube of toothpaste and pretended to squeeze make-believe toothpaste over it. The experimenter then asked what had happened.

As before, children referred to Teddy's pretend action (e.g. 'squeezed', 'put'), and the make-believe substance that he had acted on (e.g. 'toothpaste'). In addition, they referred to the target of Teddy's misdemeanour. In principle, they could identify the prop in terms of its actual identity – 'on the brick'. In practice, children almost never did that. Instead, they identified the prop in terms of its make-believe identity – 'on the banana'. When children failed to do this, they almost always pointed to the prop or remained silent. Thus, 2-year-olds realize that when a causal outcome is directed at a prop it is aimed at the object or substance that the prop stands for, and not at the prop itself, and this realization is directly reflected in the language that they use to describe what has happened (Harris and Kavanaugh, 1993, experiment 7). More generally, when children are absorbed in pretend play they describe what is happening in the imaginary world. They eschew literal references to the movements and props that are used to construct that imaginary world.

An Unfolding, Causal Chain

In the experiments described so far, the episodes have typically involved a single pretend action: tea is poured, or toothpaste is squeezed. In the real world, of course, actions can be combined together to execute a plan. The outcome of one action provides an enabling condition for a second action which can, in turn, permit a third action and so forth. Narrative fiction is constructed out of such causal chains. An initial event provides the starting or enabling conditions for a subsequent event, which in turn leads to a new set of conditions, and a new set of possible events. Pretend play can also incorporate these causal chains. Recall Teddy's bath once more. Turning on the taps meant that the bath was filled with water; putting Teddy in the water meant that he became wet; and rubbing him down made him dry again.

Can young children imagine not just a single causal transformation but a causal chain and describe its outcome? In particular, can they envisage the outcome of an initial pretend action, and then incorporate that outcome into their interpretation of the impact of the next pretend action? To examine this possibility, we devised episodes in which 2-year-olds watched two successive, causally connected actions. For example, at first the Duck, a hand puppet, might pour pretend cereal from an (empty) cereal carton into a bowl. Alternatively, the Duck might shake pretend talcum powder from a (sealed) can into a bowl. In either case, the Duck proceeded to feed a toy horse from the bowl with a spoon. Children were then asked what Duck had given to the horse. If they had understood the two successive pretend actions – the pouring and the subsequent feeding – they should have figured out the causal link between them, realizing that the horse was being fed either with cereal or with talcum powder depending on the initial pretend action. In two separate experiments, 2-year-olds proved adroit at understanding such interlinked actions (Harris, Kavanaugh and Meredith, 1994, experiments 1 and 2). They were usually accurate in saying what make-believe substance was fed to the horse in the second part of the episode. Similar results emerged when the causal chain involved an object substitution rather than a make-believe substance. For example, if a brick was first stipulated as either an ice-cream or a fishfinger, and a toy animal was then unceremoniously dumped on top of the brick, children drew the appropriate conclusions about what had happened in each case. They realized that the animal's feet were 'cold', 'ice-creamy', 'soggy' or 'covered in ice-cream' in the one case, but 'hot', 'burning', 'fishfingery' and even 'dinnery' in the other (Harris et al., 1994).

In summary, these experiments show that 2-year-olds can sustain a causal chain in their imagination and describe its outcome. Their descriptions are based on a realization that the result of one pretend change is the starting point for the next, whether the outcome involves a purely imaginary substance, such as talcum powder 'shaken' from a can, or a substitute prop, such as the placement of a brick standing in for some ice-cream.

A Theoretical Model

I began by describing a prototypical episode of pretend play, Teddy's bath. It should be clear by now that a 2-year-old who follows such an episode, and eventually joins in by drying Teddy, must be able to appreciate each of the four components of pretence that I have underlined. The child needs to grasp the way that the bath, the tap and the soap are stipulated into existence by the partner's remarks and actions; that these various stipulated entities have the causal powers of their real counterparts – for example, the make-believe tap can deliver water and the make-believe soap can be used to wash Teddy; that Teddy can be appropriately described or depicted as 'wet' in the pretend world, even though he is objectively dry; and that his final state is the outcome of an unfolding, causal chain in which the bath was filled with water, Teddy was then immersed in that water, and became wet as a result. The various experimental results that have been described show that 2-year-olds understand all four components.

Armed with these conclusions, we may start to build a theoretical account of young children's ability to engage in shared pretence. A couple of cautionary remarks are in order before doing so. The results that I have described were obtained with 2-year-olds. By contrast, children below 2 years have more difficulty in responding accurately and appropriately (Harris and Kavanaugh, 1993). It is plausible that a major cognitive reorganization underpins this age change. In particular, it is likely that there is an emerging ability not just to join in with a partner – after all, cooperative social play without a pretend element is already apparent among children well below the age of 2 years (Howes, 1985; Howes and Matheson, 1992) – but precisely to engage in joint pretence, by responding appropriately to the stipulations and transformations introduced by a partner. It is also important to notice that even among the 2-year-olds that we tested, there was variation in performance. Some of this variation might be tied to differences in motivation or in linguistic skill, but it is equally possible that children differ in their capacity to enter into and keep track of a pretend world. I take up the issue of individual differences in pretend play in more detail in the next chapter, particularly since there is increasing evidence that such differences are stable and consequential for the child's later cognitive development.

Turning now to the theoretical model, an initial assumption is that by the age of 2 years, children must be attuned to the special forms of activity that pretend play involves. For example, in the course of a pretend game of tea-parties, a mother may 'pour' from an empty teapot into a cup, then pick up the cup and hand it to the child, saying, 'Give Dolly some tea'. The mother's actions and utterances are obviously deviant in several ways: normal pouring involves a transfer of liquid, but in this case no liquid emerges from the teapot; standard requests to give someone tea do not typically focus on an empty cup for their realization; and dolls cannot drink tea. Young children are not bewildered by such actions and utterances. They respond appropriately to them by joining in with the game of pretend. By implication, young children can be easily prompted by a play partner to adopt a shared pretend stance toward a play episode.

Having adopted this stance, children must go on to interpret the particular stipulations made by their partner. For example, when a partner lifts an empty carton and tilts it, children must recognize the stipulation that the carton contains a liquid that can be poured. When a partner gives an animal a brick, saying that the animal likes 'banana', they must recognize the stipulation that the brick is to be treated as a banana. These stipulations must also be remembered for the duration of the episode. To solve these problems, I propose that children do two things: having adopted a pretend stance, they suspend processing the actions and utterances of their partner according to normal rules. In particular, they stop scanning the immediate environment for situations that literally fit the utterances being produced or ways to comply literally with the requests that are being made. They recognize that a special mode of processing is called for in which the situation implied or requested by their partner is to be constructed through pretence. In addition, children compose mental 'flags' or reminders, encoding the information implied in the partner's various stipulations. For example, watching their partner 'pour' tea from an empty teapot, they encode the stipulation that: 'This teapot contains tea'. Hearing their partner talk about one of several yellow bricks as if it were a banana, they encode the stipulation that: 'Yellow bricks are bananas'. The force of these flags is restricted by linking them to the pretend stance under way. Effectively, each flag is prefaced by the cautionary statement: 'For the duration of this play episode, pretend that . . . '. So long as the episode is under way, the flags are retrieved and treated as valid. Once the episode comes to an end, and the pretend stance is abandoned, the flags, and the information that they encode, cease to guide the child's reactions and the child reverts to normal, literal processing.

These proposals mean that when the child joins in with a partner's pretence, actions directed to particular props are guided by the stipulated as opposed to the real status of the prop. For example, before acting on a brick, the child consults any relevant, flagged information. As a result, the child thinks of the brick as a banana, as a sandwich or as a bar of soap, depending on what has been stipulated, and then acts on the brick accordingly. Indeed, the child thinks of other props of the same type in the same way. For example, other yellow bricks nearby may also be treated as bananas. Yet the child does not end up with any long-term confusion about the nature of bricks. Once the pretend episode is over, the flagged information that is stored as part of the pretend episode is no longer activated, and the prop reverts to being a humdrum brick.

Children's understanding of the causal consequences of a pretend action can now be seen as a routine by-product of a simple processing rule: to understand the consequences of a pretend action, assume that the entities or substances whose existence is stipulated in the flagged information (e.g. 'banana', 'soap', 'tea' and so forth) are subject to the same causal principles as their real-world equivalents.[1] Consider, for example, the episode in which Naughty Teddy tilted an (empty) carton of milk in front of a toy pig; the make-believe milk in the carton should be regarded as subject to the same causal laws as real milk. When the carton is tilted, the child consults the encoded stipulation ('This carton contains milk') and assumes that the make-believe milk will behave like real milk.[2] It will pour out from the spout of the carton, fall onto a surface below, and wet that surface. Once such outcomes have been imagined, they should then be encoded in much the same way as the stipulations that set the pretend episode in motion. For example, the child should now flag the information that: 'The floor is wet'.

This will allow children to understand the causal chains that make up a pretend episode. Consider, for example, the episode in which a (sealed) can of talcum powder is held above a bowl and shaken. The child watching this pretend gesture should end up flagging the information that: 'The bowl contains talcum powder'. When the spoon is dipped into the bowl and lifted up to feed the horse, the child consults that flagged information and infers that some talcum powder will be carried in the spoon to the horse's mouth.

By consulting the flagged information, children can also provide a description or choose a picture of a pretend change. When the experimenter asks: 'What happened – what did Teddy do?', their response does not reflect what they actually saw. When the teapot was lifted and tipped, they saw no tea emerge, and no visible consequences for the monkey. Nevertheless, given the processing rules introduced above, children will have flagged various pieces of information: 'Tea poured from the spout . . . onto the monkey . . . and made him wet'. By referring to this information in describing what happened, children can offer a description of the pretend episode as opposed to a description of what they actually saw, namely Teddy holding the empty teapot above the monkey and tilting it.

In the light of this account, we may consider two wider theoretical issues concerning pretence: the extent to which children aim to represent reality when they engage in pretend play, and the extent to which their pretend play ends up being a distortion of reality.

Pretence and the Representation of Reality

The proposals that I have made imply that 2-year-olds understand some of the essential ingredients of drama and fiction. They recognize the existence of episodes that are not to be construed as events in the real world but as events occurring within a make-believe framework. This point is especially obvious if we think back to children's picture choices and to their descriptions of the pretend episode. In each case, children ignored what they had actually seen and chose a picture or description that conveyed the make-believe outcome that the adult had enacted with the help of props and pretend gestures, even if that make-believe outcome was objectively invisible.

It is worth emphasizing how this characterization of pretend play departs from Piaget's approach. Piaget construes pretend play as a representation of reality. He claims that the child who is pretending, for example, to go to sleep is using that pretend act to signify the real act of going to sleep (Piaget, 1962, p. 101). Even when the child can use a prop (or 'signifier' – to use Piaget's terminology) that bears little resemblance to what is signified – for example, instead of pretending to go to sleep on a pillow the child lays her head on the tail of a toy donkey (Piaget, 1962, observation 64(a)) – Piaget assumes that what is being signified is reality itself, namely the act of really going to sleep on a proper pillow.

I believe that this analysis is misleading because it conflates two different issues, the inspiration for an act of pretence and what it is meant to signify. It is certainly plausible that real episodes and real objects inspire children's pretend play, but that does not mean that pretend play is intended to signify reality. The distinction can be illustrated by reference to works of fiction. Tolstoy's *War and Peace* was inspired by Napoleon's unsuccessful invasion of Russia. This event is described at length in the novel. Yet it would be a mistake to think of Tolstoy's novel as a history of the actual invasion. Even if the fictional invasion is described in a manner that is broadly consistent with actual historical events, the particular fate that befalls the central characters has no real-world counterpart. When we become immersed in the novel, we become immersed in a set of fictional episodes rather than in a historical event. Thus, we need to distinguish between the inspiration for a novel, which may be an actual event, and the central episodes of the novel, which remain fictional notwithstanding that inspiration.

There is an artistic gap, to say the least, between the drama of Teddy's bath and that of *War and Peace*. Nevertheless, there are important parallels in their conceptual and psychological status. Children, like novelists, are inspired by actual events. Their everyday routines of going to sleep, getting dressed, having a bath, and so forth all provide material for their imagination. Piaget, for example, describes how Lucienne at 31 months made up a lengthy game that involved washing and drying her dolls' sheets and giving the dolls a bath (Piaget, 1962, observation 82). That does not mean, however, that she was referring to any actual episode. Equally, when children join in a game of pretend with an adult, whether it is bathing Teddy or watching his mischief-making with a variety of other toy animals, we need not suppose that they think of these episodes as signifying some real event in which Teddy actually was bathed or made real mischief.

My claim that early pretend play, including joint pretend play with an adult, makes no direct reference to real episodes can be further illuminated by exploring the contrast between pretend play undertaken in the context of a make-believe framework and those occasional acts of pretence – undertaken outside that framework – that *are* intended to refer to a real episode. Consider a child who has just accomplished some new challenge, such as diving into the swimming pool. In telling a parent what she did, the child might briefly re-enact her bodily movements – she might stand on tip-toe, hold her arms above her head and lean forward, as if about to dive. In this case, the child is not pretending to dive in the context of a make-believe framework – her pretence is a re-enactment and a reference to a particular action that she carried out earlier. It helps her to communicate more effectively just what she did. In this case, the inspiration and the action that her pretend movements signify are one and the same: her successful dive into the swimming pool. Here, we have a case that fits the analysis of pretend actions offered by Piaget: the pretend act is intended to signify the real act. Yet, such a re-enactment is different from ordinary pretend play where there is typically no intention to refer to any actual event – even if, as I acknowledge, children draw on their everyday experience of actual events for inspiration when they enact a pretend episode.

Does the Child Distort Reality?

In drama and fiction, the twists and turns of the plot can introduce elements that are novel and iconoclastic, as compared to ordinary, real events. Such elements were included in the experiments described earlier. Nonetheless, to understand that toothpaste might be squeezed onto a banana or a pig's tail, children need to draw on familiar, real-world causal principles, even if they end up imagining an outcome that is improbable, non-existent or even forbidden in the real world. Thus, by drawing on their understanding of causal regularities in the real world, 2-year-olds have the ability to imagine outcomes that they have never actually witnessed. At the same time, when children enter into a make-believe framework, there is no indication that they end up distorting the underlying causal fabric of the real world, even if they conjure up various specific novel outcomes that they would not encounter in that real world.

Piaget concedes that children do sometimes use pretend play to represent non-existent possibilities, including possibilities that are forbidden or that are otherwise impossible. For example, as described in the previous chapter, Jacqueline aged 28 months, having been told that she could not play with the water intended for washing, stood beside the tub and pretended to pour water with an empty cup. Similarly, at 30 months, she folded her arms and pretended to carry her baby sister, an activity that she was not allowed to engage in at that time (Piaget, 1962, observation 84). At 47 months, she created a hybrid creature ('aseau') – half-bird and half-dog – and the creature's movements by flapping her outstretched arms and by crawling on all fours, growling: 'It's a kind of dog' (Piaget, 1962, observation 83).

Nevertheless, Piaget draws an essentially negative conclusion about these episodes. Such episodes should not be seen, he argues, as part of the child's developing imagination because

> the subsequent evolution of symbolic imagination will consist in its decrease in favour of representational tools more adapted to the real world. The striking feature of these symbolic combinations is the extent to which the child reproduces or continues the real world, the imaginative symbol being only a means to increase his range, not an end in itself. In reality, the child has no imagination, and what we ascribe to him as such is no more than a lack of coherence, and still more, subjective assimilation. (Piaget, 1962, p. 131)

By implication, the child who is truly imaginative will be unfettered by reality. To the extent that the child merely reproduces or recombines elements from reality, Piaget denies that genuine imagination is at work.

Once again, my analysis departs from Piaget's. If we took Piaget's yardstick seriously, we would end up dismissing most works of fiction, *War and Peace* included, as unimaginative. Inevitably, such works reproduce and recombine elements from the real world. The laws of physics, biology and psychology are normally respected in fiction, even if certain genres – fairy stories, science fiction or magical realism – can intrigue us with occasional departures from some of those regularities. Moreover, as I shall argue in later chapters, readers of fiction presuppose those everyday causal regularities in seeking to make sense of what they read. Thus, contrary to Piaget, I conclude that children do possess a genuine imagination – the type of imagination that we all exercise when we entertain fictional possibilities. Just like readers of fiction, they deploy their understanding of the causal regularities of the real world to make sense of the novel possibilities that occur within that make-believe framework. Indeed, I would argue that the evidence from children's pretend play suggests that the disposition toward fiction is remarkably deep-rooted. It begins to emerge toward the end of the second year, at around the same time as speech itself. I return to that intriguing conjunction in the final chapter.

Conclusions

It is possible to construe pretend play as an early attempt to assimilate or represent reality, but one that fails, given the child's limited objectivity. Then, once greater objectivity is attained, pretend play is increasingly suppressed. This is essentially the developmental sequence that Piaget proposes. In this chapter, I have argued for an altogether different sequence.

In the first place, pretend play does not emerge in early infancy. It emerges in late infancy, around the same time as language. By that time, the child has gained a limited but functional understanding of the way that the world works. Children exploit a good deal of that already established conceptual knowledge in their pretend play. In particular, they begin to deploy their causal understanding of everyday transformations. In the second place, despite its conceptual fidelity to reality, it is a mistake to construe pretend play as a representation of reality. It does not even involve playing with reality. The episodes and events that are represented in the course of pretend play are fictional rather than real. Children's pretend play is not an early distortion of the real world but an initial exploration of possible worlds. Moreover, as they think about those alternatives, children consider them in a coherent and consequential fashion. In that sense, pretend play is not an activity that is doomed to suppression but the first indication of a lifelong mental capacity to consider alternatives to reality.

Notes

1   When we think of make-believe entities such as witches and monsters, it is tempting to assume that children invest them with powers that *defy* the causal relationships that obtain in the real world. This is probably true of older children who do contemplate magical possibilities in their pretend play. However, this chapter is concerned with more prosaic entities, make-believe tea, bricks that stand in for cake, and so forth. The magical dimension of make-believe will be discussed in chapter 8.
2   A superficially plausible objection to this line of argument is that the make-believe milk does not behave like real milk because it is invisible. However, this objection confuses the objective status of the make-believe milk – which is indeed invisible – with its status within the make-believe framework, where it is deemed to be visible. For example, other participants in the episode would be expected to 'see' it, to wipe it up, and so forth.

3

Role Play

... if a Sparrow come before my Window I take part in its existence
and pick about the Gravel
John Keats, letter to Benjamin Bailey, 22 November 1817

Introduction

In the last chapter, we saw that 2-year-olds can imagine causal transformations that do not actually take place. The transformations in
question mainly involved the physical environment – the pouring of
milk, or the squeezing of toothpaste. Yet an agent and a victim were
often involved in these physical transformations. In this chapter, I examine how children incorporate animate beings into their pretend play.
More specifically, I examine children's ability to imagine and act out
the role of a person or creature. This type of play is produced during
solitary pretence, or together with an adult partner, but its most frequent context is with other children, especially siblings or familiar
peers (Dunn and Dale, 1984). Indeed, from the age of 2 years and
upward, complementary role play in which children adopt different
but related roles – for example, bus driver and passenger or mother
and baby – appears to be a key form of interaction between friends.
Successful cooperation in this type of play calls for considerable flexibility and sensitivity. Not surprisingly, young preschoolers who engage in a high proportion of this type of role-taking are perceived as
more likeable by their peers and as more sociable by their teachers
(Howes, 1988). Below, I discuss these individual differences in children's participation in role play in more detail. I also explore the cognitive processes that lie behind children's production of a given role
and consider what these cognitive processes might augur for children's
later imaginative life.

Before going any further, it will be useful to set out a working definition of the type of play that I have in mind. I define it as pretend play in which the child temporarily acts out the part of someone other than the self using pretend actions and utterances. The child need not explicitly announce or assign a given role – such overt stage management tends to emerge only at around 3 or 4 years (Howes and Matheson, 1992) – but it should be possible to infer the role from the child's pretend activities, or from acquiescence to proposals made by a play partner. My definition is deliberately wide-ranging. It includes those familiar cases where the child adopts a role or identity for the self, for example by impersonating a mother or a soldier. However, it is not critical that the child set aside his or her own identity and personally adopt another identity. My definition also covers cases in which the child creates and enacts a role but, instead of assigning that role to the self, projects it onto a doll or toy that serves as a prop for the role. Finally, my definition includes cases where the child invents a creature or person but does not rely on the support of any props at all. Figure 3.1 illustrates the various possibilities covered by this broad definition.

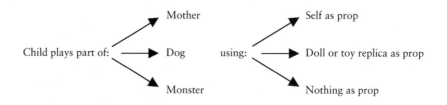

Figure 3.1   Role play showing how any given role might be enacted using three different vehicles.

Role play is striking because children temporarily immerse themselves in the part that they create. They frequently start to act on the world and to talk about it as if they were experiencing it from the point of view of the invented person or creature. This perspectival shift is manifested in various ways. First, children use the terms of reference, including deictic terms that are appropriate to the role that they have adopted.

Consider the following examples, drawn from children of 3 years or younger: Jacqueline (aged 28 months) has assumed, and is acting out, the role of her mother. Approaching her father, she says: 'It's *Mommy* . . . come kiss *Mommy*' (Piaget, 1962, observation 79). A 37-month-old says to her male playmate as she places an Indian doll on an ironing board: '*Our* baby . . . let me lie it down' (Miller and Garvey, 1984, p. 109). These playful remarks are so natural and self-evident that it is easy to miss the subtle indications of role enactment. In the first example, the child refers to the self not as 'me' or 'Jacqueline' but as 'Mummy'. In the second example, the child sees herself as one of two parents when she refers to the doll as 'Our baby'.

Children also shift to the mood and tone of voice that is appropriate to the part that they are playing. A 29-month-old girl, adopting the role of mother, lays down a doll and says sternly: 'Baby, you have to go to bed' (Miller and Garvey, 1984, p. 122). Mary, aged 38 months, addresses a boy playmate (whom she has called 'Daddy') in the whining tone of a demanding child: 'I want my teddy bear' (Miller and Garvey, 1984, p. 111).

Children also give expression to the emotions, sensations and needs that are appropriate to the adopted role. For example, J at 21 months develops a new pattern of interaction with his Jack-in-the-box. If, when he closes the lid, Jack still has his hand poking out, J says: 'Ouch, ouch. Boo-boo' (his word for 'hurt') (Wolf, 1982, p. 319). Carrie at 37 months, playing the part of baby, says to her playmate, who has adopted the role of mother: 'Mommy, I need to go to the bathroom' (Miller and Garvey, 1984, p. 124).

Finally, children comment on the content of the perceptual experience that is available to the person whose part they act out. J at 24 months plays with a farmer doll and a bath-like enclosure made of bricks. Having added and re-added water to the bath (by turning imaginary taps), J puts the farmer back into the bath and says: 'Oh, no, sooooo hot, too hot' (Wolf, Rygh and Altshuler, 1984, p. 197). Laura, aged 24 months, is invited by her older sister to play at Mother and to: 'Change my bottom'. Laura obliges by pulling off her sister's pants, saying: 'That's stinky', and 'Wee-wee! Wee-wee!' (Dunn and Dale, 1984, p. 141).

These various remarks suggest that when children engage in role play, they do not simply remain off-stage directors or puppeteers. They enter into the make-believe situation that they create and adopt the point of view of one of the protagonists within it. The real world recedes into the background and is replaced by the make-believe landscape and experience that would be available to that protagonist.

Imaginary Companions

Children's absorption in role play when they are 2 or 3 years of age is often transient. For a few moments, they take on the part of baby, or mother duck. However, during this same period, some children also begin to engage in an intriguing form of sustained role play. They repeatedly conjure up an imaginary person or creature whose identity can remain stable over several months. The character is invoked on such a regular basis that it becomes a kind of companion to the child. Svendsen (1934, p. 988) proposed the following influential definition of the phenomenon:

> An invisible character, named and referred to in conversation with other persons or played with directly for a period of time, at least several months, having an air of reality for the child, but no apparent objective basis.

In her investigation of such characters, Svendsen explicitly sets aside cases in which the child either impersonated a companion, or used a doll or stuffed animal as an external prop. She focused exclusively on those cases in which the child eschewed any use of props and invoked an invisible companion. However, in line with my more inclusive definition proposed earlier, this exclusion is probably unnecessary. When children invent and invoke a character over several months, they may keep it invisible, as implied by Svendsen, but they may also become the character via an act of impersonation or they may project it onto an external prop. In each case, as with more transient role play, it is the child who orchestrates the character and gives voice to his or her experience. The vehicle for that orchestration, be it a purely invisible person, the self or a stuffed doll, is ultimately at the disposal of the child's imagination. If we adopt this broad-ranging definition, we find that the invention of an imaginary companion is quite widespread. In one of the most careful, recent studies, Marjorie Taylor (1998) reports that nearly two-thirds of a sample of American children had either an invisible imaginary companion or one projected onto an external prop at some point before the age of 7. Indeed, the figure climbs to about three-quarters of the sample if those children who engaged only in impersonation are also included. Contrary to the implication of early research suggesting that the invention of an imaginary companion is characteristic of atypical children with social or interpersonal difficulties, these figures suggest that the phenomenon is widespread. Indeed, there is little consistent evidence of any difference in personality or temperament between children who do and do not invent such a companion (Taylor, 1998, ch. 3). There is, however, intriguing evidence for a cognitive difference. Before considering that evidence, it will be useful to present some examples of the various forms of imaginary companion.

First, there are cases where children enact a role by means of impersonation: they themselves became the person or creature in question. For example, from 36 to 60 months, DF pretended to be a boy. 'Mostly she was a boy named "Jimmy" and would not answer if addressed by her own name. (She) would say. "My name is Jimmy." If any request were prefaced by "Jimmy, will you . . . ?" she would accede immediately. Sometimes she was some other boy than Jimmy. Occasionally when she did something she was not supposed to do she was Shisky' (Ames and Learned, 1946, p. 157). BT pretended to be a kitten. 'At 24 months of age he visited his grandmother, who had a kitten. When he got home, he became a kitten and this continued quite consistently till he was 36 months old. He went around on all fours "meowing", lapping up milk. At 30 months he took on, briefly, an additional role, that of his best friend's dog. In this role, he went around on all fours and bit people' (Ames and Learned, 1946, p. 154).

Taylor (1998) describes a case of a 5-year-old girl who projected an imaginary companion onto a doll. The child had an interest in dolphins and had been given a stuffed toy dolphin which became the prop for an imaginary companion called 'Dipper'. When asked to describe Dipper, she did not give an objective description of her doll, but explained that Dipper was 'the size of a door, had sparkles and stripes (unlike a regular dolphin), and lived far away on a star'.

RP provides an example of a child who retained her own identity while populating her home with a variety of invisible people. 'At 33 months she talked to imaginary beings in the corners of the room. She would sit at supper and make faces at the corner of the room near the ceiling. Had long conversations with this imaginary friend and was oblivious of the rest of the family . . . two clowns she once saw were taken home (imaginatively) and were kept in the guest room for a long time. She said they made dents in the bed where they slept. She was annoyed when guests came and the clowns had to move out of the guest room bed' (Ames and Learned, 1946, p. 156). Children also create invisible non-human companions. Taylor (1998) describes a 4-year-old girl who invented two invisible birds called Nutsy and Nutsy. According to the child, they had brightly coloured feathers, were about 12 inches tall and talked incessantly. Sometimes, she claimed to be irritated by their boisterous behaviour, but they also made her laugh. The child's parents often observed their daughter playing with them, and were informed about their opinions and activities.

In sum, whether we look at examples of fleeting role play, or the more sustained invention of a pretend companion, children adopt the same trio of techniques: they use impersonation in which the self stands in for the target role; they project a character onto an external vehicle such as a doll or stuffed animal; and they create such characters out of thin air, positioning them at various points in their actual environment.

The Process of Role Play

At first glance, the process that underpins children's role play seems obvious. Children identify a character and then produce actions and remarks that fit the role or identity of that character, supplementing their pretence, if possible, with the imitation or mimicry of distinctive features of that character – such as a special voice or way of moving.

This account implies that children have encoded some kind of mental record of the remarks and actions appropriate to particular roles. For example, having entered repeatedly into a relationship with their mother, they have encoded what amounts to a mother–baby 'script' which they use as a temporary guide for their own role-based actions and remarks, whether they act out the part of mother or baby. However, this account is ultimately too restricted. Were children only following a script, we would expect their play to be quite stereotypic from one episode to the next. Indeed, role play would consist of a series of brief character sketches complete with the relevant voice and gesture. In practice, children's role play is more flexible. In the first place, they play the part of characters, such as a Jack-in-the-box or Dolphin, with whom they have had no genuine interaction, and for whom they presumably have no script. Moreover, they locate the characters that they invent and orchestrate within an unfolding drama that borrows from everyday life. Jack hurts his hand when the lid of the box is shut; the invisible clowns are obliged to move when visitors usurp the guest room. This means that children must adapt the actions and remarks of the characters to a changing situation. At this juncture, the child is going beyond a fixed script with a well-rehearsed and remembered set of actions and remarks. Rather, the child enacts the way that the characters might respond to novel and unexpected events.

To play a role in this fashion, children need an operating procedure that is more flexible than a script. The notion of 'simulation' (Goldman, 1992; Gordon, 1992; Harris, 1992) offers a plausible explanation of this flexibility. By way of illustration, suppose that the child is playing at pirates. An initial step is to imagine the situation that the pirate is currently in and to adopt – in a pretend fashion – the attitude that someone might adopt toward that situation. For example, the pirate may have found some treasure; in addition he may have enemies who might steal it. Even in this relatively simple situation, there is no standard 'pirate' script that specifies what to do next. However, the process of simulation can help the child to construct a suitable plan. Effectively, the make-believe situation (i.e., the discovery of the treasure and the threat from enemies) can be fed into the child's own knowledge and planning system, and the output of this system can be translated into a pretend action or statement. In so far as the child's mind is an analogue of anyone's mind (including a pirate's), it will simulate an appropriate plan. For example, the child is so designed that the threat of loss is likely to trigger plans for retention or concealment. Provided the child's mind can operate in a similar way with respect to a pretend threat of loss, the plan that is produced will be appropriate. So, as a result, the child might say: 'I think I know where to hide the gold so that they can't get it' (Wolf et al., 1984, p. 203).

By feeding pretend input into the child's own knowledge and planning mechanisms, considerable cognitive economy is achieved. Consider one simple but ubiquitous fact about role play. The child talks while acting in a role, occasionally mimicking the intonation or accent of the chosen character. That talk will consist of well-formed, English sentences (if that is the child's native language). In producing those sentences, which may be completely novel, children can rely on their own knowledge of the language, assuming by default that the person whose role they are adopting speaks according to the same tacit rules (Harris, 1992). Putting the same point differently, in executing a role, children need have no deep insight into the hidden psychological processes that underpin another person's production of novel but relevant sentences. While attempting to capture any distinctive, surface features of the person's speech via mimicry, they can rely on the default assumption that the hidden processes by which speech is produced are similar from one person to another.

This point has considerable generality. According to several recent accounts of cognitive development, children make use of a variety of domain-specific theories, one specialized for dealing with the behaviour of middle-sized physical objects within a spatial framework, another for grasping the regularities of the biological domain, and so forth (Hirschfeld and Gelman, 1994; Wellman and Gelman, 1998). When children adopt a particular role, the character in question will presumably subscribe to these various theories too. Thus, the character will understand how physical objects are displaced and transformed within a three-dimensional framework; and the character will also understand certain dictates of biology, that food relieves hunger, that sleep alleviates tiredness, that living things die and so forth. Arguably, when children play out a particular character, they need to have recourse to a set of meta-theories: theories about the theories that the character holds in the domains of physics, biology, psychology and so on. However, a more parsimonious explanation is that by simply recruiting their own knowledge-base, children reproduce these routine aspects of human mentation in any character that they enact.[1]

Summing up the argument so far, role play depends upon an active process of simulation in which the role player projects him- or herself into the make-believe situation faced by a given protagonist. Having fed that make-believe situation into their own knowledge-base, the role player can arrive at judgements, plans and utterances that are appropriate for the adopted role.

In the last chapter, I discussed the way that children are not bound by the physical world. They deem one thing to be another and they readily imagine various make-believe transformations. In some ways, role play is even more peculiar. Children cast aside their own identity and act the part of someone else. It is tempting to conclude that such flights of fancy gradually wane as children get older. Certainly, overt role enactment declines as a form of spontaneous play. However, I shall argue that the process of simulation which guides role play has an enduring part to play in our mental life. We should not mistake an outer decline for an inner change. As a first step in that argument, we may examine the links between role play and later psychological understanding.

Individual Differences in Role Play

Children vary in the extent to which they engage in role play. As noted earlier, this type of play, especially persistent play with imaginary companions, has been seen as a potential marker for emotional or social disturbance. Svendsen (1934), for example, reported that personality difficulties, especially timidity or a domineering manner with other children, were present in a large majority of the children with an imaginary companion that she studied. However, as Taylor (1998) has pointed out, there are flaws in this early research. The studies either did not include a comparison group of children without an imaginary companion, or they focused on a non-random sample recruited from child guidance centres or clinics, and such children might already have a heightened risk of personality difficulties. Indeed, more recent evidence suggests that children who often engage in role play, far from suffering any kind of pathology, are socially skilled in the sense that they are more insightful about mental states. In particular, they perform better on tests that call for an appreciation of the subjectivity of such states – the way in which people vary in their emotions, desires and beliefs even when faced with the same objective situation. One early and intriguing piece of evidence was reported by Connolly and Doyle (1984). Young children (ranging from 35 to 69 months) who engaged in more complex pretend play with other children proved to be more skilled in assessing how people might feel.

Research on this link between pretend play and mental state understanding began to pick up momentum with the advent of better tools for assessing children's grasp of mental states, especially beliefs. In one well-known task, children watch as a puppet places an object in a cupboard, and then leaves the scene for a short time. During this interval, a second puppet enters, surreptitiously moves the object to a new location, and leaves. When the first puppet returns, children are questioned to find out if they understand that the returning puppet will mistakenly think that the object remains where it was put in the first place. A key feature of this task is that if children are to solve it, they must differentiate between where they themselves know the object to be (in the new location) and where the returning puppet believes it is (still in the cupboard). Between the age of 3 and 5 years, an increasing proportion of children acknowledge the puppet's false belief. Until they do so, they are inclined to say that the returning puppet knows the actual location of the object, despite the fact that it was moved without the puppet's knowledge (Wimmer and Perner, 1983).

Michael Chandler and his colleagues were the first to explore and provide evidence for the link between role play and belief understanding (Chandler, Lalonde, Fritz and Hala, 1991; Lalonde and Chandler, 1995). They gave a group of 3-year-old children various tasks that assessed their understanding of false beliefs. In addition, the children's preschool teachers rated them on a variety of social and play skills, including the ability to make friends, to take turns in a game without prompting, and to share toys spontaneously. Performance on most of these items proved to have no significant correlation with false belief understanding. However, among the nine items that did display such a link, three concerned various aspects of make-believe play: engaging in simple make-believe activities with others; engaging in simple make-believe activities alone; and having an imaginary friend or playmate. Subsequent studies have begun to throw more light on this intriguing link between pretend play and belief understanding. Before reviewing these studies, however, it will be useful to consider how to conceptualize that link in theoretical terms.

Pretend Play and Mental Understanding: Theoretical Links

Some authors have argued that it is a major challenge for young children to understand the part that representation plays in our mental lives – to realize that our actions, utterances and emotions are guided not by the way things really are but by the way that we represent them to be (Perner, 1991). Pursuing this line of argument, Marjorie Taylor and her colleagues (Taylor, 1998; Taylor, Gerow and Carlson, 1993) have proposed that pretend play is a major tool for helping children to deal with this challenge. The proposal runs as follows.

First, although a person's mental representation of the world need not correspond to the way things really are in the world, it often does so. For example, mother may think that the chocolate is still in the cupboard where she put it, and it may indeed be in the cupboard. Thus, in trying to predict how she will behave, a child can frequently ignore the distinction between reality and her representation of reality. Similar predictions about what she will do can be made by consulting either. For example, if asked where she will look for the chocolate, the child can answer either in terms of where the chocolate really is – in the cupboard – or in terms of mother's mental representation of where the chocolate is. Provided she accurately represents where it is, each strategy will yield the same prediction.

The situation is different for pretend play. In making sense of pretend play, current reality is not a useful guide. For example, when mother pours imaginary tea into a cup, an appropriate continuation of that pretend initiative should not be tailored to the objective fact that the cup is empty. Rather, it is necessary to take into account the pretend tea that has been stipulated. More generally, engaging in a good deal of pretend play might help children to appreciate that pretend actions are guided not by reality itself but rather by the make-believe reality that is represented in the mind of the person engaged in the pretence. For example, if a child is pretending that an imaginary companion is seated at the dinner table, the child may be confronted by a sibling who wants to sit on that ostensibly empty seat, and another family member who graciously sits elsewhere. In such circumstances, children may be helped to make a distinction between those actions that are guided by reality and those actions that acknowledge the make-believe reality represented in the child's own mind.

Granted these points, it is possible that children who engage in a good deal of pretend play are thereby alerted to the wider role that representation plays in our mental lives. In particular, their attention may eventually be drawn to other cases in which actions are guided not by reality itself but by a representation of the way that reality might be. In particular, there are cases in which serious, non-playful actions – and not just pretend actions – fly in the face of reality. Actions that are based on false beliefs fall under this heading. Here, the actor is guided by a representation of reality that is supposed to be accurate but is actually incorrect, although in contrast to the case of pretence, this discrepancy between representation and reality is not known to the actor in question. He or she blithely takes their mental representation to be an accurate guide to reality, much as we might navigate by an out-of-date road map without being aware of its inaccuracies. For example, if a child has surreptitiously removed and eaten all the chocolate that mother put in the cupboard, she will naturally assume it is still there. An accurate prediction of where she will look for it must take into account her mistaken representation of its location. In sum, according to this line of speculation, we can predict that children who engage in a good deal of pretend play will thereby become more proficient at realizing the way that mental representations of the world, including those that misrepresent reality as it stands, may guide how someone will act.

There are, however, two obstacles in the way of this causal argument. First, it presupposes that children discover the role of mental representation rather easily in the case of pretence, and that they benefit from applying this insight to the case of false belief. As John Flavell (1993) has pointed out, both of these assumptions are dubious. First, it is reasonable to maintain that 2-year-olds, and perhaps even 3-year-olds, mostly think of pretend play as a special form of activity. For example, they could think of someone who pours pretend tea or wipes it up when it has spilled as engaged in a special type of action directed at make-believe tea rather than real tea (Harris and Kavanaugh, 1993). On this argument, children might be well aware of what they or their partner are pretending, but eschew any reflection on the mental process of representation by which that pretence is realized. In much the same way, we can work out that a mime artist is pretending to peel a banana or lift a heavy box without having to reflect on the mental process of representation that guides his or her gestures. We focus rather on the artist's gestures, and on the entity – the banana or the box – that those gestures conjure up in our imagination.

Evidence for this conservative assessment of young children's conceptualization of pretence has emerged from studies showing that even when children are told that someone lacks the knowledge necessary for a given piece of pretence, they still have difficulty in diagnosing whether the person in question is pretending. For example, 4-year-olds think that someone might be pretending to hop like a kangaroo even if the person does not know that kangaroos hop (Joseph, 1998; Lillard, 1993). By implication, young children do not understand that pretence critically depends on a well-informed representation of what is being pretended. If this conclusion is correct, pretence is not likely to serve as a stepping stone for learning about the role of representation with respect to other mental states, such as belief.[2]

In any case, as Flavell (1993) also emphasizes, even if young children are able to work out that a mental representation must underlie acts of pretence, it is not so evident that this putative insight would then help them to appreciate the role of representation in the case of mistaken belief. Instead, it might tempt them to think that someone mistakenly looking for chocolate in an empty box is simply pretending that there is chocolate in the box rather than mistakenly believing that there is chocolate there. Assimilating the case of false belief to the model of pretence could be positively misleading for a child rather than instructive.

In sum, to the extent that either of these two counter-arguments is valid, we should be cautious in accepting the proposal that pretend play will teach children about mental representation. There is, however, an alternative way of conceptualizing the beneficial impact of pretend play on children's understanding of mental states. As described earlier, children's role play suggests that they can enact what people might do in a given situation by a process of simulation: they imagine themselves in that same situation and act *vis-à-vis* that imaginary situation. For example, when pretending to be Mother, the child pretends to be confronted by a crying Baby, and ministers to it accordingly. When pretending to be a pirate, the child pretends to have discovered some treasure, and announces a plan to conceal it. We may now extend this proposal to the prediction of serious, non-playful actions and utterances. Such predictions can also be guided by a process of simulation. The child temporarily imagines facing the situation that currently confronts the person whose actions or utterances are to be predicted, formulates a plan or conclusion in relation to that imagined situation, and projects it onto the person in question.

The major difference between role play and prediction is simply the nature of the output. In the case of role play by simulation, the output is translated into overt action: the child acts out a role, voicing the thoughts of the character that he or she is playing, or acting as that character would act. In the case of prediction by simulation, the output of the simulation process is a prediction of how the other person will think or act rather than any overt role play. Simulation is taken off-line, as it were, rather than used on-line to guide pretend actions and utterances. Nonetheless, given that role play and prediction both call on a simulation process, it is likely that children who often engage in role play will be more adroit at prediction. Accordingly, we may expect children who often engage in role play to show more understanding of mental states, including false beliefs.

In summary, we have identified two different interpretations of the potential link between pretend play and mental state understanding. One interpretation predicts that various types of pretend play will facilitate an understanding of mental representation, including the representational nature of belief. This is because pretend play alerts children to the potential gap between a representation of reality and reality itself. The alternative interpretation predicts that role play improves children's simulation skills, and hence their psychological understanding.

As this brief summary implies, the interpretations differ in more than one way. They differ in the particular benefit that they ascribe to pretend play – the discovery of mental representation in the one case, and practice at the art of simulation in the other. They also differ, however, in the type of pretend play that they take to be important. The first proposal implies that any form of pretend play should be helpful for later mental state understanding because all pretend play involves mental representation. The simulation hypothesis, by contrast, implies that role play, rather than pretend play in general, should be helpful because it is only role play that calls for a simulation process.[3] With these competing interpretations in mind, we may now review studies that have examined the link between pretend play and mental state understanding, giving special attention to studies in which role play has been distinguished from pretend play in general.[4]

Role Play and Belief Understanding: Empirical Evidence

Astington and Jenkins (1995) assessed a group of 3- to 5-year-olds for their understanding of false beliefs and observed the children playing in groups of three or four. Pretend play was coded on three dimensions: (1) the overall frequency of statements that were concerned with non-literal play – whether to plan an imaginary activity, to assign a role, to substitute one object for another, and so forth; (2) the frequency with which children made joint proposals in the context of pretend play that included both the play partner and the child (e.g. 'You have to stay in my arms'); and (3) the frequency of statements in which the self or another child was assigned an explicit role (e.g. 'OK Baby, you get in the carriage'). The first measure – the overall frequency of pretend statements – was not linked to performance on the false belief task. However, both of the other two measures – the frequency of joint proposals and of role assignment – were related to performance on the false belief task, even when the potential contributions of age and verbal ability were controlled for.

A similar pattern emerged in two studies by Schwebel, Rosen and Singer (1999). They assessed 3-, 4- and 5-year-olds on various theory of mind tasks and watched them playing at their preschool. In particular, they kept track of how often the children engaged in either joint or solitary pretend play. Joint play included episodes in which joint roles were assigned ('I'm the baby, you're the mommy'), or one child responded appropriately to the pretend premise stipulated by another, for example running in mock terror when another child announced that 'a monster is coming'. As in the study by Astington and Jenkins (1995), children who engaged in more joint play, including role play, performed better on the theory of mind tasks, even after the contribution of age and verbal ability had been taken into account. On the other hand, no such connection was found for solitary pretence which mainly involved objects and props rather than role play.[5]

These two studies fit the simulation model quite well. As argued earlier, a process of on-line simulation can sustain role play in which the child acts out the response that is appropriate to a given identity or make-believe scenario; a similar process of off-line simulation can allow children to predict rather than to enact what someone might think or say. Consistent with this idea, children who often engage in role-based pretend play perform well when asked to predict what someone might mistakenly think or say. The findings are less congenial for the hypothesis that pretend play alerts children to the nature of mental representation. On that basis, the overall frequency of pretence should be just as good a predictor of performance on the false belief task, because in principle any type of pretence could illustrate how pretend actions are guided by non-veridical representations.

Still, despite this support for the simulation approach, it is important to stress that these studies only demonstrate an association between two concurrent skills – mental state prediction on the one hand, and role play on the other hand. One might reasonably object that skill at role play, especially when it involves joint planning and role assignment, is a consequence and not a precursor of the type of understanding that leads to accurate performance on assessments of mental state understanding. Indeed, this was the line of thinking that guided the investigation carried out by Astington and Jenkins (1995).

A study by Youngblade and Dunn (1995) speaks directly to this alternative interpretation. They carried out two assessments of a group of toddlers. Before their third birthday, when the toddlers were approximately 33 months, they were observed at home with their mother and older siblings. Various measures of social understanding were made at this point. In particular, children's pretend play was assessed along several dimensions, including the amount of conversation dedicated to pretend play, the diversity of pretend themes that a given child displayed, the amount of role enactment (as indexed by role-appropriate behaviour or utterances, even when the role was not explicitly identified), and the frequency with which a role was explicitly assigned (as opposed to simply enacted).

Seven months later – when the toddlers were 40 months – they were tested for their understanding of belief. A key result was that pretend play at 33 months was linked to children's belief understanding as indexed by their ability to explain why a puppet was searching in an empty container. This finding reproduces the pattern obtained in the studies just described. However, to the extent that pretend play was assessed before the children were 3 years old – at an age when most children fail false belief tasks – it is most unlikely that the variation in pretend play was a consequence of variation in false belief understanding. Moreover, and again this fits the pattern obtained in the studies described earlier, not every aspect of pretend play was linked to false belief understanding. Among the various measures of pretend play taken at 33 months, only role enactment was a predictor of false belief understanding. This relationship proved to be robust even after allowance was made for the sophistication of children's language (as measured in terms of the mean length of utterance).[6]

A final piece of evidence linking role play with false belief understanding was reported by Taylor and Carlson (1997). They assessed children ranging from 3½ to 4½ years for their disposition toward role play. However, instead of studying children engaged in joint play with other children, they checked whether children had invented an imaginary character, be it an invisible companion that they played with, or a creature that they impersonated themselves. Children provided their own report, but they were only judged to have invented an imaginary character if their parents provided independent corroboration of their self-report. Just over one-quarter of the 3-year-olds met this relatively strict criterion for sustained role play, but about half the 4-year-olds did so.

Children were also given several different tasks to tap their understanding of belief. In each case, children had to differentiate between their own currently accurate knowledge about an object, and the mistaken conclusion that they or someone else might reach on the basis of an initial, incomplete inspection. Children performed consistently across these various tasks – passing most of them or failing most of them.

Accordingly, it was appropriate to give the children a single composite score for their performance on the entire set of tasks.

Consistent with the results reviewed so far, those 4-year-olds who engaged in more role play, as indexed by their invention of an imaginary character, performed better on the belief tasks, even when the potential contributions of age and verbal ability were taken into account. No effect was found for the 3-year-olds, but few of them engaged in this type of role play, and, in any case, most of them performed quite poorly across the belief tasks. One further result is worth noting. Some of the children explained that they often impersonated a machine, such as an aeroplane. This type of pretend play was associated with poor rather than good performance on the belief tasks, and reinforces the assumption that it is only when children enact the part of an animate being, endowed with mental states, that they make any gains in mental state understanding.[7]

Taking these four reports together, we have persuasive evidence that involvement in role play, whether in the context of joint play with other children or pursued in a more solitary fashion through the creation of an imaginary character, is a correlate, and indeed an advance predictor, of later success on belief tasks. This link emerges even when potentially confounding factors such as age or verbal ability are controlled for. At the same time, the overall frequency of pretence is not linked to belief understanding. Moreover, the impersonation of a machine – an entity that would not normally have any type of mental state – is negatively related to such understanding. This pattern of results clearly supports the proposal that the process of simulation carries over from pretend role play to belief understanding, but it provides no support for the claim that pretend play in general promotes an understanding of mental representation.[8]

The Nature and Origin of Individual Differences in Role Play

The studies just reviewed underline the fact that children vary in the extent to which they engage in role play. Not all children create an imaginary companion, and when they play with others, children vary in the extent to which they enact or propose roles. So far, I have taken these individual differences for granted and emphasized their association with the concurrent or subsequent understanding of mental states.

At this point, it is worth taking a closer look at the nature and origin of these individual differences in role play.

It is obviously likely that children vary in the opportunities and encouragement that they are offered for engaging in role play. For example, this type of play is more likely to occur with siblings than with a parent. Indeed, when Youngblade and Dunn (1995) looked at factors that promoted role play, having an older sibling was an obvious support. Moreover, consistent with the idea that opportunities for role play might correlate with subsequent understanding of false belief, several studies have shown that children who have siblings, and notably older siblings, perform better on false belief tasks (Ruffman, Perner, Naito, Parkin and Clements, 1998).

Still, we should also consider the possibility that children differ not just in their opportunities for role play but also in their inclination to take up and become engaged in those opportunities. Evidence pointing in this direction emerged in research carried out by Marjorie Taylor and her colleagues (Taylor, Cartwright and Carlson, 1993). At the suggestion of an adult, children who had an imaginary companion readily pretended to speak to that companion on the telephone. They were also just as willing to pretend that a real friend was on the line, and to engage in a pretend conversation with him or her. Adults who listened in to these pretend conversations judged that most children were highly involved in them. By contrast, children of the same age who had no imaginary companion were often reluctant to start such a pretend conversation; they said that no one 'answered' the phone or they said that the friend was not available. Moreover, only a small proportion (2 out of 15) showed the high level of involvement displayed by most of the children who had an imaginary companion. Apparently, children vary in the extent to which they become absorbed in role play, even when encouraged to do so.

This study highlights the possibility that part of the variation among children in their disposition toward role play – and by implication in their disposition toward simulation – reflects a stable, underlying personality dimension. Some children engage in role play early and often, and they become absorbed in this type of pretence. Other children, by contrast, are not inclined to such play and engage in it less effectively. Longitudinal research provides support for the speculation that such individual differences emerge quite early. Linda Acredolo and her colleagues observed children engaged in free play at 11, 15, 19 and 24 months (Acredolo, Goodwyn and Fulmer, 1995). At each time-point, they measured the extent to which children played either with toys conducive to fantasy play including role play, for example a doll or toy telephone, or with toys that called for sensory-motor exploration and manipulation, for example shapes or boxes. When the children were 4 years old, those who had an imaginary companion proved to be those who had preferred playing with the fantasy as opposed to the manipulation toys.

The most persuasive evidence for early and stable endogenous differences in the disposition toward fantasy comes from children with autism. These children appear to understand the logic of pretence. For example, they can make sense of the type of pretend causal transformations that were described in the previous chapter (Kavanaugh and Harris, 1994). However, unless prompted to do so, children with autism rarely engage in pretend play themselves (Harris, 1993; Harris and Leevers, 2000b). Indeed, the absence of pretend play at 18 months of age is associated with a later diagnosis of autism (Baron-Cohen et al., 1996). Moreover, as would be expected on the above analysis, children with autism perform quite poorly on the false belief task even when compared to normal or retarded children of the same mental age (Baron-Cohen, Leslie and Frith, 1985; Yirmiya et al., 1998). In future research, it will be informative to assess whether autistic children are limited at all types of pretend play. The account that I have presented implies that it is role play in particular rather than pretend play in general that facilitates mental state understanding. Accordingly, we might expect autistic children to be especially limited in role play.

In summary, for the time being there is no firm answer to the question of why children vary in the extent and richness of their role play. It is likely that children vary in the opportunities and encouragement that they receive for this type of play. At the same time, we may reasonably speculate about the existence of stable and endogenous individual differences in this type of pretence. Such stability has been observed among normal children. Children with autism also display an enduring restriction in their pretend play, although it is not yet clear whether that restriction includes all types of pretence or whether it is particularly marked in the case of role play. Whatever the explanation for the differences among children in their disposition toward role play, that variation appears to be consequential for later cognitive development. Children who engage in more role play turn out to be better able to view a situation from another person's point of view, as indexed by various measures of mental state understanding. We may now turn to a more wide-ranging question about continuity. What happens to children's role play as they get older? Does it die away or are there analogues to be found in adulthood?

Absorption in a Pretence: Continuities Between Children and Adults

I have argued that when children enact a role, they imagine the world from the point of view of another person. Do we find anything akin to this process among adults? One likely context for such imaginative involvement is reading. Whether reading a biography, a historical narrative or a novel, adult readers are invited to view the world from a point of view that is not their own. Below, I begin to consider the intriguing parallels between children's absorption in make-believe and adults' engagement with a text in more detail.

Under normal circumstances, our everyday consciousness includes an awareness of time, space and identity as a constant backdrop. Barring a psychotic interlude, or a sudden awakening from deep sleep in an unfamiliar environment, we are aware at some level of the current time, of where we are, and of who we are (Dodd and Bucci, 1987; Neisser, 1967, p. 286). Yet when we are absorbed in a narrative, current reality is temporarily held in abeyance while we focus attention on the world of the narrative. We start to locate ourselves inside that world rather than in the real world and events that befall the protagonists loom large in our consciousness.

The information that we have about a given protagonist can vary. Sometimes, we are made privy to his or her innermost thoughts and feelings. A private monologue might reveal how the world appears to that character. At other times, we are not provided with such personal information. We share a given protagonist's knowledge of the ongoing events, but we must infer their thoughts and emotions from what they say and do. We move in the same space as them but do not have full access to their point of view. Finally, the narrative may provide us with information that is pertinent to a particular character, but as yet outside of his or her purview. Some of the most charged moments in fiction and drama occur when we have such privileged access and watch as a particular character – whether it is Little Red Riding Hood or Othello – acts in ignorance of the true situation. In short, various structural devices serve to modulate the information that is available to us about a given protagonist within the world of the narrative. Nonetheless, and this is a central assumption of this chapter, once the state of narrative absorption has been evoked, we begin to share the same spatial and temporal framework as the protagonist. What is subjectively near or far, in the present versus in the past, must now be measured not in terms of the real world but in terms of the narrative world.

Recent research on text-processing provides persuasive evidence that the concept of a subjective displacement into the narrative world is not just a loose metaphor. This research suggests that readers mentally situate themselves at a particular locus within the scene being described, typically one that is coincident with or close to a central character. From that locus, a cognitive 'spotlight' is emitted that illuminates certain objects and events in the narrative and leaves others in obscurity. Well-lit objects are more mentally available than those left in darkness. Rinck and Bower (1995) demonstrated this point by having adults remember the room layout of a building. They then read about the movements of a protagonist from one room to another within the building. In the course of the narratives, readers were probed with sentences that referred to various items of furniture and equipment in the building. The consistent finding was that probes about items near the current location of the protagonist led to faster responses than probes about more distant items – including items that had been visited earlier. By implication, readers mentally travelled around the building along with the protagonist. As they did so, their cognitive spotlight lit up an area specified by their current subjective position.

Similar results emerged in an experiment by Glenberg, Meyer and Lindem (1987). Adults read a text about a runner who either put on or removed his sweatshirt and then went jogging round the lake. If then asked whether the word 'sweatshirt' had occurred in the story, readers answered more quickly if the runner had put on his sweatshirt rather than removed it. Again, the implication is that readers move their spotlight along with the main character so that information about the sweatshirt is retrieved more readily if it falls within that spotlight rather than further back, and outside of its arc. More generally, this line of research shows that it is reasonable to suppose that readers of fiction adopt a position within the spatio-temporal framework of the text (Bower and Morrow, 1990). By adopting that mental locus, certain objects are rendered salient and cognitively accessible whereas others fade into the background.

Granted that readers situate themselves mentally with the same spatio-temporal framework as the story protagonist, is there any sense in which they also come to adopt the same point of view as that protagonist? Recall that children do appear to engage in such perspective-taking when they engage in role play: they frequently give voice to the perceptual experiences, sensations, needs and emotions of a protagonist.

One suggestive piece of evidence was reported by Black, Turner and Bower (1979). Readers were introduced to a story character by the following simple sentence: 'Bill was sitting in the living room reading the paper'. If readers adopt the same point of view as Bill, they should find it easier to process and remember sentences that describe subsequent events from that point of view. Suppose that a second protagonist, John, makes his way to the living room. From Bill's point of view, John would be seen as entering the living room rather than leaving the adjacent room. So, if readers share Bill's point of view, they should find it easier to process the sentence if it continues with a deictic verb which fits that point of view – as in (a) but not (b).

(a)   '. . . when John *came* into the room.'
(b)   '. . . when John *went* into the room.'

The same claim can be extended to other deictic verbs of motion, such as *bring* and *take*. If we read a sentence such as: 'Fred was just sitting down by the fire' and we then mentally settle down alongside Fred, we should find it easier to process the sentence if it continues in a fashion that is consistent with that point of view – as in (a) but not (b).

(a)   '. . . when his faithful dog *brought* him his slippers.'
(b)   '. . . when his faithful dog *took* him his slippers.'

In line with these predictions, adults read the critical final sections of the sentences more quickly if they included the verb that was consistent rather than inconsistent with the protagonist's viewpoint. Figure 3.2 illustrates this pattern of results.

Readers were also more accurate in remembering the verb if they were asked to recall sentences like (a) as opposed to (b). By implication, readers adopted the protagonist's point of view so that a movement into the same room as the protagonist was encoded as *coming* rather than *going*. Accordingly, even if the story stated that someone

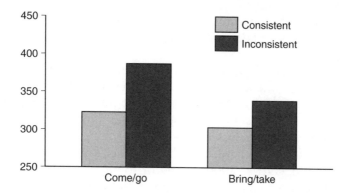

Figure 3.2 Reading time per syllable by verb type and consistency.

went into the same room as the main character, readers mentally converted it into an entry as opposed to an exit, and substituted the verb *came* in their recall.

Overall, these findings provide encouraging support for the idea that there are important continuities between children's role play and adults' reading of fiction. First, both the role player and the reader mentally locate themselves inside an imaginary space. Second, the particular point of view that they adopt within that space appears to depend on the main protagonist. Both the role player and the reader view events from the point of view of a fictional protagonist. There is, however, a powerful objection to this line of speculation. A long tradition of research, dating back to Piaget's early research on egocentricity, suggests that young children are quite firmly anchored in their own point of view. When asked to imagine how a scene might look to another person with a different perspective, they frequently claim that the other person would have the same view as themselves. Admittedly, more recent experimental work, using less complicated scenes than the one used by Piaget (Flavell, 1978; Flavell, Everett, Croft and Flavell, 1981) and posing the questions in the more familiar context of hiding from another person (Hughes and Donaldson, 1979), has suggested that even preschoolers have some ability to imagine another person's perspectives. Still, the notion that such perspectival shifts are a robust and stable disposition, initially manifested in children's role play – as illustrated in the examples given at the beginning of this chapter – and eventually deployed in adults' story comprehension, scarcely fits the standard developmental assumption that young children are prone to egocentricity.

One way to place the assertion of continuity on a more secure footing is to find out whether very young children approach narratives in the same way as adults. Do they also adopt the point of view of the protagonist and view subsequent actions and movements as if from that point of view? To answer this question, we embedded test sentences in stories about characters who were well known to young children (Rall and Harris, 2000). Parts of these stories maintained a consistent point of view, whereas others did not. Compare, for instance, example (a) with example (b):

(a) 'Little Red Riding Hood was sitting in her bedroom when her mother *came* in and asked her to go to Grandmother's house.'
(b) 'Cinderella was sitting on the chair by the fireplace, dreaming about the ball. Then her fairy godmother *went* into the cottage.'

Children aged 3 and 4 years were asked to recall what they had heard. We looked at their recall efforts to see whether they managed to recall the verb verbatim, whether they switched verbs by substituting one member of a verb pair for the other (e.g. switched 'came' and 'went' or 'bring' and 'take'), introduced a neutral verb with no deictic component (e.g. 'walk') or made no response at all. Figure 3.3 shows how often children produced a response in each of these four categories depending on whether the verb in question was or was not consistent with the point of view of the protagonist.

Figure 3.3 shows that verbatim recall was much more likely when the verb was consistent with the point of view of the protagonist. Conversely, switched verbs were much more likely when the verb was inconsistent with the point of view of the protagonist. The other two response patterns (the introduction of a neutral verb and the failure to make a response) were not affected by the consistency of the verb. Thus, 3- and 4-year-old children shift their point of view when listening to a story, just like adults. This evidence reinforces the claim that young children can solve simple visual perspective-taking tasks. At the same time, it shows that such perspectival shifts are not just an occa-

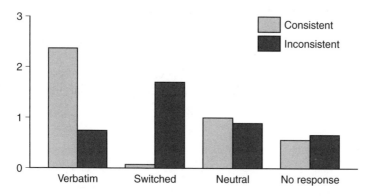

Figure 3.3   Mean number of four types of recall responses by consistency.

sional strategy that children deploy to override their predominantly egocentric stance. Rather, they spontaneously and tenaciously maintain an alternative point of view because they switch inconsistent verbs so as to render them consistent with that alternative perspective.

These results provide encouraging support for the proposal that there is an important continuity from early childhood into adulthood. In their early role play, young children situate themselves in an imagined world and process events from the point of view of a pretend protagonist. Similarly, when they start to listen to narratives, children mentally locate themselves within the narrative world and process events from the point of view of the narrative protagonist. This same altercentric mode is found among adult readers and regulates the ease with which they take in narrative information. These experimental findings bear out our subjective experience of fiction. Even when a fictional scene is not described in graphic detail, our absorption can lend it a subjective immediacy. As a result, the apparent proximity of our actual surroundings fades. Indeed, when we stop reading, it may take a few moments before the landscape of the narrative world recedes from consciousness, and the familiar contours of the actual world reassert themselves.

Admittedly, there are also certain obvious discontinuities between role play and narrative absorption. Role play is not regulated by input from an author in the way that narrative absorption is: children themselves typically invent the roles that they play, or at least elaborate on the suggestions of older siblings and caretakers. In addition, role play involves the production of actions and utterances whereas narrative absorption has no overt consequences. Still, these differences should not mask the basic continuity: in each case, there is absorption into an imagined world so that what counts as centre-stage, or here and now, is temporarily recalibrated. In the next chapter, I examine the emotional repercussions of such absorption.

Conclusions

In this chapter, I have described a form of pretend play that is both common and surprising: role play in which the child acts out the role of Mummy or Pirate. Even 2-year-olds engage in this form of pretend play, especially with siblings and friends, and in so doing they display, through a variety of indices, their absorption in the pretend role: they use terms of reference that are appropriate for that new identity; they adjust their tone of voice; and they express the sensations and emotions appropriate to that role.

According to simulation theory, there is a close link between the process that underpins role play and the process that yields a solution to classic theory of mind tasks. In each case, children must view the world through the eyes of another person, temporarily setting aside current reality. Granted this conceptual link, simulation theory predicts that individual differences in the frequency of role play will correlate with performance on theory of mind tasks, especially assessments of belief. Recent studies confirm this association.

The nature and origin of these individual differences in role play remain uncertain. They may reflect variation in environmental support, especially in the encouragement toward joint role play provided by older siblings; they may reflect stable and endogenous variation in the tendency to be absorbed in an imagined role; or they may reflect a mix of both factors.

Research on narrative comprehension with adults points to an equivalent process: readers mentally travel alongside a protagonist and view the landscape from that projected point of view. Preschool children, despite their alleged egocentricity, readily engage in such perspectival shifts when they listen to a story. The implication is that children and adults alike are equipped to set reality aside and to take up the point of view of a protagonist situated in an imagined landscape.

Notes

1 For further discussion of the argument that such meta-theories are implausible and unparsimonious, see Harris (1992).

2 These studies show that preschool children do not realize that knowledge about the content of a given piece of pretence is a necessary condition for carrying out that pretence. This does not mean that they are altogether incapable of finding any link between pretending and thinking when prompted to do so. For example, Bruell and Woolley (1998) found that 3-year-olds could use information about an actor's thoughts, illustrated in the form of a thought bubble, to infer what the actor might be pretending. Similarly, Custer (1996) found that 3-year-olds could use information about an actor's pretence to infer what he or she was thinking, as illustrated in a thought bubble. Moreover, they performed better on this task than a closely matched assessment of false belief understanding – again involving thought bubbles. Taken together, these experiments show that 3-year-olds can infer the thoughts that accompany a given act of pretence, and vice versa. However, the children were provided with a highly unusual access to the actor's likely thoughts, namely a thought bubble, and each study began with training in the use of thought bubbles.

When children are asked about pretending in a less artificial context, the pattern of findings is mixed. Rosen, Schwebel and Singer (1997) report that 4-year-olds could recognize acts of pretence – for example, most of them correctly judged that Barney and friends (depicted on video) were just pretending to gallop like a horse – but only a minority correctly inferred the thoughts (e.g. thinking about being a horse) that would accompany such pretending. Indeed, 4-year-olds were less accurate at inferring pretend thoughts than mistaken beliefs on standard theory of mind tasks. A different pattern was obtained by Hickling, Wellman and Gottfried (1997). Three-year-olds were more accurate at inferring pretend thoughts than mistaken beliefs in two closely matched tasks.

Summing up, there are some indications that 3-year-olds are able to identify the thoughts that typically accompany an act of pretence. In that sense, they appreciate that pretence typically combines acting and thinking. At the same time, the results of Lillard (1993) and Joseph (1998) show that 3-year-olds and even 4-year-olds do not regard the presence or absence of particular thoughts as a constraint on what an actor can pretend. Hence, it is not clear that their understanding of the role of thinking in pretence is sufficiently systematic and robust to help them understand the wider role of mental representation, especially in the context of belief-based action. In that latter context, the child does need to understand that thoughts are not simply a typical accompaniment to action but that it is precisely the presence or absence of particular thoughts that constrains what an actor will do.

3   Peter Carruthers (personal communication) has proposed a third way to think about the relationship between role play and false belief understanding, based on a modular account of children's developing understanding of mind. He suggests that when children engage in role play, they need to recruit a module which (amongst other things) processes goal-directed agency. This module – dubbed SAM by Baron-Cohen (1995) – is assumed to feed into and activate ToMM, a module that processes beliefs. Thus, given its dependence on SAM, frequent role play serves as a catalyst for ToMM. A straightforward prediction of this modular account is that greater activation of SAM – indexed, for example, by greater frequency of desire talk – should eventually cause a greater activation of ToMM – indexed, for example, by greater frequency of belief talk. However, existing data provide, at best, dubious support for this prediction. Bartsch and Wellman (1995, p. 133) found no evidence that children who talk more about desire early on subsequently talk either more often or at an earlier age about belief. Moreover, a more demanding assessment of children's talk about desire – the frequency with which they couched their *explanations* in terms of desire – also showed no relationship to either the later frequency or the age of onset of belief talk. Only one tantalizing relationship between desire and belief talk was found: the age of onset of desire explanations was correlated with the age of onset of genuine references to belief. Yet even this correlation provides only equivocal support for a modular account. A simpler interpretation is that some children acquire language more quickly than others, and therefore pass various language landmarks earlier than others. A modular account would be supported only if it could be shown that the relationship between the onset of desire explanation and subsequent reference to belief remains robust, even when children's overall language ability (as indexed by MLU, for example), is partialled out.

A further proposal made by Carruthers is that role play (in common with other forms of early activity such as interaction with siblings) might provide input requiring an interpretation by ToMM. Hence, role play provides a type of exercise or training ground for ToMM. However, without further specification concerning the way that role play provides direct input for ToMM to set to work on, it is not clear how this proposal differs from the two proposals discussed in chapter 3.

4   Some researchers have looked for, and found, a correlation between pretend play and mental state understanding, but they have used an omnibus measure of pretend play in which no differentiation is made between role play and object-directed pretend play (e.g. Hughes and Dunn, 1997).

5   Schwebel et al. (1999) report a link with understanding the distinction

between reality and appearance, but not with understanding false belief. However, in each study children were given more than one false belief task, and may have become confused or inattentive because a sizeable proportion failed control questions.

6   Youngblade and Dunn (1995), unlike Astington and Jenkins (1995), found no link between explicit role assignment (which they refer to simply as role play) and false belief understanding. However, this discrepancy can probably be explained by the difference in the age at which pretend play was assessed: 33 months in the case of Youngblade and Dunn (1995); and approximately 51 months, range = 37 to 65 months, in the case of Astington and Jenkins (1995). Explicit role assignment is rare among 2-year-olds (Dunn and Dale, 1984; Howes and Matheson, 1992), so that little variance would be expected at this age. Consistent with this suggestion, the toddlers observed by Youngblade and Dunn (1995) rarely engaged in explicit role assignment (3 per cent of their pretend bouts), whereas the preschoolers observed by Astington and Jenkins (1995) did so more often (14.6 per cent of their pretend bouts).

7   Given that children with autism have difficulties with the false belief task (Yirmiya, Erel, Shaked and Solomonica-Levi, 1998), it is interesting to note that clinical reports of such children pretending to be a machine are not uncommon. I thank Maureen Dunne for this observation.

8   Two unpublished studies provide additional evidence. Nielsen and Dissanayake (in press) examined the correlation between several types of pretend play and belief understanding among 3- and 4-year-olds. They found that the tendency to attribute animate properties to a doll (e.g. by talking for it, or to it) was associated with good performance on belief tasks but, contrary to the present hypothesis, object substitution was also correlated. On the other hand, Dockett and Smith (1995) gave preschoolers (with an average age of 4 years 3 months) training in socio-dramatic play (Christie, 1985). Although such training includes a variety of elements, it is likely to promote the type of role play that I have emphasized. Consistent with the present hypothesis, this training led to sharp improvements (relative to a pre-test, and relative to untrained controls) on a variety of belief tasks. In future research, a comparison of the effects of different types of training study is likely to be especially informative in assessing the contribution that pretend play makes to later mental state understanding.

4

Imagination and Emotion

In chapter 2, I claimed that young children can construct a make-believe world that is causally coherent. I also intimated that they grasp the distinction between the make-believe world and the real world even if they attribute the same causal structure to each. This portrait of young children as imaginative but clear-eyed may strike some as overdrawn. Surely, pretence and fantasy is a context in which children's hopes and fears carry them to the point where they begin to confuse fantasy and reality.

In support of this more sceptical line of argument, consider the phenomenon described in the previous chapter: many children invent an imaginary companion with whom they play for a sustained period of weeks or months. In the course of such play, they often act as if the playmate had taken on an independent life of its own, with all the emotional repercussions that that might entail. For example, children express anger at various misdemeanours allegedly carried out by imaginary companions, or they engage in arguments with them (Taylor, 1998, p. 25). One child insisted that the television be turned on when the house was left empty so that an imaginary companion would not be lonely or bored (Taylor, Cartwright and Carlson, 1993). When a 3-year-old with an imaginary pony as a companion was taken to an actual horse show, the child's day was ruined because he 'discovered' on arriving at the show that the imaginary pony had made other plans and was not there (Taylor, 1998, p. 212). The child was unable to solve the problem by simply pretending that the pony was there. In these various cases, the companion invented by the child appears to take on an independent existence and to drive the child's emotional reactions, be they anger, concern or disappointment.

Consider also children's fear of monsters and other imaginary creatures. Jersild (1943) observed that this type of fear is relatively uncommon at 2 years of age but becomes more widespread at around 5 years of age. The fear appears to be genuine – children are not simply finding an excuse to avoid going to bed. Indeed, such fears can intrude in the daytime and restrict children's movements. For example, Newson and Newson describe a 4-year-old who had imagined monkeys living in the cellar. 'That's why he won't go down in the cellar, because they might get him', his mother explained (Newson and Newson, 1968, p. 184). Such fears are not usually amenable to rational argument. They persist despite repeated verbal reassurance from the parents that there are no monsters – or ghosts – or witches (Jersild and Holmes, 1935). On the other hand, children can sometimes overcome their fear by creative redeployment of their imagination, for example when a parent or therapist joins the child in a game of make-believe and carefully incorporates the feared creature into an imagined scenario that is less threatening (Jersild and Holmes, 1935; King, Cranstoun and Josephs, 1989).

So, in the case of both imaginary companions and monsters, children's emotional reactions can be vigorous. They may become distressed at a meeting that fails to take place, even though the companion and the meeting are entirely fictitious, or they may fear an encounter even though the monster and the potential encounter are both a product of their imagination. A plausible implication is that children create an imaginary entity, elaborate on their invention – 'My companion is not there' or 'The monster might be waiting for me in the dark' – and start to react as if these fictitious premises were literally true by becoming distressed or fearful. Such an interpretation implies that children's fantasy life is not always tagged in a clear and unequivocal fashion as mere fantasy: the possibilities that have been conjured up begin to be treated as emotionally charged actualities.

There is, however, an alternative way to interpret these emotional reactions. Consider the impact of the theatre or the cinema. Even as adults, we may experience a quickening of our heart rate when the heroine enters alien territory. We know full well that she and the dangers that she faces are mere fictions. Yet these imaginary premises can drive our emotional system, including its physiological components. We must admit, therefore, that adults can react with strong emotion to a situation that is definitely recognized as make-believe. This raises the possibility that children might be aware that their absent companion or the monster waiting in the dark are purely imaginary even as they react with distress or fear. This interpretation denies that young children conceive of the relationship between fantasy and reality in a radically different way from adults. It implies instead that even if children and adults alike are able to maintain an epistemic distinction between the domains of fantasy and reality, emotion can be activated by material from each domain.

In summary, we have two different accounts of children's emotional reactions to imaginary entities. On the one hand, perhaps misled by the fertility of their own imagination, children invest its products with a quasi-reality. Alternatively, they know full well that what they miss or fear is imaginary but remain sad or fearful nonetheless, their emotion being aroused narrowly and directly by the imaginary input. As a first step in assessing these two accounts, we can begin by asking whether children do confuse fantasy with reality, as the first hypothesis implies.

Confusion of Fantasy and Reality?

In the previous chapter, I considered a somewhat contentious issue about young children's understanding of pretence – do they realize that someone engaged in pretence is *ipso facto* entertaining a particular mental representation of whatever it is that they are pretending? I concluded that children of 2 or 3 years of age might be able to engage in pretend play, and indeed understand their partner's pretence, without understanding the role of mental representation. Here, we consider a separate and more straightforward issue. Do young children realize that the creatures and events that they invent in their pretend play are purely imaginary and not real? Several studies are now available to answer this question. In a series of experiments, Henry Wellman and his colleagues (Wellman and Estes, 1986; Estes, Wellman and Woolley, 1989) told children about two different objects, a real object on the one hand, and a 'mental' object on the other. For example, the children might be told about two different story characters, one who actually has a dog and another who is only pretending to have one. The children were then asked to make various judgements about what the two characters could do. Even 3-year-olds correctly judged that only the character who actually had a dog could touch it, see it and so forth. Overall, this line of research shows that preschool children have a firm grasp of the difference between a real object and an object that is merely being conjured up by the mind. They appreciate that real objects are available to perceptual inspection, whereas mental objects are not, and conversely that mental objects can be transformed by an act of the imagination, whereas real objects cannot.

At first glance, these findings immediately rule out the first account. They imply that young children grasp the non-real status of imaginary creatures including monsters and imaginary companions. The way seems clear, therefore, to explore the second account. However, this conclusion would be premature. The entities that Wellman and his colleagues asked children about were everyday objects with no obvious emotional cathexis. Perhaps children can be quite clear about the distinction between fantasy and reality with respect to prosaic objects but equivocate with respect to more emotionally charged objects.

To explore this possibility, we asked children to imagine special and potentially frightening creatures: a monster, a ghost and a witch (Harris, Brown, Marriott, Whittall and Harmer, 1991, experiment 1). To do this, children were encouraged to 'make a picture in their head' of the creature in question. Next, children were asked to make two judgements about each imagined creature: *Was it real? And could it be seen by the experimenter?* Two control conditions were included for comparison purposes, one in which the children were asked to imagine everyday, neutral objects (a balloon, a cup and a pair of scissors) and a second in which they were shown those same everyday objects. In each case, questions about reality and visibility were posed. In line with the findings of Wellman and his colleagues, we expected children to differentiate between these last two conditions, agreeing that the everyday objects that they had been shown, but not those that they imagined, were real and visible. The interesting question was how children would judge the special and potentially frightening objects, the imagined ghost, witch and monster. Would children judge them to be like the real, everyday objects that they were shown or like the everyday objects that they merely imagined?

Figure 4.1 shows the proportion of 'realist' (i.e. positive) judgements that children made in the three conditions. They were scored for the number of realist replies that they made (out of a possible total of 6). Our expectations for the two control conditions were clearly borne out. Children gave many realist judgements about the everyday ob-

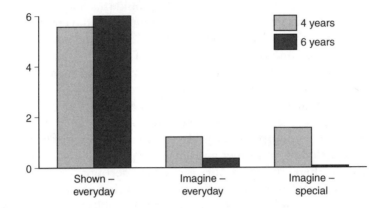

Figure 4.1   Mean number of realist responses by age and type of object.

jects that we had shown them. They agreed, for example, that the cup or the pair of scissors could be seen by the experimenter and were indeed real. Conversely, when they imagined such everyday objects, they denied that the experimenter could see them, and they denied that they were real. The critical result was their judgement about the special and potentially frightening objects that they had imagined. The children were quite systematic in denying that these creatures were real or could be seen. In fact, their judgements were very similar to those that they made for the everyday objects that they had imagined. The implication is, therefore, that children's ability to distinguish fantasy from reality includes not just everyday objects that are emotionally neutral, but extends to more exotic and fearsome creatures as well.

Still, one might reasonably ask whether the special entities that the children imagined were truly frightening. Imaginary creatures, such as a monster, might be associated with fear under some conditions, but not in the context of the experiment as it was carried out. Children were seated in a familiar, well-lit classroom and they were interviewed by an adult who had spent some time at the school getting to know them. All they were asked to do was to 'make a picture in their head' of a monster, ghost or witch as the case might be. Under these circumstances, children might have felt no fear.

Accordingly, in a follow-up experiment, we attempted to make the

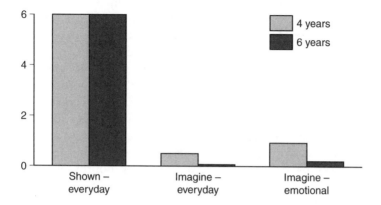

Figure 4.2 Mean number of realist responses by age and type of object.

situation somewhat more frightening (Harris et al., 1991, experiment 2). We deployed the children's own imagination to this end. Specifically, the first experiment was repeated but with one important change. Having imagined one of the special creatures – the witch, or ghost or monster – children were asked to imagine the creature chasing after them as they ran away.[1] It was assumed that this supplement would be mildly frightening for the children in the same way that a fairy story can be frightening if it describes scenes in which a child protagonist is threatened by a witch or monster. To check the effectiveness of this manipulation, children were asked to say whether or not they felt frightened.

The results for children's judgements are shown in figure 4.2. It is evident that the pattern is very similar to the one that we found in the first experiment. Children again distinguished sharply between the everyday objects that they were shown and the everyday objects that they imagined. They also continued to judge the imagined ghost, witch and monster in much the same way as the imagined cup, balloon or pair of scissors. Nevertheless, children often acknowledged that they felt afraid when they imagined the creature chasing after them. Every child did not make this acknowledgement on every occasion, but it was made often enough to suggest that the manipulation had had an effect.

As a final check on children's grasp of the fantasy–reality distinction, we carried out a study of children with imaginary companions (Goy and Harris, 1990). In the experiments that I have described so far, we had selected children from a variety of schools in terms of their age. We made no special effort to identify children who were especially imaginative, or who were afraid of monsters and ghosts. Arguably, confusion between fantasy and reality might be particularly likely among children who are prone to invent imaginary creatures rather than typical of all young children. Confusion might also be more probable if the imaginary creature has not just been conjured up in the last few minutes, as in the experiments described so far, but has been part of the child's make-believe world for weeks or months, as is often the case for an imaginary companion. For these reasons, our assessment of children with imaginary companions was especially interesting. With the help of parents' reports, we identified children falling in this select group, and asked them about the status of their imaginary companions. In addition, we interviewed a comparison group of children equivalent in age but lacking an imaginary companion.

The full experiment involved three parts. In an initial phase, the children were shown pictures of two children and told that one had just been given a puppy, whereas the other one was just pretending to have one. They were asked which child could really stroke her puppy, and which child could only pretend to do so. In addition, they were asked whose puppy they themselves could stroke if they 'went to visit these children'. In a second experimental phase, the same procedure was used, except that questions were posed about two children, one of whom had a real little brother, whereas the other had only a pretend brother and the questions were about holding hands. The third phase was administered only to the children with imaginary companions. They were shown two pictures of themselves. In one picture, the experimenter described them as playing with their best friend at nursery school, and in the other playing with their imaginary friend. Children were then asked to say which friend they could really hear, and which friend they could only pretend to hear. In addition, they were asked which friend the experimenter could really hear.

Whether or not they had an imaginary companion, children proved to be very accurate in answering all the questions that they were asked. Only one or two children ever made any errors. We found no evidence that the children with imaginary companions formed a special group. Whether we asked them about pretending to have a puppy, about pretending to have a brother, or directly about their own imaginary companion, they were clear about the status of such make-believe companions – just as clear as the children with no history of an imaginary companion. Taylor et al. (1993a) subsequently obtained similar results. Irrespective of whether they had an imaginary companion, 3- to 5-year-old children could differentiate between the properties of a pretend as compared to a real entity.[2]

Overall, this series of experiments tells a highly consistent story. Preschool children can distinguish between reality and make-believe. They realize that an object that they can see is real and is open to inspection by others, whereas an imaginary creature is not, even if it arouses feelings of fear or attachment, and even if it has been part of their imaginative life for weeks or months. We can therefore reject our first hypothesis: when children show an emotional reaction to an imaginary creature, it is not because of any confusion on their part about what is real and what is imaginary.[3]

Fiction and Emotion

We may turn now to the alternative interpretation, the proposal that fictional entities can arouse our emotional system at any point in the life cycle, even when they are recognized as fictions. If a distinction between the real world and the pretend world is established early in life, this second interpretation becomes attractive. We may spell out this interpretation in terms of the following, more detailed hypothesis. Children and adults alike have the capacity for 'absorption' in a pretend world. Phenomenologically, we are all familiar with this state of absorption. It occurs when we become lost in a good film or novel. In the previous chapter, I argued that both as young children engaged in pretend play, and also as readers of a text, we can take up a vantage-point within an imagined spatio-temporal framework. That vantage-point is normally specified by the locus of the main protagonist and it determines what we judge to be in the foreground, to be close in time or space. This hypothesis offers a plausible explanation of the way that imagined, as opposed to actual, inputs impinge on our emotional system. Temporarily, we set aside the current world with its anxieties and problems, and we live instead in the imagined world. Once we enter that state of absorption, it is the events occurring within the imagined world that drive our emotional system. Indeed, our emotional response to those events is heightened by their being viewed alongside, or from the perspective of, the main protagonists. We share their aspirations and disappointments.

Contemporary accounts of emotion assign a key role to the appraisal process by which the ongoing situation is coded for various critical attributes, such as the likelihood of loss or gain. The present hypothesis assumes that once absorbed into an imagined world, these appraisal processes are set to work on the events of that world. They will be appraised from the particular vantage-point that has been adopted within it. More specifically, we do not appraise the inputs from a perspective outside of that imagined framework, although in principle such a stance is available to us. Thus, any distinction that we might potentially make between imagined and actual input is not fed into the appraisal system. As a result, our appraisal of imagined input is, in key respects, equivalent to that for actual input. Both types of input are conveyed directly to the appraisal system. Admittedly, imagined input can be analysed for its ontological status. We can judge it to be 'just a story', 'a remote possibility in the future' or 'something that could have easily happened but didn't'. However, on the present hypothesis, the results of that ontological analysis do not necessarily impinge on, or redirect, the appraisal processes. Figure 4.3 illustrates this hypothesis in terms of a flow diagram. It shows how an event can be independently analysed for its ontological status on the one hand, and appraised for its emotional implications on the other.

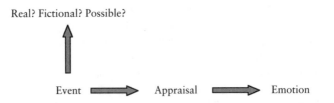

Figure 4.3   A flow diagram showing how an event can be appraised for its emotional significance independent of the status of the event

As we shall see, this hypothesis needs some refinement and elaboration. For the moment, however, its simplicity makes it worth exploring. An important implication is that, for much of the life cycle, human beings respond to imagined input with a pattern of cognitive and emotional processes that mirrors their response to the equivalent, real input. We may consider various sources of evidence for this claim:

cognitive processes as indexed by reaction times, and emotional processes as indexed by autonomic activation and by the modulation of simple reflexes.

Cognitive Processes

A straightforward prediction from figure 4.3 is that when adults process an imagined event, they work out its emotional implications, and more specifically, they work out its emotional implications from the point of view of the protagonist who is currently in focus. Research on story comprehension by adults has mainly concentrated on the processing of causal and spatial information rather than emotional information. Nonetheless, recent studies provide good support for this prediction. For example, Gernsbacher, Goldsmith and Robertson (1992) asked adults to read stories in which the main protagonist was likely to feel a particular emotion. One such story was as follows:

> Joe worked at the local 7–11 to get spending money while in school. One night, his best friend, Tom, came in to buy soda. Joe needed to go back to the storage room for a second. While he was away, Tom noticed the cash register was open. From the open drawer Tom quickly took a ten dollar bill. Later, Tom learned that Joe had been fired from the 7–11 because the cash in the till had been short that night.

Readers were then probed with emotion terms that they had to pronounce as quickly as possible. The key finding was that readers were faster to pronounce the emotion term if it coincided with the likely emotion of the protagonist in focus at the end of the story, namely Tom. For example, *guilt* was pronounced more quickly after the above story than less appropriate terms such as *proud* or *shy*. By implication, before the term was explicitly presented, readers had appraised the situation from Tom's perspective so that the concept of guilt was activated, or at least rapidly accessible.

In the previous chapter, I argued that readers not only adopt a similar point of view to a given protagonist, but they also mentally 'track' that protagonist as he or she navigates through the imagined landscape. If we extend that assumption to the processing of emotion, we should expect readers to update their appraisal of the protagonist's emotional state as the plot unfolds. De Vega, León and Díaz (1996) examined this issue by composing stories with two successive episodes. In 'cumulative context' stories, both the first and the second episode made it likely that the main protagonist would feel a particular emotion. For example, in one story a man receives an invitation from an attractive woman, and subsequently a great deal of attention from her, so that he is likely to feel *flattered* rather than *insecure* throughout. In 'shifting context' stories, the second episode produced an unexpected turn of events so that the protagonist's emotional state would be likely to change. For example, the protagonist initially receives an ambiguous invitation from an attractive woman, but subsequently she gives him her undivided attention, so that initially he is likely to feel *insecure* but then *flattered*. Across both 'cumulative' and 'shifting' episodes, adults were quicker to read sentences if they attributed an emotion, or even an expressive behaviour (e.g. smiling or gaze-aversion), that was consistent rather than inconsistent with the protagonist's probable current state. Taking these two studies together, they suggest that readers monitor the unfolding narrative, keeping track of its cumulative or shifting emotional implications for the protagonist who is centre-stage.

Persuasive evidence for the central role of the protagonist in guiding this monitoring process has emerged from narratives in which the protagonist is not yet fully aware of a twist in the narrative situation. The device of the 'naive' protagonist is common in all sorts of genres. Little Red Hiding Hood, for example, does not realize that she is facing a wolf when she enters her grandmother's house. Othello does not realize that Desdemona's fidelity is unswerving when he accuses her. In such cases, the emotion that is felt by the protagonist does not depend on the objective situation – the danger that confronts Little Red Riding Hood or Desdemona's devotion to Othello – but on their ill-informed appraisal of that situation. Accordingly, we may ask how readers deal with such narratives. Do they focus on what the protagonist ought to feel, in the light of the objective situation, or on what the protagonist will feel, granted his or her point of view? To explore this question, we gave adults three types of narrative to read (Harris and Martin, 1999). In *standard* narratives, the protagonist was about to have a meeting with clear emotional implications – for example, to meet with a medical specialist to discuss the results of a brain scan. In *informed* narratives, the protagonist was given information ahead of the meeting that dramatically altered its emotional implications – for example, the protagonist was told that the scan had ruled out any danger of a tumour. Finally, in *uninformed* narratives, the protagonist did not yet have access to such information – for example, the reader, but not the protagonist, was made aware of the reassuring outcome of the scan. In all three narratives, readers encountered a sentence that attributed an emotion to the protagonist, for example *relieved* or *anxious*.

Figure 4.4 shows how quickly adults read these sentences, depending on whether the emotion in question was or was not consistent with the actual situation. As would be expected from the findings described so far, in both the standard and the informed narratives, adults read the emotion attribution faster when it was consistent with the emotional implications of the objective situation. In the standard narrative, for example, they were quicker to read the target sentence if it described the protagonist as anxious – after all, the outcome of the scan remained unclear; in the informed narrative, they were quicker if it described the protagonist as relieved – given that the outcome of the scan was reassuring.

With the uninformed narratives, readers behaved differently. They were quicker to read the sentence if it attributed an emotion that was inconsistent with the objective situation, but was nonetheless warranted by the protagonist's ill-informed point of view. So, for the uninformed narrative above, readers were quicker to read the sentence if it described the protagonist as anxious rather than relieved, even though the objective situation (which readers already knew about) meant that

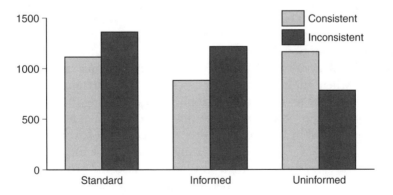

Figure 4.4 Mean reading time (msec) as a function of story version and whether the attributed emotion is consistent or inconsistent with the objective situation.

there were no objective grounds for anxiety. A plausible interpretation is that adults kept the point of view of the protagonist in mind as they read the narrative, even if that point of view ignored or ran counter to what they knew about the emotional implications of the objective situation.

Autonomic Activation

The evidence reviewed so far fits the idea that adults who entertain an imagined world appraise events from the point of view of a central protagonist within that world. Nevertheless, the findings are perfectly consistent with a 'cool' or non-empathic analysis. Readers might work out the implications of an imagined event and then attribute the relevant emotion to a protagonist in a purely cognitive fashion, without feeling any concurrent emotion themselves. On this interpretation, the output from the appraisal process is used to activate only the concept or idea of an emotion. Although a particular emotion, for example guilt, might be temporarily accessed and attributed to the protagonist in the imagined situation, thereby speeding reaction times to inputs that match, or are related to, that emotion, the emotion itself is not felt by readers themselves.

This cold-hearted analysis is plausible for many narrative encounters, but our everyday experience suggests that the act of imagining a situation sometimes provokes genuine emotion, and not merely the idea of an emotion. Is our everyday experience simply an illusion? Research that has used physiological measures rather than reaction times shows that under certain conditions the description of a hypothetical but emotionally charged scene can indeed move us, even at a visceral level. For example, Lang (1984) reviews various studies showing that when adults read a text describing a frightening encounter and they use the text as a set of prompts for deploying their imagination, some of the visceral accompaniments to fear (i.e., heart-rate acceleration and skin conductance) are triggered. Indeed, when they are given passages of descriptive text ranging from least to greatest fear content, they respond with a gradient of visceral arousal (Lang, Melamed and Hart, 1970, experiment 2). An increase in heart rate is especially likely if the text makes the encounter all the more vivid by including references not just to a frightening situation but to the reactions that normally accompany fear (e.g. muscle tension and rapid breathing), and if readers have been previously trained to imagine such reactions, and not just the situation itself (Lang, Kozak, Miller, Levin and McLean, 1980).

The imagery-based reactions of individual readers mirror the reactions that they would produce when confronted by an actual situation equivalent to the one being imagined. For example, if readers are given a text that prompts them to imagine an encounter with a snake, an increase in heart rate is especially marked among snake phobics – people who would display a similar pattern of cardiac acceleration when shown a live snake – but less marked among social phobics who are especially fearful of public speaking rather than snakes (Lang, Levin, Miller and Kozak, 1983).[4] More generally, when people write out a description of a situation that is of particular personal relevance to them, and then imagine being in that situation, they report more emotion, and they show more visceral signs of emotion, than if they imagine being in a situation presented to them by an experimenter (Velasco and Bond, 1998).

Taken together, these findings show that adults can drive their emotional system by an act of the imagination. If they are presented with a description of an emotionally charged situation, and they imagine experiencing that situation, presumably in the full knowledge that what is being described is not actually taking place, some of the standard physiological accompaniments to emotion, such as an increase in heart rate or changes in skin conductance, can be detected. Those visceral changes are especially likely when the description prompts them to focus on the responses and bodily sensations that typically accompany the emotion in question, and when it refers to a situation that is of personal relevance. Finally, as might be expected on the present account, it is worth noting that such physiological changes are especially evident among adults who score high rather than low on a paper-and-pencil test of role-playing ability (Gollnisch and Averill, 1993).[5]

Reflex Reactions: The Startle Response

A change of emotional state can reveal itself not just through autonomic responses such as an accelerated heart rate but also through an alteration in the strength or latency of basic reflexes. For example, when an animal or human being is fearful, they are more readily startled by a sudden stimulus (Lang, Bradley and Cuthbert, 1992). In com-

mon parlance, we would say that fear makes someone jumpy or jit-
tery. Accordingly, if we are able to provoke a genuine change to our
emotional state simply by imagining a frightening experience, then we
should observe a comparable alteration to our reflex startle reactions
– for example, we should react more intensely to a sudden loud noise.
Such a change in reactivity would provide strong evidence that a real
encounter and an imagined encounter can have an equivalent effect on
our emotional state. After all, it is possible to argue that adults can
somehow contrive deliberately to alter their heart rate to mimic the
reactions that occur when they are frightened, but it is less plausible to
argue that they can deliberately alter the magnitude of a sudden, brief
reaction such as the startle reflex.

Prima-facie evidence for the equivalence of fear that is provoked by
a real encounter and fear that occurs in the context of an imagined
encounter is provided by a familiar ploy of movie-makers. They create
a suspense-laden scene (the hero or heroine enters the haunted house
and climbs the stairs), and then introduce a sudden, but harmless,
stimulus – a window that slams shut or a cat that hisses. Against the
backdrop of prior suspense, the sudden stimulus precipitates a startle
reaction from the audience. A similar phenomenon can be reproduced
in the laboratory.

Vrana and Lang (1990) asked adults to study and remember two
different types of sentence. One type described a state of emotional
tension or fear, for example: 'I tense as the nurse slowly injects the
sharp needle into my upper arm and beads of sweat cover my fore-
head'. The other type described a state of pleasant relaxation, for example: 'I am relaxing on my living room couch looking out of the
window on a sunny autumn day'. Participants were then prompted to
recall either one or the other type of sentence. As they did so, they
were sometimes startled by a loud click. Startle responses were stronger
if they were concurrently in the process of recalling the sentence with
frightening as opposed to pleasant content. Particularly important for
the argument being developed here is the fact that the size of this increase in the startle reflex depended on the exact way that participants
recalled the sentences. Reflexes were especially marked if participants
had been instructed not to recall the sentence passively but to imagine
themselves undergoing the frightening experience described by it; they
were not so marked if participants had been instructed to repeat the
sentence silently to themselves, and weaker still if they had been instructed simply to ignore the sentence and relax.[6]

Thus, when adults are safely seated in an armchair but reading a text with emotional content, what they read has an impact on several cognitive and emotional processes. The idea or concept of the relevant emotion becomes more accessible. In addition, especially when they actively imagine themselves undergoing the emotional reaction described in the text, readers begin to reproduce some of the autonomic changes that normally accompany the emotion in question. For example, in the case of a frightening experience, their heart rate quickens. Finally, changes in their emotional state can be detected at a reflex level: if they imagine a tense or fearful situation, they are more readily startled by an unexpected stimulus. All of this evidence lends credence to the claim that adults resemble children in their emotional reaction to imaginary events. Even if they are aware that the input is purely fictional, it can nevertheless drive the emotional system.

Control Processes

I have proposed that when someone is absorbed in an imagined world, the events within that world are processed in the same way as real events.[7] That proposal makes sense of a considerable number of findings, but at the same time it offends common sense. When we are lost in a film or a book, we are indeed moved by fictional events, but their non-real status surely does impinge at some point on the way that we feel about them. When we remind ourselves that a fictional event is no more than a fiction, we appear to attenuate our emotional reaction. At the very least, we set in motion some type of override that moderates the standard functioning of our ordinary appraisal processes. Figure 4.5 illustrates how we might conceive of this regulatory process. As in figure 4.3, the direct link between input and appraisal allows for the fact that, in the absence of any regulatory process, imagined events and real events are appraised in the same way. However, figure 4.5 also introduces the possibility that the appraisal system can be subjected to control processes. Specifically, information about the status of the input – for example, whether it is real or fictional – is fed into the appraisal system, and modifies its output.

In an effort to explore young children's ability to engage in such a regulatory process, we told 6-year-olds a sad story (Meerum Terwogt, Schene and Harris, 1986). It described how a family was about to move to a new city, obliging the main character to say goodbye to a

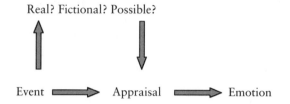

Real? Fictional? Possible?

Event ⟹ Appraisal ⟹ Emotion

Figure 4.5   A flow diagram showing how an assessment of the ontological status of an event can be fed into the appraisal process.

close friend for the last time. To increase the likelihood that children would identify with events and emotions described in the story, the main character was presented as being of the same age and gender as themselves.

Children's ability to regulate their emotional reaction to the story was examined by dividing them into three groups, with each group receiving a different set of instructions. One group was given instructions likely to increase absorption: they were asked to become involved with the story, and to feel sad along with the main character. Another group was given instructions likely to diminish absorption: they were asked to remain detached, to listen to the story in such a way 'that you won't become sad yourself'. Finally, a third, control group was given no instructions, except 'to listen carefully' to the story.

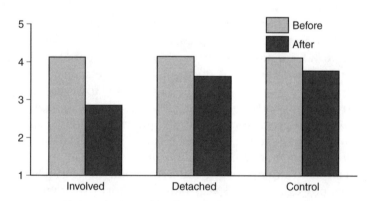

Figure 4.6   Self-report of emotional state by the three groups before and after the story.

Children's responsiveness to these instructions was measured in three different ways. First, they were asked to report on their mood before and after listening to the story. All three groups reported feeling cheerful before they listened to the story. Afterwards, children reported a decline in their emotional state, but this was especially evident among children in the involved group. These results are illustrated in figure 4.6.

We also studied children's responsiveness to the instructions by looking at the way that they later retold the story. All three groups tended to focus on key elements of the story rather than details, and the length of their narratives was similar. Despite this overall similarity, children in the involved group were more likely to refer to sad elements of the story: in their retelling, they used more words for emotion (e.g. 'sad', 'shocked' or 'crying') or phrases that connoted emotion (e.g. 'he lay down on his bed crying'). This variation among the groups is illustrated in figure 4.7. Moreover, across the three groups, there was also an overall association between mood and recall: children who reported themselves to be sad after hearing the story were more likely to produce an emotionally charged narrative.

Finally, although a sad mood led children to recall more of the sad elements of the story, this was not because it had provoked a general improvement in memory performance. Those children who reported themselves to be sad after hearing the story tended to perform poorly on a standard memory task that required them to study a sequence of picture pairs, to remember one of each, and to re-identify it later.

Summing up, the instructions that children were given before listening to the story modulated its impact: the children who were asked to involve themselves in the story reported a sadder mood after listening to it, focused on more of the sad elements in their recall, and performed worse on a standard memory task. By contrast, the children who were asked to remain detached or were left to their own devices reported only a slight change of mood, were less likely to refer to the sad elements of the story, and performed normally on a standard memory task.

To discover more about how children in the involved and detached groups had tried to follow the experimenter's instructions, they were interviewed at the end of the experimental session. Many children had difficulty in articulating what they had done. Alternatively, and these replies were quite common in the involved group, children said that they did not need to do anything because involvement was a natural

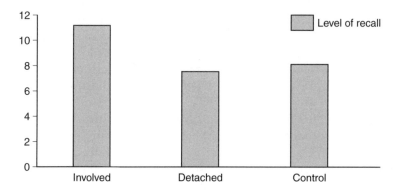

Figure 4.7   Mean recall of emotional elements by the three groups.

attitude. Nevertheless, replies from the minority of children who did succeed in putting their strategy into words were informative. Children in the involved group mentioned a family of techniques likely to increase their absorption or engagement in the fate of the story character: they mentioned pretending that the story events were happening to them, or to someone close to them, or they linked the story events with a similar experience of their own. By contrast, children in the detached group mentioned strategies likely to disengage them from the story character's fate: they talked about reminding themselves that it was 'just a story' or 'not real'.

These findings support the central proposals of this chapter. First, they reinforce the claim that an imagined situation has the capacity to arouse emotion. Children, especially those in the involved group, were often moved by the fate of the main character, even though they knew that they were just listening to a story. Second, the findings confirm that the impact of fiction depends upon the stance or point of view that is adopted. Children in the involved group referred to strategies that were likely to increase their psychological proximity to the perspective of the protagonist and their absorption within the make-believe framework. By contrast, children in the detached group referred to strategies likely to lift them outside of that framework: they reminded themselves of the fictional status of the story. Finally, as we shall see below, there are important continuities across the life cycle: the 6-year-olds often echoed, almost verbatim, the strategies that adults endorse.

One of the most informative programmes of research investigating the way that adults regulate their emotions was carried out by Richard Lazarus and his colleagues. In an early study, they found that when adults watched a disturbing film of an initiation ritual that included a painful incision, they responded to a greater or lesser extent at the autonomic level depending on whether the accompanying commentary prompted a more involved stance by highlighting the pain and cruelty of the ritual, or an intellectualized stance by providing a detached 'anthropological' description (Speisman, Lazarus, Mordkoff and Davison, 1964). In a follow-up study, Lazarus and his colleagues asked whether the same pattern would emerge if participants were simply given direct instructions to adopt a detached or involved stance before the film began rather than guided to do so during the film by the accompanying sound track (Koriat, Melkman, Averill and Lazarus, 1972). Adults were repeatedly shown a film about industrial safety. As in the earlier study, the film included various disturbing scenes, such as a finger laceration or amputation. Prior to the later screenings, adults given detachment instructions were asked to attend to the film but to remain detached and unemotional, much as a surgeon might do; adults given involved instructions were asked to 'let themselves go' – to become as emotionally involved as possible; finally, a control group was asked to watch the film attentively but given no instruction about what attitude to adopt toward it. Physiological measures taken as they watched the film showed that viewers asked to become involved were more aroused, as indexed by an acceleration in heart rate, than those asked to remain detached. As might be expected, these differences in arousal emerged during the disturbing parts of the film but not during the more benign interludes. After each screening, viewers indicated how they had felt during the film and these reports were in line with the heart-rate findings. Those who had been asked to become involved during the later screenings reported that they felt as aroused by the film as they had on the initial showing. By contrast, those asked to remain detached reported that they felt considerably less aroused than on the initial showing.

Participants were also given a list of strategies that they might have used to comply with the instructions and asked to say which ones they had actually used. Identification with the events and people in the film (e.g. 'I tried to imagine that it is happening to me') was the most widely endorsed strategy for achieving involvement. By contrast, a focus on the status or production of the film was the most widely endorsed strategy for achieving detachment: participants said that they constantly reminded themselves that: 'it was a film rather than a real occurrence', or that they concentrated: 'on the technical aspects involved in its production'. Moreover, participants who claimed to have used these latter strategies proved to be less aroused during the film.

In summary, these findings provide further support for considerable continuity between children and adults. Adults achieve involvement by staying within the make-believe frame, and by narrowing the subjective distance between the self and the protagonist – they imagine that the events in the film are happening to themselves. Detachment, on the other hand, is achieved by inhibiting that process of identification, and by feeding into the appraisal process reminders that the input is not real – it is just a film that simulates reality by various technical tricks.[8]

A Developmental Hypothesis

We can now advance a plausible developmental hypothesis about the impact of make-believe fictional material on young children. Tentatively, we can say that the initial mode for processing such input is to become absorbed by it, to appraise it as if it were real, and to respond to it as if the self were really involved either as actor or witness. This hypothesis is consistent with the absorption of preschool children in pretend play, and their frequent emotional reactions to the characters and creatures that they themselves create. This absorbed stance is also typical of the way that children approach stories and films. As mentioned earlier, children often state that such an involved attitude is both natural and difficult to explain.

In the course of development, this initial mode of processing can be moderated by techniques that increase or decrease involvement. This proposal has several implications. First, and most obviously, it predicts that the standard response of very young children to fictional material will be one of absorption or engagement with the material, as if it were real. Accordingly, among children of 3 or 4 years, fictional material is likely to provoke feelings of curiosity, excitement, fear, attachment, and so forth, depending on the content of the material in question. The hypothesis does not imply that children of this age cannot distinguish between imaginary and real entities or events. The evidence discussed at the beginning of the chapter strongly suggests that they are aware of that difference. Instead, the hypothesis implies – in line with figure 4.5 – that this ontological distinction is not deployed in processing make-believe or story episodes. Nevertheless, the distinction can be deployed by older children and by adults to modulate an emotional reaction. A plausible implication is that in the course of the preschool years and probably beyond, children gain an increasing facility in regulating their involvement with episodes or entities that they know to be imaginary.

Consider the child who starts to play a game involving a pretend monster. If the above hypothesis is correct, such a fantasy is likely to be processed in the same way as real input. In consequence, the child will, depending on the size, ferocity and proximity of the imaginary monster, begin to feel afraid. This emotional arousal can, however, be moderated in several different ways. First, the child can stop feeling afraid by simply withdrawing from the game of pretend. In terms of the diagram presented in figure 4.5, input is no longer fed into the appraisal system. Second, the child can continue the game but recast it to reduce the threat posed by the monster; for example, the child can imagine wielding a magical weapon that repels all monsters. In this case, imaginary input is still fed into the appraisal system but the nature of that input is elaborated to make it less threatening. Third, children can remind themselves that the material is simply imaginary. Effectively, in terms of figure 4.5, the same material is fed into the appraisal system but children make use of information about the ontological status of the material to modulate the output of the appraisal system. Thus, in the case of a monster, the child can remind him- or herself that: 'I'm just imagining a monster – it's not a real monster'. According to the findings described earlier, children can be prompted to do this by 6 years of age, and may increasingly do this spontaneously as they get older, with no external prompting. Given the increasing deployment of these various tactics for altering the output of the appraisal system, we can reasonably expect emotional engagement with an imaginary creature, whether it is fear of an encounter or distress at its absence, to decline with age as children become more adroit at recruiting an appropriate strategy whenever their emotional reaction becomes too intense.

Implications

I have argued that children and adults alike, despite a firm grasp of the distinction between imaginary and real situations, can be swayed in their emotional state by the contemplation of an imagined situation. Far from being a peculiarity of childhood, children's susceptibility to emotional engagement in imagined material is a characteristic of the human species throughout the life cycle, rather than a short-lived phenomenon of the early years. This claim raises two important issues. First, it suggests a way of conceptualizing the so-called aesthetic emotions, the emotions that we feel in response to the dramatic episodes of films, stories and plays. Second, the phenomenon occurs with sufficient frequency and ubiquity that it calls for some functional analysis. Why, as a species, are we so emotionally responsive to imagined events as well as real events? What purpose might such responsiveness serve? I take up these two issues in turn.

The Paradox of Emotional Reactions to Drama

Discussions of emotion have frequently touched on, but never resolved, an interesting paradox. It is tempting to conclude that our emotional reactions are nicely correlated with the apparent reality of their target. When we hear the fire alarm, we feel afraid; informed that it is a false alarm, our fear dissipates. In such cases, the strength of our emotional reaction is proportionate to the perceived reality of the threat. If there is no longer any genuine threat, our fear rapidly dissipates. Indeed, some have ventured to erect this graduated nature of our emotional response into a psychological law. Frijda (1988) formulates 'the law of apparent reality' as follows: 'emotions are elicited by events appraised as real, and their intensity corresponds to the degree to which this is the case'. Under some circumstances, this means that our emotional response will be insufficient, at least from a rational point of view. The full horror or sorrow of a situation will not be immediately apparent. When first told of a death or impending separation, we may not fully grasp the reality of the situation. In line with Frijda's law, our initial emotional reactions in such cases should be muted, and only become more intense as all the implications are understood.

Despite its plausibility, there is an important problem with Frijda's law that is clearly identified by Walters (1989). As argued at various points in this chapter, dramatic events embedded in works of fiction such as films, plays and stories have the capacity to arouse our emotions. If that point is granted, it raises a paradox. How can such episodes provoke emotion if we know from the outset that their apparent reality is illusory, that they depict only imaginary events. Why do we not react to them as we react to a defective alarm bell that signals, at best, a fault in the electric circuitry but not a genuine fire?

We have three options at this point. First, we can deny that art elicits genuine emotion; if art elicits only pseudo-emotions, then Frijda's law need offer no explanation. Alternatively, we can allow that art elicits genuine emotion, but insist that art does, in some important sense, have an apparent reality, consistent with Frijda's law. Finally, we can acknowledge that emotional responses to art really do violate Frijda's law, at least in its current formulation, and seek to reformulate it. Let us consider each of these options in turn.

The first option is distinctly unpromising. The tension and suspense that we feel as we watch a fictional combat appear to be qualitatively similar to our feelings as we watch a genuine combat, be it a race, an election or a battle. Moreover, it is difficult to maintain that the tears that we shed at the theatre are different from the tears that we shed in real life. Thus, even if our subjective distress is less intense or less persistent, the physiological changes appear to be qualitatively equivalent. Indeed, if tearjerkers never brought a lump to the throat, and thrillers never thrilled, it seems unlikely that they would be so popular. Finally, as described earlier, experimental materials that describe various imaginary situations, although scarcely amounting to works of art, can nonetheless elicit genuine emotion, as indexed via self-report, autonomic arousal and changes in reflex reactivity.

Should we argue then that art does have an apparent reality, so that the fact that it provokes emotion is fully consistent with Frijda's alleged law? This second option is, at first sight, more promising. Consider, in more detail, the contrast between the faulty alarm bell in real life, and the alarm that becomes ever more strident and insistent as the film heroine struggles to quit the spacecraft before it self-destructs. In the case of the faulty alarm bell, experience has taught us that the apparent threat is actually no threat whatsoever; the alarm is triggered by a power surge in the electric circuit, and not by the presence of a fire or an intruder. The reality that we come to recognize over time is that there is nothing to be afraid of. By contrast, the alarm on the spacecraft signals danger with more and more urgency as the seconds tick by. So there is genuinely something to be afraid of in this case, albeit something that might happen in the fictional world of the film rather than in the real world. Thus, we might save Frijda's law by saying that our emotional response to fictional events is calibrated to the implications, or 'apparent reality', that they have within the fictional world. Plausible though this analysis is, it ultimately ducks the critical issue. It is true that the fictional world throws up various potential dangers and threats. However, by designating these as an 'apparent reality' we appear to save Frijda's law, but we do so without providing any account of why such fictional realities can amount to apparent realities. As Walters (1989) points out, one possible account is to claim that we *pretend* that the film or drama that moves us is real. However, this is a rather tortuous defence of Frijda's law. It amounts to the proposal that having accepted that something is not real and is, therefore, not emotionally charged (according to Frijda's law), we nevertheless treat it as if it were real so that it does evoke an emotional response. Such a manoeuvre saves the law but it becomes fairly implausible when we try to use it to explain young children's emotional responses to their pretend inventions. It implies that children first of all pretend that there is a monster chasing them, or that their imaginary companion is lost, and then having created that imaginary situation take the further step of pretending that their pretence is real. It seems fairly unlikely that 3- and 4-year-old children are capable of any such cognitive acrobatics. We need a simpler and more persuasive account of the apparent reality of fictional input.

Finally, we may consider the third possibility, a reformulation of Frijda's proposal. According to the analysis presented so far, fictional material can be processed in a default mode, as illustrated in figure 4.3. When that mode is operative, knowledge that the input is fictional is not used to dampen or modulate the emotional response, even if it is available. On this hypothesis, therefore, art moves us not because we *pretend* that it is real but because thoughts about its ontological status are not fed into the appraisal system. Such considerations are only fed into the appraisal system when the material is graphic or disturbing and we seek to remind ourselves that it is merely fictional, as illustrated in figure 4.5.

We may now examine more carefully the distinction between the alarm bell that is judged to be a false alarm in real life, and the alarm aboard the fictional spacecraft. In the first case, there is no question of its being designated as a fictional alarm. It is processed as a real event. Nonetheless, the appraisal system that comes into play may arrive at the conclusion that the alarm can be safely ignored because it is faulty, and no emotional reaction ensues. Frijda's law highlights this type of appraisal: an assessment of the likely implications of an event for the concerns of the self. However, figure 4.3 introduces the idea that, independent of that appraisal system, there is another decision-making system, which can code input as real or fictional. In the default mode, output from this evaluation system is not fed back into the appraisal system: fictional input is simply treated as ordinary, real input, and is sent on to the appraisal system to be analysed in the usual way. If, on the other hand, this evaluation system is used as an override, its output is fed into the appraisal system and leads to the blockage or attenuation of emotional reactions to purely imaginary or fictional material, as illustrated in figure 4.5.

This account elucidates a point that Frijda (1989) concedes: there is not a single type of reality assessment. We need to distinguish between two different types of assessment, each involving a dedicated system. On the one hand, there is a system dedicated to evaluating the ontological status of an event as real, or fictional, or possible, and on the other hand, there is an appraisal system dedicated to figuring out the extent to which an event (be it real, fictional or possible) has genuine or only spurious implications. Figure 4.8 (based on figure 4.3) emphasizes this distinction.

The law of 'apparent reality' formulated by Frijda is mainly concerned with the work of the appraisal system. It reminds us that emotional reactions will be commensurate with the implications (i.e., 'the apparent reality') of an event. However, to the extent that the law does not separate such appraisal processes from ontological evalua-

Ontological Evaluation: Real? Fictional? Possible?

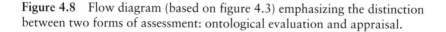

Figure 4.8 Flow diagram (based on figure 4.3) emphasizing the distinction between two forms of assessment: ontological evaluation and appraisal.

tion, it offers no explanation for the way that art can move us. It moves us because this latter type of reality assessment – although it can be used to remind us of the fictional nature of a play or story – is not usually fed into the appraisal system.

The Function of Emotional Involvement

Having offered an account of emotional reactions to imagined material, including monsters, imaginary companions, fiction and drama, we are left with a paradox to consider. It is clearly possible for the emotional system to be finely tuned to the implications of an event. As argued above, our apprehension dissipates once we establish that the fire alarm is a false alarm rather than genuine. Granted this possibility for fine-tuning, why are we so designed as human beings that imagined inputs readily drive our emotional system? Why is information about whether an event is real or imaginary not automatically deployed to fine-tune our emotional reactions? Figures 4.3 and 4.5 imply that this latter type of calibration is available but certainly not automatic. Rather, it is something that is superimposed on the default mode – an added extra that is achieved in the course of development. When operating in default mode, we are a species that thrills to fictional dangers or sheds tears for imaginary heartbreaks. We may ask, therefore, what the biological pay-off might be for not feeding in information about whether the event being contemplated is purely imaginary, especially when in other respects our emotional system is finely calibrated. Below, I discuss two speculative answers to this puzzle before re-examining the nature of the puzzle itself.

Speculation I

One answer emerges in the context of decision-making. The ability to entertain hypothetical situations and to assess what emotional reactions they might evoke is useful when we have to choose between two alternative courses of action (Harris, Johnson, Hutton, Andrews and Cooke, 1989). For example, I might be trying to decide whether to move to a new job abroad or to remain where I am. To help make that decision, I might visualize moving to the new environment and seek to gauge how stimulated, contented or lonely I would feel in that new environment. Needless to say, this type of simulation may not always be accurate. Still, it might help me to come to a view about the relative costs and benefits involved.

Although this model of decision-making is plausible, it remains ambiguous with respect to one key feature – the exact way in which we gauge how we feel. One possibility is that we make assessments of how we would feel in a purely cognitive and cold-blooded fashion. For example, I might know that the new job is less secure than my current job and I might also know from past experience that I am averse to most forms of risk. As I contemplate resigning and accepting the new job, I might draw the conclusion that I should not do something that is likely to make me quite anxious. Alternatively, such assessments might be made in a more engaged and visceral fashion. Thus, even as I contemplate resigning, I might not just anticipate my eventual anxiety, I might already begin to feel anxious. Such current apprehension – as opposed to some apprehension that I anticipate feeling in the future – might be a strong signal that I should stay where I am. Is there any evidence that this second mode of decision-making is associated with better decisions? One way to gather such evidence is to compare the decisions of those people who respond in a cold-blooded, cognitive fashion when they contemplate a hypothetical situation with those who produce a more visceral reaction to such situations.

Damasio and his colleagues report evidence suggesting that adults with damage to the frontal cortex might belong to the former group, whereas normal individuals, and individuals with damage outside of the frontal cortex, belong to the latter group. In one study, they showed participants a series of pictorial slides (Damasio, Tranel and Damasio, 1991). Most of these slides were unexceptional, depicting bland scenery or abstract patterns. Occasionally, however, the image of a disturbing event or scene was included. Normal individuals and patients with brain damage outside of the area of the frontal cortex each showed an autonomic reaction to these occasional, emotionally charged pictures: a marked skin conductance response. The frontal patients, on the other hand, showed no reaction at all. This was not because their autonomic system was damaged. When these same patients were exposed to stimuli such as an unexpected sound or flash of light, they did display a reaction, as measured via a skin conductance response, in the same way as normal subjects. Interviews with the frontal patients also showed that their failure to react was not because they did not appreciate at a cognitive level the emotional significance of the disturbing pictures. They could appropriately comment on the type of emotional reaction that such emotionally charged pictures would normally arouse, be it disgust, or sadness, or fear. However, this emotional knowledge did not translate into any emotional reaction on their part.

Damasio and his colleagues went on to study such patients when they were confronted by a decision-making task that mimicked the choices and risks that we face in real life. They played a gambling game in which they could choose to examine cards from one of four decks. Depending on which deck they chose, and the value on the card that they turned over, they either received a sum of monopoly-type money or had to give some back. Over a long run of choices, two of the four decks proved good bets because they led to modest rewards and occasional, manageable losses, whereas the other two decks proved to be bad bets because they led to more substantial rewards but occasional, punitive losses. This long-term pattern of outcomes was not explained to participants, but it did become apparent at least to normal participants in the course of the experiment: typically, they would try all four decks, but eventually shift the bulk of their choices to the good decks – the less rewarding but less dangerous choices. By contrast, the frontal patients concentrated on the high-risk decks (Bechara, Damasio, Damasio and Anderson, 1994). This lifelike experiment reproduced in a concentrated format a pattern that had occurred in the real lives of many of the frontal patients: they had persisted with risky ventures that did not work out.

In a further study, Damasio and his colleagues looked more closely at the relationship between the autonomic reactions of the players and the decisions that they made. The evidence described so far suggests that such a link is plausible: frontal patients fail to show an autonomic reaction when they contemplate a disturbing scene that is illustrated in a picture, and they also continue to choose cards that are risky. Normal controls, on the other hand, do show an autonomic reaction and they avoid cards that are risky. A plausible interpretation is that when normal subjects contemplate making a risky choice, they thereby evoke an autonomic reaction that serves as a signal, and inhibits them from making risky choices. To validate this interpretation, Damasio and his colleagues monitored the autonomic reactions of players as they made their choices (Bechara, Damasio, Tranel, and Damasio, 1997). Clear differences between the groups emerged as the game proceeded. In an initial phase, before they encountered any losses, each player sampled all four decks and a slight preference for choosing the high-risk decks emerged. Then, in an intermediate phase, having encountered a loss, the normal players began to produce anticipatory skin conductance responses as they contemplated choosing from the high-risk decks and, in the course of further choices, they voiced a 'hunch' that these decks were indeed more risky and directed the majority of their choices to the low-risk decks. During this intermediate phase, by contrast, the frontal patients did not produce skin conductance responses, did not express a hunch, and showed no preference for the less risky decks. In a final phase, most but not all of the normal players could articulate the differences between the high- and low-risk decks. However, all of them, irrespective of whether they could express this conceptual knowledge, preferred the low-risk decks. By contrast, none of the frontal patients showed anticipatory skin conductance responses or showed a preference for the low-risk decks, even if they could express a conceptual understanding of the relative risks involved.

The implication of these findings is that autonomic responses are important for wise decision-making. When normal players contemplate making a choice that has been associated with loss, an autonomic response is triggered. That autonomic response guides their choice, even in advance of a full rationale for that choice. Among frontal patients no such autonomic response is triggered, and even though they may eventually arrive at a cognitive rationale for a low-risk choice, it does not actually guide their choice. In sum, when players are trying to decide what to do, and contemplating a risky choice, the autonomic system appears to play a key role in pushing them to avoid that choice.[9]

It is worth noting that a related pattern of results has emerged within another group of people who characteristically make reckless decisions – criminal psychopaths. Lang and his colleagues asked criminal psychopaths to imagine either fearful or neutral scenes, guided by appropriate descriptive sentences (Patrick, Cuthbert and Lang, 1994). Prisoners with relatively low scores on an index of anti-social psychopathy showed the expected increment in heart rate and skin conductance when asked to imagine fearful as opposed to neutral scenes. By contrast, prisoners with relatively high scores on the same index showed a much smaller increment. Thus, anti-social psychopaths respond with little emotion, at least as measured at the autonomic level, when they imagine a potentially alarming situation. As yet, there has been no research on the way in which this deficit might affect their decision-making. However, based on the findings of Damasio and his colleagues, we would expect them, like frontal patients, to fail to show anticipatory autonomic reactions when contemplating a dangerous course of action, and to adopt that course of action, even if at an intellectual level they can articulate the risks involved.

We may now offer a more explicit, albeit speculative answer to the question asked earlier: why is it that human beings, children as well as adults, are prone to display a fully fledged emotional reaction, not just when they are confronted by an actual situation, but when they imagine a possible situation? The findings that have been reviewed suggest that human beings have evolved a planning system in which felt emotion plays a critical role. By imagining what we might do, we can trigger in an anticipatory fashion the emotions that we would feel were we to actually do it. If we strip this planning process of emotion – if we let it run in a cold-blooded fashion – then inappropriate decisions are taken, even though we can make a rational calculation of costs and benefits. Patients with frontal lesions and criminal psychopaths are notoriously poor at making appropriate decisions. Thus, as Damasio (1994) has argued, decision-making cannot be reduced to rational calculation. To make the 'right' decision we have to feel as well as know the implications of a possible course of action.

The evidence that I have presented suggests that this same linkage of imagination and emotion is engaged by fiction. When we imagine ourselves facing the same situation as the fictional protagonist, we do not simply make a rational calculation of the costs and benefits for the protagonist. Our appraisal of the situation from the protagonist's point of view drives our emotional system, even though we can judge, at an intellectual level, that this situation is not one that we are facing or ever likely to face. More generally, this line of argument suggests that imagination and emotion are brought together both when we make hard decisions and when we are absorbed in fiction. Had we not evolved a decision-making system in which the contemplation of possible lives and possible futures engaged our emotions at a somatic level, we would be less prone to spend as many hours as we do absorbed in fictional worlds.

Speculation II

The second speculative answer has less empirical evidence to back it up, but it has a wider range. At some point in our evolutionary past, we began to acquire a capacity for language. It is likely that this capacity was initially deployed for communication about the here and now:

to call attention to interesting objects and events, to make comments on them; and to regulate joint activity. Certainly, this is the type of pragmatic function that language first serves in ontogeny (Harris, 1999).

Whatever its exact origin, language eventually turned into a tool for conversing about the not-here and the not-now. This type of displaced communication meant that our forebears could gather information about events that they themselves had not witnessed, provided that other people in their community had done so. A great deal of evidence – some of which was reviewed earlier in this chapter – indicates that we, and presumably our ancestors – construct in our imagination a mental model of the scene and events that are described in such narrative reports. [10]

We may make one further assumption. The bulk of displaced testimony is likely to concern real events displaced in time and space from the utterance itself – such events might have taken place in the recent past, they might be recurrent, or they might be imminent. Stated differently, there is no reason to suppose that displaced communication developed in the service of pretence, fabrication, fiction or myth, though it might have rapidly included those genres. Rather it developed primarily in the context of honest testimony about actual events. If this proposal is correct, it suggests that mental modelling is a process that helps us to understand reports of events that we are obliged to imagine, but it also underlines the fact that such events need not be imaginary. They are simply events for which we build a mental model based on testimony from others, in the absence of having witnessed the events ourselves.

It seems plausible that such testimony would include emotionally charged events. Indeed, the more intense the emotion, the more the experience giving rise to it is likely to be shared and shared persistently (Rimé, 1995). We come now to the nub of this speculative proposal. Suppose that information gathered by testimony left us cold: told of a calamity or an unexpected boon, we would remain unmoved. Only by virtue of observing these events with our own eyes would we react to their emotional implications. Such a dissociation between the emotional impact of information gained first-hand and information gained by testimony would clearly imply a considerable impoverishment, not just to our decision-making capacities as outlined in the previous speculation, but also to our social engagement with an interlocutor. We would simply fail to register the emotion that he or she felt, or indeed the emotion that it might be appropriate for us to feel ourselves to the extent that our lives are intertwined with that of the interlocutor. On the other hand, if our interlocutor's emotionally charged eye-witness report kindles in us the same emotion as the events themselves aroused in him or her, we end up being in tune with our interlocutor and alerted to events beyond our immediate horizon.

This proposal implies that our engagement in fiction and drama is ultimately a function of our heritage as a language-using species, and more specifically as a species that can acquire information by testimony. The apparatus that underpins such information acquisition – our ability to build mental models – is primarily directed at the processing of honest testimony with all its emotional and interpersonal ramifications. That same apparatus can be engaged by a different kind of input, namely fictional input, whether it is a pretend scenario that is acted out, a story that is narrated, or even a lie that is peddled. When it is so engaged, the appraisal system and the emotional system are activated in the usual way. But our engagement with art and drama might be a small evolutionary price to pay for our emotional sensitivity to eye-witness testimony.

Is There Really a Puzzle?

Both of the speculative proposals that I have outlined offer an explanation for an apparently puzzling link between imagination and emotion. Thus, I have tried to offer an explanation for the fact that when we imagine a state of affairs – either because we are trying to make a decision about whether to bring about that state of affairs or because we are being told about an actual state of affairs by somebody who witnessed it – that simple act of the imagination can activate our emotional system. However, it could be argued that this link between imagination and emotion is not very surprising, and scarcely in need of explanation in evolutionary terms. If simple organisms such as rats and pigeons can 'generalize' an emotional reaction from one stimulus to another, similar stimulus, there is nothing very surprising about the way that human beings 'generalize' their emotional reactions from a state of affairs that they actually encounter to an equivalent state of affairs that they only contemplate in their imagination. Indeed, there is considerable neuropsychological evidence that common neural pathways mediate the processing of an actual visual stimulus and the processing of a visual image (Farah, 1988; Kosslyn, 1988). By implication, there might be no special advantage – or disadvantage – associated with our tendency to respond emotionally to an imagined state of affairs. Much more surprising – and much more in need of an evolutionary explanation – is the distinctive ability of human beings to deploy their imagination in such a wide-ranging and flexible fashion – to engage in pretend play, to adopt another person's perspective, to contemplate a future course of action, and to envisage some event that they learn about via testimony. I return to this issue in the final chapter. Meantime, in the chapters that follow, I explore other, relatively neglected ways that young children use their imagination.

Notes

1 Experimental work with adults has shown that embellishment of an imagined, frightening situation, especially through the addition of response-imagery such as running away, is likely to heighten the emotional impact of such imagery (Lang, 1984).

2 In an initial exploration of this issue, Taylor et al. (1993a, study 1) found that young children – whether or not they had an imaginary companion of their own – often claimed that a pretend friend could be seen and/or touched, suggesting that they might have been confused about the status of this pretend person. However, the authors concluded that children probably assumed that they were being asked whether the pretend friend could be seen and touched in a make-believe fashion. In line with this interpretation, some children spontaneously cautioned that the pretend friend was 'not here for real'.

3 Although children may realize that the products of their imagination are no more than that, there are, of course, many other fantasies that are collectively sanctioned – Santa Claus, the Tooth Fairy, the Easter Bunny, ghosts, witches, and so forth. Children may think of these collective representations as real, simply because they have been given misleading or partial information about them (Taylor, 1997).

4 There is a long tradition of research in behaviour therapy that relies on the fact that phobic patients display similar emotional reactions whether they encounter an actual phobic object (e.g. an actual snake) or merely imagine such an encounter (Marzillier, Carroll and Newland, 1979). Under certain conditions this equivalence can be used in therapeutic programmes aimed at desensitization. For further discussion, see Dadds, Bovbjerg, Redd and Cutmore (1997).

5 It is worth emphasizing that the paper-and-pencil test used by Gollnisch and Averill (1993) focused on various aspects of role playing, mimicry

and fantasy involvement but did not include items that referred to emotions or feelings. For more details, see Fletcher and Averill (1984).

6   Using a very similar design, Vrana, Cuthbert and Lang (1989) examined the effect of sentence processing on heart rate. Consistent with findings for the startle reflex, they found that heart rate increased when subjects recalled frightening rather than neutral sentences, and this acceleration was most evident for subjects instructed to imagine the sentence rather than to repeat it or ignore it.

7   Needless to say, insofar as an event in real life is part of a larger series of real-life events and a fictional event is part of a larger series of fictional events, our response to a real incident and an equivalent fictional incident are unlikely to be exactly the same because the context in which they are embedded will differ.

8   The exact conditions under which adults can successfully reduce physiological activation in response to a disturbing film is not yet clear. A replication study by Dandoy and Goldstein (1990) confirmed the results obtained by Koriat et al. (1972): instructions to adopt an intellectual stance reduced physiological markers of stress. On the other hand, Steptoe and Vögele (1986) found no such reduction in another replication study involving medical students. However, medical students, unlike ordinary students, might spontaneously adopt a detached attitude toward accidents and bodily injuries – independent of the experimenter's instruction. Nevertheless, the composition of the subject group is unlikely to be the full explanation for the pattern of results. In a further attempt to replicate and extend the findings of Lazarus and his colleagues, Gross (1998) observed a reduction in subjective feelings of disgust among a group of (non-medical) students who had been briefly instructed to adopt a detached attitude toward a 1-minute film depicting an amputation, but no reduction in physiological activation. In summary, this mixed pattern of findings points to the conclusion that for some film materials the default reaction – in which the film is appraised in much the same way as a real encounter (as illustrated in figure 4.3) – is not easily overridden. For further discussion, see Gross (1999).

9   Bechara et al. (1997) are inclined to argue that the autonomic signal is processed at an unconscious level, but more research is needed to establish this claim. Certainly, players who shifted toward the less risky decks expressed a 'hunch' that the high-risk decks were indeed risky, even if they could not explain why they were risky. By implication, they had some awareness, however inarticulate, of the 'bad vibrations' associated with the high-risk decks.

10   Recent research has shown that deaf children who invent their own system of signs with which to communicate (so-called 'homesign') are capable of using that system to refer to displaced events, even if such references

to displaced events emerge more slowly than they would among normal, speaking children (Morford and Goldin-Meadow, 1997). Hence, in referring to a possible link between mental model construction and displaced language, I do not assume that the medium of communication is necessarily speech.

5

Reasoning, Make-believe and Dialogue

Father: 'If you have blood you'll die.'
Mark (aged 4 years 3 months): 'Do dinosaurs have blood?'
Father: 'Some blood.'
Mark: 'Some blood – then they die.'

(MacWhinney, 1991)

By 1934, Alexander Luria had completed two expeditions to Uzbekistan in Central Asia. He wrote a short promissory note from Moscow to the *American Journal of Genetic Psychology*, briefly describing the psychological tests that had been carried out, and summarizing the findings in a very general fashion (Luria, 1934). The note ends hopefully: 'The works of the first and second psychological expeditions will be ready for press and prepared for publication by Professor Luria within the next year'. In the event, publication of the results was blocked by political censorship for almost 40 years.

On these two expeditions, Luria had tested traditional, uneducated peasants from remote villages. The results suggested that the Soviet reforms, which included an abrupt change from family-based farming to the planned economy of collective farming, together with various educational programmes, were bringing about important cognitive changes, especially in the process of reasoning, among the traditional peasants. Nonetheless, the research was attacked for presenting those same peasants, and more specifically a national minority, in an unfavourable light. The theoretical approach, it was alleged, echoed the earlier claims of Lévy-Bruhl regarding the existence of a pre-logical mentality among pre-literate people. Luria was forced to give up the research programme and after requalifying in medicine, he took up a new career in neuropsychology. Only in the 1970s, when the ideological climate had changed, was he able to publish a full report of the expeditions (Luria, 1971, 1976). Even after such a long period, the findings were provocative, if not politically, then theoretically. They did indeed revive the concept of a primitive mentality rooted in, and restricted by, everyday practice and experience.

As a colleague of Vygotsky, Luria was sympathetic to Vygotsky's theoretical position that the way we think is deeply influenced by our cultural and historical milieu. Vygotsky claimed that a psychological function is acquired at first in the context of a social practice before it is internalized and used autonomously by the individual. Observing the rapid sociocultural changes taking place in Central Asia during the 1920s and early 1930s, Vygotsky and Luria realized that a huge, real-life laboratory for testing this thesis confronted them. They speculated that the radical changes in the lifestyle of the peasants, notably their increased access to education and their incorporation into Stalin's agricultural collectives, should produce dramatic cognitive changes. Vygotsky and Luria conceived of those changes not just in terms of a cultural comparison but in terms of a historical process. Effectively, the communist revolution was compressing into a few short years an economic, educational and cognitive transformation that might otherwise take decades or even centuries.

With this theoretical expectation in mind, Luria had led the two expeditions to Uzbekistan. Logical reasoning problems were included in the test battery and these produced some of the most striking results. Consider the following propositions: 'Precious metals do not rust' and 'gold is a precious metal'. When these propositions are brought together, we can draw the straightforward conclusion that gold does not rust. Such a logical scheme allows us to go beyond our direct experience to arrive at a new conclusion. Is the ability to use such a scheme a basic capacity of human cognition or is it a skill that is activated by a particular cultural milieu? Luria anticipated that his research would provide an answer.

He compared two groups of adults. One group had not been touched by the Soviet reforms. They were illiterate peasants with no schooling, working in a traditional, non-technological economy that included gardening, cotton raising and animal husbandry. The other group, by contrast, had received one or two years of basic education and had been involved in collective farming.[1]

One type of reasoning problem proved fairly easy for both groups, namely those problems in which the initial proposition fitted in with their own experience, even if the second proposition did not. For example, they might be told: 'Cotton grows well where it is hot and dry. England is cold and damp. Can cotton grow there or not?' The first proposition would be familiar and acceptable for all the peasants – because cotton was grown in the surrounding region and the climate was indeed hot and dry. All they needed to do was to apply this well-known generalization to the unfamiliar location mentioned in the second proposition – England – by making use of what the interviewer had told them about the climate there. Although the traditional, uneducated peasants occasionally resisted making such an extrapolation, with prompting they usually succeeded. For example, one 30-year-old first replied: 'I don't know if there's cotton there or not'. When the interviewer encouraged him to focus on the wording of the problem: 'But, from my words, what do you think?', he drew the appropriate conclusion: 'If it's chilly, if there is snow, then there won't be any there, of course'.

A second type of problem proved more difficult for the peasants with no education. In these problems, the initial proposition fell outside their experience. For example, 'In the Far North, where there is snow, all bears are white. Novaya Zemlya is in the Far North. What colour are bears there?' In response to this problem, the man quoted earlier protested: 'You've seen them – you know. I haven't seen them, so how could I say!?' As with the problem about cotton, the interviewer encouraged him to focus on the wording of the problem: 'But on the basis of what I said, what do you think?', and restated the problem. This repetition met with the same refusal: 'But I never saw them, so how could I say?' By contrast, a 26-year-old who had lived for two years on a collective farm managed each of the two syllogisms. Asked about cotton growing in England, he immediately replied: 'No, if it is humid and chilly, it won't grow'. Asked about bears in the North, he replied: 'You say that it's cold there and there's snow, so the bears there are white'.

Luria drew two conclusions from these findings. First, given some prompting to focus on what the interviewer had said, even adults with no formal education could use a general premise that matched their own experience as a basis for reaching new conclusions. In the first interview quoted, the 30-year-old used his knowledge about cotton to draw an inference about what can be grown in England, a place that he had never visited. Despite this inferential capacity, uneducated peasants balked at reasoning from an initial, general premise that lay outside their experience. Even with prompting from the interviewer, they often either refused to accept the problem, or they failed to treat the general premise as universally applicable.

A different pattern emerged among the adults who had received some education through the agricultural reforms. Luria found that they managed to solve both types of problem equally well and they required minimal or no prompting from the interviewer. Education appeared to have taught them to adopt a different logical stance. They confidently accepted the general statements made by the interviewer as a valid basis for reasoning. By making use of a logical scheme, even if the elements inserted into the scheme were unfamiliar, they were not only able to extrapolate from personal experience, they could also reason from premises that lay outside their experience.

For Luria, these results were a direct confirmation of the theoretical position that he had developed with Vygotsky. Although we might assume that logical reasoning is immune to cultural influences, the results of the expedition suggest that logical reasoning, especially from unfamiliar premises, emerges within a particular social and historical context. Traditional peasants, with little experience outside of their traditional practices, are reluctant to venture beyond the generalizations that those practices have repeatedly confirmed. Less traditional peasants, who have expanded their horizon by learning to read and by involvement in collective farming, are willing to place some credence in generalizations that lie outside their experience. As I mentioned, Luria was obliged to abandon this line of research, so that he could not study such cultural influences any further. American investigators took up his findings many years later.

The Role of Schooling

Michael Cole worked with Luria in Moscow and learned about his pioneering cross-cultural research at first-hand. Impressed by Luria's findings, he and his colleagues gave equivalent reasoning problems to members of the Kpelle community in Liberia, West Africa (Cole, Gay, Glick and Sharp, 1971). The results were remarkably similar. Indeed, the replies given by the Kpelle often bore an uncanny resemblance to those that had been given so many years earlier by the Uzbeks. Further studies in Liberia and in Mexico, where children as well as adults were interviewed, produced a highly consistent pattern. Within each culture, participants with no schooling made many mistakes, but as little as two or three years of schooling led to a sharp improvement in performance (Scribner, 1977).

Subsequent research carried out among the Vai, a people in the northwest of Liberia, permitted an assessment of the contribution of literacy as distinct from schooling. In the nineteenth century, the Vai had developed their own system of writing and about half of those who learn to read using that script have never been to school. This enabled Scribner and Cole (1981) to ask whether the acquisition of literacy alone, without the normally correlated factor of schooling, would have the same effect on reasoning style. The question was theoretically important. On the strength of historical and anthropological comparison, Goody and Watt (1968) claimed that certain modes of thought are much more feasible in the context of written as opposed to oral language. In particular, the analysis of relationships among successive statements is facilitated. Indeed, Goody and Watt (1968, p. 68) went so far as to claim that: 'The kinds of analysis involved in the syllogism and in other forms of logical procedure are clearly dependent upon writing'.

Using logical problems akin to those put to the Uzbeks and to the Kpelle, Scribner and Cole (1981) tested a large group of Vai adults who varied considerably in their exposure both to the Vai script and to schooling. The results were clear-cut: there was no sign of any association between literacy and reasoning performance, whether assessed in terms of the number of correct replies or the way that those replies were justified. On the other hand, both measures were positively linked to schooling, and negatively linked to involvement in traditional practices such as agriculture. We can summarize nearly 50 years of research by concluding that disengagement from a traditional, agricultural way of life, and a relatively short exposure to schooling, brings about an intellectual transformation in the process of reasoning.

Sylvia Scribner (1977) developed a helpful analysis of this transformation. She argued that children and adults adopt either of two quite different orientations toward the reasoning task. In the absence of schooling, they adopt an 'empirical orientation': they use their own experience to supplement, to distort, or even to reject the premises supplied by the interviewer; they reason instead on the basis of their empirical experience. After two or three years of schooling, they adopt what might be called a 'theoretical' or 'analytic' orientation instead:

they focus on the claims encapsulated in the premises of the problem, even when those premises do not fit into their everyday experience and they confine their reasoning to what follows from those premises.

This difference in orientation emerged especially clearly when participants were asked to justify the conclusion that they had reached. Those who adopted what I shall call an analytic orientation justified their conclusion by referring back explicitly to what the interviewer had said, using phrases like 'From your words . . .' or 'If you say that . . .'. By contrast, those who adopted an empirical orientation mentioned some observation that they had made that justified their conclusion. Alternatively, they insisted that they lacked the relevant knowledge to reach any conclusion: 'If I know him in person, I can answer that question, but since I do not know him in person I cannot answer that question'.

Signs of both orientations can be discerned if we look back at the spontaneous remarks made by the peasants that Luria interviewed. Some, especially those who had received some education, prefaced their conclusion with the phrase: 'To go by your words' or 'If you say that . . .', whereas others clearly adopted an empirical orientation. Recall the protest of the traditional peasant quoted earlier who was asked about the colour of the bears in Novaya Zemlya: 'You've seen them – you know. I haven't seen them, so how could I say?!' Another traditional peasant tackling the same problem explicitly pointed to the role of empirical experience in reaching a conclusion: 'A person who had travelled a lot and been in cold countries and seen everything could answer; he would know what colour the bears were'.

Using this distinction between an empirical and an analytic orientation, Scribner was able to reach two important conclusions. First, the empirical orientation, in which justifications are couched in terms of experience, is predominant among those who have never been to school, whereas the analytic orientation, in which justifications refer back to the interviewer's words, is predominant among those who have had some schooling. Second, when people adopt an empirical orientation they may or may not reach a logically correct answer; their accuracy depends critically on the extent to which their empirical experience leads them to reason from premises consistent with those set out in the problem that they have been given. By contrast, when people adopt an analytic orientation they focus on the problem as it has been stated – irrespective of its fit with their empirical experience – and they almost always reach a correct answer.

On the basis of this analysis, Scribner argued that schooling does not teach people to reason as such. Even adults with no schooling reason quite accurately from those premises that they are willing to accept as a starting point. Nonetheless, schooling does bring about a profound change in intellectual orientation. It teaches people to adopt an analytic attitude. In particular, it teaches them to adopt an analytic attitude to reasoning problems where their empirical experience might otherwise interfere. In explaining that influence, Scribner speculates that logical problems form a special genre in much the same way that jokes or stories form a special genre: each genre has its own conventions and listeners are expected to know and accept those conventions when they listen to material belonging to it. Logical problems differ from ordinary conversation because the implications that they carry are governed strictly by what follows from explicitly stated premises. In trying to work out what follows from the premises, we should not draw in our empirical experience to amplify what has been said. Everyday conversation, on the other hand, often carries implications that emerge only when supplemented by our empirical knowledge. We typically fill out what someone says to us by spontaneously adding in assumptions or generalizations of our own. Ordinary comprehension is a constructive process; we do not confine ourselves to an analysis of the implications of what has been explicitly stated.

Presumably, people learn about a genre through exposure. Thus, children who are told a lot of stories learn the conventions that are peculiar to that genre. Similarly, children exposed to the logical genre come to appreciate its conventions. Yet in the normal course of a school day children are rarely, if ever, given logical syllogisms – so how do they learn the conventions of such problems? A plausible answer is that children in school receive tasks that are not syllogisms in the strict sense but have an equivalent formal structure. Consider a simple arithmetic problem: the child is told that one pumpkin costs 20 cents, and that a man buys one dozen. From these two premises, the child can work out how much the man will have to pay for the 12 pumpkins. In solving this task, the child should set aside various empirical considerations: she may doubt whether a pumpkin can be bought for 20 cents; she may wonder why anyone would want 12 of them. Such concerns are irrelevant to an arithmetic solution, which should be based on the premises as stated, however unfamiliar or unlikely.

Scribner's analysis, therefore, provides us with a plausible explanation for the much greater accuracy of schooled subjects on reasoning problems. In school, children are exposed to a variety of problems with a formal structure similar to that of the syllogism, and they can learn the appropriate analytic orientation. As a result, they abandon the empirical bias when faced with a reasoning problem and adopt an analytic orientation instead.[2]

The Origins of the Analytic Orientation

The discussion so far has suggested that the analytic orientation is something that needs to be cultivated in the context of specific, cultural practices. Admittedly, adults who have never been to school are not totally incapable of adopting that orientation. They sometimes bracket off what they know and confine their reasoning to the problem as stated, but as Scribner points out: 'More often than not, traditional villagers fail to do just that, under conditions in which educated subjects almost always do just that'. Accepting that the analytic orientation is something that does not come naturally, Scribner concludes that adults differ in their internalization of the logical genre. Some appear to ignore the genre completely. Most show some grip on it but, depending on their education, they exhibit it in either a transient or systematic fashion. Ultimately, therefore, Scribner's final conclusion is very much in the tradition of cultural psychology espoused by Vygotsky and Luria (Cole, 1990): 'For the psychologist, the leading developmental question becomes that of specifying under what circumstances and as a result of what experiences individuals possessing this genre internalise it as a schema available for cognitive activities' (Scribner, 1977, p. 500). More generally, Scribner's conclusion implies that human beings, without the scaffold that is provided by schooling, remain stuck in their daily experience: the empirical orientation comes naturally whereas the analytic orientation, in which empirical knowledge is suspended or bracketed off, is an unnatural attitude that depends on cultivation. A similar conclusion was reached by Martin Braine: 'Artificially setting aside part of what you know is an academic game, and there is no reason to assume that our ancestors' life conditions would lead them to acquire much skill at that game' (Braine, 1990, p. 136).

I shall argue for a different conclusion and for a different set of questions. Borrowing Scribner's helpful distinction between the analytic and the empirical orientation, I shall claim that young children, even those who have not been to school, are not confined to the empirical orientation. Under certain circumstances, they consistently adopt the analytic orientation. The implication is that neither schooling nor any other type of environmental exposure is needed for the 'internalization' of the analytic orientation. Rather, schooling leads to the extension and cultivation of a mode of thought that comes quite naturally before the child enters school.[3] Ironically, the seeds of these claims are implicit in Vygotsky's sensitive remarks on play which he made in the course of a lecture in 1933, not long after the two expeditions to Uzbekistan had been completed. In the context of play, he argued, even preschool children can liberate themselves temporarily from perceiving and acting on the basis of empirical reality. They can create an imaginary situation, distinct from reality, and subordinate their actions and judgements to that imaginary situation (Vygotsky, 1978, ch. 7).[4]

Make-believe Worlds

Although the analogy might seem far-fetched at first, there are several interesting parallels between children's attitude toward the imaginary situation that they create during make-believe play and the analytic orientation. When engaged in make-believe play, children routinely set aside certain obvious facts. For example, as described in chapter 2, 2-year-olds ignore the fact that the table is actually dry and they readily wipe up some make-believe liquid when asked to do so. In describing the outcome of a pretend transformation, they refer to what has happened in the make-believe world, not to what has actually happened. Clearly, involvement in pretend play calls for the suspension, however transient, of the empirical orientation; otherwise the implications of the make-believe situation could not be responded to or described.

With this analogy in mind, we attempted to deploy children's facility at make-believe in a reasoning task. We gave 4- and 6-year-old children problems that were similar to those used by Luria (Dias and Harris, 1988). Particularly crucial were those problems that started off with a premise that contradicted something that the children knew. For example, we might tell them: 'All fishes live in trees'.[5] We then stated the so-called minor premise – for example, 'Tot is a fish' – and finally we asked the critical test question: 'Does Tot live in the water?'

Notice that an empirical approach to this question would prompt the answer 'yes' – after all, fishes generally live in water and so, if Tot is a fish, then he presumably lives in water as well. On the other hand, if the child accepts the initial premise, even though it runs counter to his or her empirical knowledge, then the logically correct answer is 'no': Tot, like all his fellow fishes, must live in a tree.

The children were presented with problems like these in one of two ways. Either the interviewer stated the problem with a normal matter-of-fact intonation. Alternatively, to prompt children to set aside their empirical orientation, the interviewer gave several signals that the problem should be treated as a kind of make-believe game. She started off by saying: 'Let's pretend that I am in another planet', and went on to state the problem with a dramatic intonation, just as one might in telling a story (Dias and Harris, 1988, experiment 4). This intervention produced a clear change in children's pattern of responding. Within each age group, the make-believe presentation led to more logical replies than the matter-of-fact presentation. Admittedly, the 6-year-olds were more accurate in general than the 4-year-olds. However, the more important finding was the impact of presentation on both age groups, illustrated in figure 5.1.

Further evidence that a make-believe presentation encourages an analytical approach emerged when we asked children to justify their answers. As shown in figure 5.2, children were more likely to give analytic justifications for the make-believe presentation. They referred to what the interviewer had said, not to their own knowledge. For

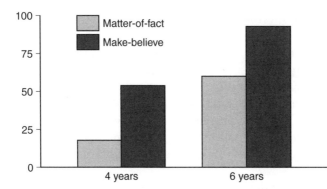

Figure 5.1   Percentage of logical replies by age and presentation.

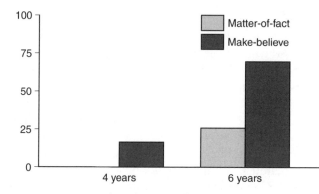

Figure 5.2   Percentage of analytic justifications by age and presentation.

example, they might say: 'Because we're pretending that fishes live in trees' or 'You said that fishes live in trees'. This type of justification was rare for the standard, matter-of-fact presentation but much more common for the make-believe presentation, especially among the 6–year-olds who were generally more willing to offer justifications than the 4-year-olds.

Given that none of the children had received much formal schooling, these findings suggested that the ability to reason, even about premises that run counter to empirical knowledge, might be an early and natural disposition. To strengthen this conclusion, Dias (1988, experiment 6) carried out a further study in Recife, in north-east Brazil, where she tested 5-year-old children who had never been to school and were illiterate. The findings were very similar to those obtained in Britain. Once prompted to use their imagination, children accurately solved problems that included a major premise that flatly contradicted their empirical knowledge. Figure 5.3 shows the proportion of logical replies and analytic justifications that the children offered when they were given the problems in the standard, matter-of-fact fashion, or alternatively with prompts to treat them in a make-believe fashion. The clear difference in performance, especially with respect to the number of logical replies, demonstrates that schooling is not necessary for children to adopt an analytic orientation.

In subsequent studies, we looked more carefully at the conditions under which children adopt the analytic orientation. As a first step,

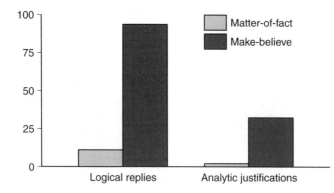

Figure 5.3 Percentage of logical replies and analytic justifications by presentation.

we analysed the various ways that children could be prompted to adopt a make-believe attitude (Dias and Harris, 1990, experiment 1). As before, one group of children was given the problems in the standard, matter-of-fact fashion. Other children were given various types of cue likely to prompt a make-believe attitude. One group, for example, heard the problems presented with a dramatic, story-like intonation; a second group was told that the problems were stories about a far-away planet; and a third group was instructed to use imagery – children were asked to 'make a picture in their head' of, for example, fishes living in trees, or black snow.[6] As compared to the standard, matter-of-fact presentation, all three make-believe cues proved effective in boosting the proportion of correct replies and the proportion of analytic justifications, as figure 5.4 illustrates.

Apparently, children will adopt the analytic orientation after a variety of quite disparate prompts. The use of a dramatic intonation, references to a distant planet and instructions to use imagery have no surface features in common. Nevertheless, they have a similar effect on children's approach to the reasoning problems. A plausible interpretation is that these various make-believe cues, notwithstanding their heterogeneity, all converge in producing a similar psychological stance. They prompt children to treat the problems as descriptions of an imaginary world; this imaginary world contains creatures and events that violate their everyday knowledge – fishes that live in trees and cats that bark. Yet precisely because

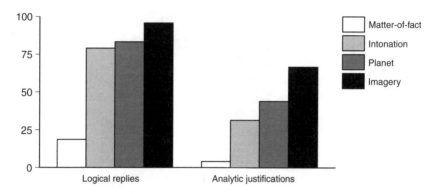

Figure 5.4   Percentage of logical replies and analytic justifications by presentation.

children have knowingly entered an imaginary world, empirical considerations are set aside and do not interfere with their acceptance of the initial premise.

Long- or Short-term Effects?

The pattern of findings reported so far appears to be quite robust. Indeed, it has been reproduced with still younger children, including 2- and 3-year-olds (Richards and Sanderson, 1999). Nevertheless, there is an important restriction to be considered. In each case, children were prompted to use their imagination by the interviewer, using one or more make-believe cues. By contrast, the change in intellectual orientation that is brought about by schooling appears to be more far-reaching. After two or three years of schooling, children spontaneously bring an analytic orientation to the task of reasoning; it does not need to be prompted or coaxed by an interviewer. The findings presented so far show that young children who have had little or no formal schooling can briefly display an analytic orientation in the context of a dialogue with an adult. However, they may not be able to display such an orientation over a longer period or do so without external support.

To evaluate this sceptical interpretation, we carried out a simple training study (Leevers and Harris, 1999, experiment 2). In the first test session, all the children were given a brief introduction to the prob-

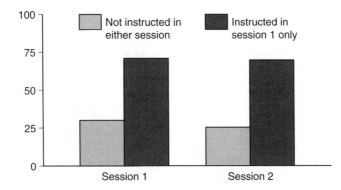

Figure 5.5 Percentage of logical replies by session and presentation.

lems, but half of them were also instructed to make a mental image of the incongruent major premise. Approximately one week later, the children were re-tested. They were briefly reminded of the earlier set of problems that they had been given, and then given a new set of problems. Unlike the initial session, none of the children were given any additional instructions. Figure 5.5 shows the pattern of results. To our surprise, children who had been given further instructions in the first session performed better than their uninstructed peers, not just in the first session, as we expected, but also one week later in the second session. They spontaneously applied the orientation that they had initially adopted to the new set of problems.

To check on children's stance toward the problems in more detail, we classified them into three groups: 'analytic', 'empirical' and 'mixed'. Analytic children combined high accuracy in replying to the problems with a predominance of analytic justifications. Empirical children combined low accuracy in replying to the problems with a predominance of empirical justifications. Children assigned to the mixed group showed a mixture of these two orientations. Figure 5.6 shows that when children were not instructed in either session, they were mainly classified as 'empirical' across the two sessions. On the other hand, when they were given instruction in the first session, they were mainly classified as 'mixed' or 'analytic' across the two sessions. Scrutiny of individual children confirmed that their orientation remained stable: they almost always received the same classification in each session.

These results show that a modest intervention can have more than

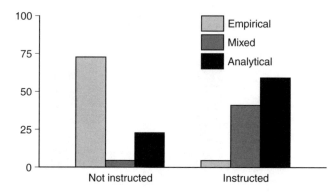

Figure 5.6   Percentage of children adopting each of three strategies by presentation.

just a transient effect. Children were likely to adopt the analytic orientation in the second session even though they were not prompted to do so. Indeed, in a follow-up study, we found that the effect of an intervention could be detected over a longer period of two to three weeks, and could be found not just among normal 4-year-olds but also among older, handicapped children whose verbal mental age was equivalent to that of the normal group (Leevers and Harris, 2000).

Adopting a Pretend Stance?

Earlier, I set out what appeared to be a plausible interpretation of the effect of make-believe cues. They prompt children to adopt a pretend stance toward the initial premise, treating it as a description of an imaginary world. Having adopted that stance, children set their empirical knowledge to one side and use the premise as a basis for reasoning, even though it contradicts what they know to be the case. This interpretation works well for the short-term effects produced by a story intonation, by references to another planet, or by instructions to use imagery. However, there are three reasons for not being fully satisfied with the proposal (Harris and Leevers, 2000a).

First, as we have just seen, such cues do not have only a short-term impact – they alter children's orientation one, two and even three weeks later. It makes little sense to claim that make-believe cues prompt children to adopt a pretend stance, and that they then hold onto that stance or attitude until they meet the interviewer again. Conceivably, the second encounter with the interviewer might somehow reactivate a pretend stance. For example, children might think of the interviewer as a kind of storyteller or mythmaker, but this interpretation is post-hoc, at best.

A second reason for dissatisfaction with the proposal that children adopt a pretend stance and set aside their empirical knowledge harks back to some findings that emerged in the series of experiments reported above, but which we did not at first recognize as problematic. Instead of being given premises that ran directly counter to their everyday experience (e.g. 'All fishes live in trees' or 'All snow is black'), some children were given premises similar to those that Luria had used in Uzbekistan. Thus, they were given unfamiliar premises that lay outside their experience (e.g. 'All molluscs live in shells' or 'All leukocytes are white'). Before presenting the problems, we confirmed that children were unaware of these facts. Provided they were first prompted with make-believe cues rather than presented with the problems in the ordinary, matter-of-fact fashion, we found that children also did better on problems with such unfamiliar premises. This boost in performance contrasted with the pattern that emerged for premises that were familiar to the children (e.g. 'All fishes live in water' or 'All milk is white'). Children performed quite well on these problems irrespective of the way that they were presented. Figure 5.7 shows the results (Dias, 1988, experiment 6).

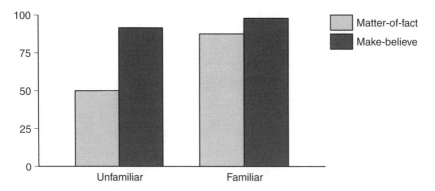

Figure 5.7 Percentage of logical replies by type of premise and presentation.

In a subsequent study, using made-up premises (e.g. 'All pongodaps have stripes on their backs' or 'All mib is black'), we again observed more accurate performance if children were presented with the problems following prompts to use the imagination rather than in an ordinary, matter-of-fact fashion (Leevers and Harris, 1999, experiment 3). Clearly, these findings with unfamiliar or made-up premises are inconsistent with the proposal that a pretend stance promotes an analytic orientation by prompting children to set aside empirical knowledge of the real world that might interfere with their encoding of the premises. In the case of both unfamiliar and made-up premises, children have no potentially interfering experience to set aside. For example, they know nothing about leukocytes or pongodaps. Hence, any benefit that is brought about by make-believe cues must have a different explanation.

A third and final reason for dissatisfaction with an emphasis on the adoption of a pretend stance is that it makes it difficult to elucidate the parallels between the effect of schooling and the effect of make-believe cues. After all, it makes little sense to say that a long-term effect of schooling, whether in Central Asia or West Africa, is the induction of a more or less stable pretend stance. Yet the parallels between the effect of schooling and of make-believe cues are clear and worth explaining. In each case, children shift toward an analytic orientation, and in each case that orientation can be characterized in terms of an increase both in the number of logical replies and in the number of justifications where children refer back to the wording of the premises. Given that equivalence, it would be illuminating to find a common explanation for the effect of schooling and of make-believe cues.

An Alternative Account

Because of these various doubts about our original emphasis on the adoption of a pretend stance, we developed a different account. The starting point was an obvious but nonetheless critical feature of the reasoning process (Leevers, 1997). When children are given a reasoning problem that starts with a familiar fact – for example, 'All fishes live in water' – it is not strictly necessary for them to take account of the initial premise. Even if they ignore it, and concentrate on the second premise and subsequent question – 'Tot is a fish. Does Tot live in a tree?' – they can provide the correct answer from their general knowledge. On the other hand, to reason accurately from a premise that either runs counter to previous experience or that introduces some new or made-up fact, it is vital to take the initial premise as a starting point and to coordinate later premises with it. For example, if children are told: 'All molluscs live in shells. Tot is a mollusc. Does Tot live in a tree?', encoding and acceptance of the initial premise is critical for a correct solution. If, instead, they focus only on the second premise and the follow-up question, they will be obliged to guess at the answer because they know nothing about molluscs. By implication, cues that prompt children to focus on an initial premise, and accept it as a starting point for what comes afterwards, are likely to improve the reasoning process whenever the initial premise states something that is either false or unfamiliar.

Hitherto, I have emphasized the way that a pretend stance might encourage children to set their empirical knowledge aside. There is, however, an additional feature of pretend play, especially joint pretend play, that was considered in detail in chapter 2. When children start to engage in joint pretence, they must be alert to the stipulations that their play partner introduces. These stipulations can fly in the face of reality – they can imply that an empty teapot contains tea. Alternatively, they can introduce hitherto unknown facts. Recall the episode involving Richard and his older sister. Richard was told that the train needed some more petrol. It is unlikely that he knew that trains need fuel, let alone petrol. Nonetheless, he went along with this premise and duly put more petrol in the train. Thus, pretend play is a very early context in which children are called on to accept premises introduced by their partner, and to respond in a consequential fashion. An alternative interpretation, therefore, of the effectiveness of make-believe cues is that they alert children to the importance of accepting the premises introduced by their interlocutor as a consequential starting point for the subsequent dialogue. Thus, looking back at the various make-believe cues that we employed – the use of a dramatic intonation, the reference to a far-off planet, the instruction to use imagery to make a mental picture of the initial premise – all these cues were likely to prompt children to treat that initial premise as an important starting point – a stipulation or premise that needed to be accepted as true, however temporarily. By contrast, when the interviewer began with a false or unfamiliar statement presented in a matter-of-fact tone, children may not have realized that the statement was an important presupposition for what was to follow, and failed to integrate it with the premises that followed.

This interpretation shifts attention away from the issue of whether children adopt a pretend as opposed to an empirical stance toward the material. It focuses instead on children's judgement about the nature of the dialogue, and more specifically on their encoding of the initial premise. To test this new interpretation, we looked at the efficacy of a cue that highlighted the first premise, but did not explicitly invite children to think of that premise as part of an imaginary or pretend world (Leevers and Harris, 1999, experiment 1). In the first session, children were presented with the problems in one of four ways: (1) they were given no special instructions; (2) they were given imagery instructions similar to those used in earlier experiments; (3) they were given imagery instructions plus a rationale, namely that using imagery would help them to solve the problems; (4) finally, they were simply asked *to think about* the first premise and what would happen if it were true. This last cue was intended to prompt children to accept the first premise as a starting point for the rest of the problem. In the second session one week later, all children, irrespective of the type of presentation that they had received in the first session, were given a new set of problems with just a minimal introduction but no further instruction.

Figure 5.8 shows that children given instructions produced more logical replies than children who received no instruction. Moreover, consistent with the long-term effects described earlier, these benefits from instruction were evident in the second session one week later. Especially important, however, is the finding that instructions to think about the initial premise were just as effective as instructions to use imagery. The clear implication is that when young children are led to accept the initial premise as a starting point for the subsequent premises, they reason more accurately. That acceptance can be brought about in various ways. It can be brought about in a relatively indirect fashion by prompting children with make-believe cues. Alternatively, it can be achieved by explicit instruction to focus on the first premise. In either case, children appear to reinterpret the nature of the exchange between themselves and the experimenter. Rather than rejecting the first premise as false or bizarre, they accept it and integrate it with the subsequent premise.

We may now step back and assess the extent to which this emphasis on children's ability to think about and accept the initial premises addresses the three findings discussed earlier: the persistent, long-term effect of instruction; the finding that performance is improved both for premises that violate ordinary experience and for those that lie

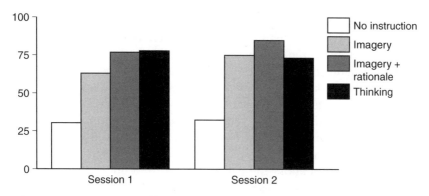

Figure 5.8 Percentage of logical replies by session and presentation.

outside it; and the parallel effects of brief instruction on the one hand, and of schooling on the other.

To the extent that brief instruction does not simply induce a pretend or make-believe attitude but instead alerts children to the initial statement and its implications, the stable effect of instruction is less puzzling. We have no need to suppose that children maintain a pretend attitude over the course of a week or more. Rather, when confronted with a similar set of problems, they reinstate their earlier insight into the way that the initial statement of the problems should be handled and apply that insight to the new problems.

Second, if children were prepared to think about the implications of the critical first premise, that would increase the likelihood of an analytic approach for various types of problem. More specifically, if children accept the first premise as a starting point for the reasoning process, no matter whether it strikes them as either false or unfamiliar, they should appropriately integrate that information with the next premise. For example, if they accept the initial premise that 'All fishes live in trees' or that 'All molluscs live in shells', they can use that information when they encode the second premise. If they learn that 'Tot is a fish' or that 'Tot is a mollusc', they can draw an inference about where Tot lives. Thus, irrespective of whether children know something that contradicts the initial premise or whether they find it altogether unfamiliar, an acceptance of the first premise and its integration with subsequent information would lead them toward a correct conclusion.[7]

Finally, this alternative interpretation suggests an explanation for the parallels between the effects of brief instruction and schooling. We have suggested that brief instruction leads children to adopt a different stance toward the dialogue that they have with the experimenter. Instead of ignoring statements that contradict or lie beyond what they know, children start to adopt a receptive stance – they accept and integrate such statements with later information. We may speculate that the impact of schooling is more profound but ultimately similar. It changes the way that children construe adult discourse. More specifically, children increasingly see it as a context where they will be given information about the world that lies beyond or does not fit in with their everyday experience.

It is true that children will already have encountered this type of information before they go to school. Such encounters are likely to take place when children engage in a one-to-one dialogue with an adult about some question that puzzles them.[8] For example, when they are at home with a parent, children have frequent opportunities for posing questions that can lead to a dialogue in which new information is supplied (Tizard and Hughes, 1984). Indeed, as illustrated by the exchange quoted at the beginning of this chapter, it is precisely in the context of this type of dialogue that children are likely to engage in a reasoning process – with the adult supplying all or some of the premises and the child supplying the conclusion (Scholnick and Wing, 1991, 1995).

This type of dialogue is likely to be less frequent and less sustained when children leave home and enter the classroom. Children pose many fewer questions at school than at home, and the difference is especially obvious for questions that are motivated by curiosity (Tizard and Hughes, 1984, p. 271). In school, children are increasingly exposed to a new type of discourse: the didactic monologue. In this type of discourse, even though they have not asked for it, children are provided with information about the world that goes beyond their everyday experience. Indeed, whether it is about the visit of the Magi, the demise of Tyrannosaurus Rex or the wartime evacuation of children, the information may be as outlandish as anything that children have encountered in fiction. Nevertheless, it is delivered in a matter-of-fact fashion. Thus, from the child's point of view, the didactic monologue is likely to be a hybrid. The content may be as exotic as a fairy tale but it is delivered with a matter-of-fact tone of voice. A plausible effect of schooling, therefore, is gradually to teach children to extend the receptive stance that they adopt during joint pretend play or during a dialogue that is initiated by their own curiosity to the didactic monologue that they first encounter in school. They start to become receptive to information that they have not asked for so long as it is delivered with authority.[9]

In conclusion, this chapter has provided evidence for two claims. First, the ability to adopt an analytic orientation is not something unusual or unnatural. Contrary to the conclusion reached by Luria, Scribner and Braine, we should not think of the analytic orientation as a fundamentally new capacity that is the product of schooling.[10] Children come to school already capable of adopting that orientation even if they are sometimes disinclined to use it, especially when they are presented with exotic information in an ordinary, matter-of-fact fashion. Second, the effect of brief instruction is not to get children to adopt a temporary, pretend attitude toward information that contradicts their experience. Rather, it provides them with a relatively stable insight into the nature of a particular type of dialogue – a dialogue in which they are expected to be receptive to premises that do not fit their experience or lie outside it. That receptivity is displayed by 2- and 3-year-old children when they engage in pretend play. It is displayed by preschool children when they engage in a one-to-one dialogue with a parent. It is also expected in school. In that context, children will often be confronted with information that cannot be easily assimilated into their everyday experience. Such information will be increasingly offered not when children pose a question, but in the context of a didactic monologue. Effectively, children begin to acknowledge their teacher as an authority – someone who expects their claims to be heeded, even if they sound implausible or strange.

Notes

1 Luria and Vygotsky viewed the changes in economic practice and in educational provision as closely intertwined sociocultural changes. Hence, no effort was made to disentangle their influence. Subsequent replication work by Michael Cole and his colleagues has focused on the impact of schooling and literacy, while holding economic conditions approximately constant.

2 This line of thinking raises the interesting possibility that participation in collective farming might have a similar impact independent of formal schooling. According to Luria's brief description, the collectivization pro-

gramme called for group decision-making about the future production of the farm. Such planning, like school arithmetic, requires the invocation of hypothetical values, and the calculation of their consequences.

3　Other commentators have also been disinclined to accept the claim advanced by Luria, and largely endorsed by Scribner, namely that the analytic attitude involves a new mode of thought. For example, Cole (1977, p. xv) reaches the following, cautious conclusion: 'What Luria interprets as the acquisition of new modes of thought, I am more inclined to interpret as changes in the application of previously available modes to particular problems and contexts of discourse represented by the experimental setting'. However, Cole does not discuss evidence for the earlier availability of these modes, or describe the contexts in which they are engendered.

4　Vygotsky even implies that an incapacity for distancing oneself from empirical reality, especially in the context of dealing with language, is symptomatic of pathology. Citing the findings of Goldstein (1948), he refers to a patient with a speech disturbance who was incapable of repeating anomalous phrases such as 'snow is black'.

5　Children's empirical knowledge about the claims made in the initial, major premise of each problem was established in a pre-test. For example, they might be asked: 'Where do fishes live?' or 'What noise do cats make?' Children were highly accurate in answering these questions. As a result, we could be confident that the initial premise of each problem did run counter to their empirical knowledge.

6　The full experiment (described in Dias and Harris, 1990, experiment 1) contained eight conditions: a baseline condition and seven experimental conditions. The seven experimental conditions involved the presence or absence of one or more of the three make-believe cues: Intonation, Setting and Imagery. The three experimental conditions described in the text were those that included a single make-believe cue (e.g. Imagery).

7　This explanation can also go some way to explain an anomalous finding of Scribner and Cole (1981). In a smaller-scale follow-up to their major survey of the Vai, they found considerable use of the analytic mode even among unschooled, illiterate subjects. Although none of the background variables, including schooling and literacy, was associated with good performance, one procedural variable was associated: participants who tackled the logical problems at the end of the interview, after a conversation about grammar or words, did better than those who tackled them at the outset. A plausible interpretation of this finding, in the light of the present interpretation, is that the prior interview led participants to focus more carefully on exactly what the interviewer claimed in the opening premise, even if it sounded bizarre (e.g. 'All women who live in Monrovia are married' or 'All men living on the moon do not have three heads').

8   Children are also likely to be given information that conflicts with, or lies outside, their experience in the context of prescriptive as well as descriptive discourse. For example, they will be informed of the conditions under which they may or may not engage in a given course of action. This type of discourse has several interesting and distinctive features which will be discussed in more detail in chapter 7.

9   There are, of course, differences among these contexts. In the case of joint pretence, the child's receptivity should involve a willingness to treat the stipulations introduced by a play partner temporarily as if they were true. By contrast, in the context of a dialogue that is sparked by the child's questions, or a didactic monologue encountered in school, the child's receptivity should involve a willingness to believe – and not just temporarily to entertain – the information that is introduced by an interlocutor. Nonetheless, in all three cases, there is the common requirement that an initial premise (or stipulation) is treated as a starting point for the integration of subsequent information.

10 An important but unanswered question is how adults who have had no formal education whatsoever (i.e., adults equivalent to those tested by Luria) would respond to the various prompts that successfully elicited an analytic orientation among young children. Arguably, uneducated adults would display a similar receptivity to unfamiliar or false premises if they were suitably prompted. An alternative possibility, however, is that when adults have no schooling and have passed their entire life engaged in a restricted and very localized set of subsistence activities, their receptivity to such premises may be reduced – despite prompting. Recall that the uneducated peasants that Luria interviewed often balked even when he sought to elicit a more analytic answer by prompting them to attend to his words ('But on the basis of what I said, what do you think?').

6

Counterfactual Thinking

In previous chapters, I described how children can imagine a non-existent situation and the way in which that situation might unfold. I also argued that children may become absorbed in that imaginary situation and its emotional implications – often, to the neglect of what might be happening in the real world. Admittedly, in going on that imaginary journey, children take with them causal knowledge based on the real world, knowledge that allows them to make sense of their make-believe encounters. However, they do not look back over their shoulder at the real world and compare it with what they have imagined.

In the course of the next two chapters, I attempt to correct this emphasis on children's absorption into an imaginary world. Sometimes, children mentally travel back and forth between the imagined and the real world. I shall argue that children's interpretation of what has actually happened is constantly infused by their ability to consider what might have happened or should have happened but did not. In that respect, the landscape of reality may look different after they return from an excursion into the counterfactual world. In this chapter, I focus on an important but somewhat unexpected role for such counterfactual thinking: its contribution to causal judgement. Young children are able to compare an observed outcome with what might have occurred had events taken a different course, and they make causal judgements about reality in the light of such comparisons.

Hume and His Critics

What is our everyday conception of a causal connection? According to Hume (1978), we observe a regular succession between two events A and B, and by dint of an ensuing association in our mind between the two events, we come to infer a causal connection between them. For example, we see someone blowing at a lighted candle, and almost immediately we see the candle flicker and go out. After observing this sequence several times, an association between blowing at the candle and its going out is formed in our mind, and we infer the presence of a causal connection between the two events. Hume pointed out that the empirical evidence does not justify our inference. We have seen a regular sequence but we have not observed any causal link. Hume's primary philosophical goal was to lay out the case for scepticism concerning the foundation and validity of our causal judgement. At the same time, he provided a vivid psychological analysis of the process of causal thinking and his account has had a marked influence on subsequent psychological investigations.

Nevertheless, modern philosophical analysis has suggested that whatever the merits of Hume's sceptical arguments about the true nature of causality, his characterization of our everyday causal thinking captures only part of the psychological process involved. Mackie (1974) has provided an especially important critique. He proposes that our ordinary conception of causality is based not just on observation of a regular sequence, but also on a consideration of what we imagine would have happened had circumstances been different. Consider again the candle that is extinguished. On the one hand, we do indeed observe a sequence of events. Yet we are also able to imagine a different sequence of events. We can imagine that no one blows at the burning candle, and it remains alight. Mackie proposes that our inclination to ascribe a causal role to blowing at the candle is based on a comparison between the observed sequence, and a sequence that we did not actually observe but we can easily imagine as an alternative to what did happen, namely no one blowing at the candle and its remaining alight. Indeed, as Mackie points out, when we see a candle extinguished, the alternative sequence is easily imagined – if we cast our mind back to an earlier point in time when the candle burned uninterruptedly, we have a compelling example of that alternative sequence.

Mackie acknowledges that our conception of causality includes other features. We assume an asymmetry between cause and effect, and some kind of causal mechanism. Nevertheless, his analysis of our everyday thinking about causality is distinctive in ascribing central importance to our contemplation of what might have occurred but did not, and our comparison of that counterfactual sequence with the actual sequence. Effectively, we carry out a thought experiment in which we compare an observed sequence with an imagined sequence, holding other background factors constant. In the observed sequence, a given outcome is present, whereas in the imagined sequence it is eliminated. In so far as the outcome only occurs when a particular antecedent is present, we feel justified in ascribing a causal role to it.

One advantage of Mackie's analysis is that it helps to explain why on different occasions we may offer a different causal account of the same type of outcome. His analysis implies that our causal conclusions will vary depending on the type of counterfactual case that we are prompted to bring to mind. A hypothetical example described by Hart and Honoré (1985, p. 35) provides a convincing illustration of this point. When a fire breaks out in a factory, we might attribute the fire to the dropping of a lighted cigarette, but we would not find it satisfactory to attribute it to the presence of oxygen – even though the presence of oxygen is obviously a necessary condition for the fire to have occurred. We do not deem oxygen to be the cause of the fire because – unlike the lighted cigarette – it would also be present on countless occasions when fire did not break out. The possibility of its being absent does not occur to us. Consider now a different case. If a fire breaks out in a factory where special precautions are taken to exclude oxygen during part of the manufacturing process, we might well attribute the fire to the presence of oxygen. In explaining the fire, we would have in mind the contrast between the exceptional case – when for whatever reason oxygen is present – and the counterfactual but normal case when oxygen is excluded. This example shows how for a given observed sequence, the particular counterfactual alternative that we bring to mind for comparison purposes may vary – with concomitant effects on the causal conclusions that we reach.

Empirical Research on Causal Judgement

Recent research with adults provides empirical support for the proposals made by Mackie (1974). Wells and Gavinski (1989) presented adults with two versions of a story about a fatal accident and asked them to make various judgements about how the accident had happened. The story described a celebratory meal eaten by Karen and her boss, Mr Carlson. Because he had been to the restaurant several times before, Mr Carlson ordered for both of them. In one story version, he wavered between *moules marinière* – mussels in a wine sauce – and another fish dish with no wine sauce. He eventually decided on the mussels, with disastrous results. Unbeknown to him, Karen suffered from a rare hereditary disease that made her allergic to fermented drinks such as wine or liqueurs. Having enjoyed her meal, Karen began to feel ill, was rushed to hospital and died. In an alternative version of the story, Carlson also chose the mussels but in this case he hesitated between the mussels and another fish dish with a wine sauce.

Thus, the two story versions were identical with respect to the dish that was actually chosen – mussels – and also with respect to the immediate cause of Karen's death – the presence of a wine sauce. They differed only in the alternative possibility considered by Mr Carlson when he was ordering. Nevertheless, the participants in the study came to different conclusions about the causal role played by the choice of dish in these two versions. When the alternative dish did not contain wine, they were more likely to judge that the ordering decision played a causal role, more likely to list that decision among the key causes, and more likely to mention that decision in listing ways the accident could have been avoided. In assessing the causes of the accident, participants appeared to think back to an alternative antecedent that would have prevented it. When the story rendered such an alternative salient – as it did when the alternative choice was a harmless dish with no wine – the actual choice was deemed more critical. This analysis implies that a causal judgement can involve two separate and successive phases: (1) a scanning of the train of antecedent events for a salient counterfactual alternative that would have led to a different outcome, and (2) a focus on the actual antecedent that such a salient alternative could have replaced as a key element in the causal sequence. More generally, this analysis implies that counterfactual thinking can precede and influence causal judgement.

Support for this two-stage model emerged in a follow-up study in which adults read one of two versions of a story about a car accident involving a taxi-driver (Wells and Gavinski, 1989, experiment 2). Participants were asked to (1) think about possible ways in which the accident could have been avoided and (2) make a causal judgement about the behaviour of the taxi-driver. However, the order of these two tasks was varied – some people first listed ways in which the accident could have been avoided and then carried out the causal judgement task, whereas others did the reverse. Consistent with the notion that counterfactual thinking can influence causal judgements, participants judged that the taxi-driver's behaviour had played a more important role in the accident if they had previously thought about how the accident might have been avoided. Further support for the two-stage model was reported in a reaction-time study. Participants read a story about a student doing poorly in an exam after a night of heavy drinking. They then answered a series of questions, of which two were critical – a question that invited counterfactual thoughts about how the student might have done better in the exam, and a question about what had caused his disappointing performance. Consistent with the two-stage model, participants who answered the counterfactual question first were quicker to give an answer to the causal question, whereas the reverse type of facilitation did not occur (Roese and Olson, 1997, pp. 38–9). By implication, the prior engagement of counterfactual thinking meant that participants were helped on their way to a causal judgement.

These findings show the role of counterfactual thinking in a convincing fashion. Effectively, we ask ourselves: under what circumstances might this outcome have been avoided or prevented? Such an emphasis on counterfactual thinking allows us to make sense of two important features of our causal judgement. First, depending on what counterfactual situation we bring to mind, we can arrive at different conclusions about the cause of an outcome. At the same time, our use of counterfactual thinking may lead us to ignore certain factors that indubitably do play a causal role. We are unlikely to imagine a world in which fire is avoided by a temporary absence of oxygen. Hence, we do not normally cite oxygen as a causal factor in most fires, even if we are capable of doing so under exceptional circumstances.

Children's Causal Judgements

Within developmental psychology, Hume's emphasis on regular, successive events has had a marked influence. For example, children's sensitivity to the temporal and spatial contiguity between cause and effect has been a major focus of research (Bullock, Gelman and

Baillargeon, 1982). Even those investigators who have been inspired by Michotte's (1963) proposals concerning innate or maturational constraints on our perception of causality – and who might therefore be expected to dissent from Hume's empiricist approach – have focused on the role of temporal and spatial contiguity in the perception of causality (Cohen and Oakes, 1993; Leslie, 1982; Leslie and Keeble, 1987; Millar, 1972; Millar and Schaffer, 1972).

However, if Mackie's analysis of everyday causal thinking is correct for adults – and the findings just described lend support to his analysis – we may reasonably ask whether this mode of causal thinking emerges in childhood. Is it a mode of thought that is elementary and foundational? Alternatively, is it a relatively sophisticated and late-emerging adjunct to the alleged sensitivity of babies and young children to events in close temporal and spatial proximity? Mackie himself took the former position. Like Hume, his aim was to analyse causal thinking not just among adults but among children and even animals: 'although we express this kind of thinking in words, its development need not have waited for the development of language. It is not essentially tied to verbal expression, and there is some reason to suppose that other, non-verbal animals share this capacity with us' (Mackie, 1974, p. 55).

To decide whether young children are able to make causal judgements in the way that Mackie describes, we start with a very basic question: do young children ever acknowledge that reality might have turned out differently? If they do, we may go on to ask whether they are able to entertain an alternative antecedent to one that they have actually observed and anticipate its consequences. Finally, we may ask if they ever bring that mode of counterfactual thinking to bear in making causal judgements. In particular, do they compare what might have happened with what actually did happen?

Thinking About How Reality Might Have Turned Out Differently

At first glance, one might think that the previous chapters have provided abundant evidence that very young children can think and talk about ways in which reality might have taken a different course. For example, in chapter 2, I described 2-year-olds' ability to watch and then report on a pretend episode. In particular, children were able to describe the outcome of pretend mischief such as pouring make-believe tea over a toy animal: they realized that the victim would end up 'wet' or 'soggy' or 'teaey'. These episodes appear to include a counterfactual premise: children go along with the supposition that tea has been poured from the teapot (when nothing, in fact, emerged) and they also recognize the causal outcome: the pouring of the tea causes the victim to end up 'wet' etc.

However, the type of suppositional thinking that is deployed in pretend play is importantly different from the counterfactual thinking that may be directed at reality itself. In the case of pretend play, children do not set up a contrast between an imaginary event and an actual event. They simply invent, watch, or describe an imaginary event; the imaginary event has no close cousin in reality with which it contrasts. At best, the imagined situation may include certain incidental parallels with the actual situation, parallels that can be exploited – for example, make-believe tea can be poured into a real cup, if there happens to be a real cup available in reality. The existence of a cup, both in the make-believe world and in the actual world, is fortuitous. It is simply the result of the pretend player's 'looting' of reality to furnish the make-believe world. Such exploitation is not prompted by any consideration of how reality itself might have turned out differently. Pretend events are essentially self-contained; they are not set up as departures from actual events. Indeed, consistent with this analysis, a game of pretend can turn on a situation that happens to coincide with the way things really are. For example, Sully (1896, p. 48) describes the case of two sisters, who played at being sisters. Similarly, Vygotsky, following Sully's example, reported that he successfully elicited this type of play by having a child 'play' at being a child while the child's mother 'played' at being mother (Vygotsky, 1978, pp. 94–5).

Given this analysis, we need to define our domain of search a bit more precisely. Rather than seeking evidence for children's ability to engage in suppositional thinking in general (including pretence), we seek evidence for their ability to think about what might have happened as an alternative to what really did happen. To obtain evidence for this mode of thinking, it is helpful to look at the way that children talk about causal outcomes. It is true that children do not often produce well-formed counterfactual, conditional statements (e.g. 'If you had been awake, you would have heard the owl') until 4 or 5 years of age (Kuczaj and Daly, 1979; Reilly, 1986). On the other hand, their more succinct comments about what has happened betray an appreciation that something different might well have happened instead. This is especially obvious when they talk about events that *almost* happened.

If we watch someone rapidly gain on the front runner in the home stretch of a race but just fail to reach the finishing line first, we are apt to say that the loser almost won (Kahneman and Varey, 1990). We anticipate an outcome that does not actually materialize and in describing what has happened, we pick out this unrealized possibility. Do young children make such extrapolations when they are shown a sequence in which a particular outcome almost happens? To answer this question, we showed 2- and 3-year-olds scenes involving two toy animals; one animal came much closer to a particular outcome than the other, although neither animal suffered the outcome in question (Harris, 1997b). For example, one toy horse was made to gallop to the very edge of the table so that it almost fell off, whereas the other stopped well short of the edge. We then asked children: 'Which horse almost fell off the table?' Note that the test question referred to an outcome that had not materialized for either horse: both came to a halt on the table and neither fell off. Nevertheless, children appeared to understand the question and they were more likely to indicate the animal that came close to the unrealized possibility rather than the one that never approached it.

In the next study, 2- and 3-year-olds watched a single animal that almost suffered a mishap. For example, a toy bear was marched across the table wearing a hat perched somewhat precariously on his head. The experimenter brought the bear to a halt, announced that: 'Just then there was a big puff of wind', and blew mightily at the bear – almost making his hat fall off. Children were then asked: 'Did you see that? What happened?' In offering a description, children frequently mentioned the outcome that came close to happening. For example, a 28-month-old said: 'It blowed off' and a 40-month-old said: 'His hat nearly fell off'. As these two replies illustrate, older children were more likely to include an explicit marker such as *nearly* or *almost*. Nevertheless, both age groups made references to the unrealized outcome they had not actually seen.

Finally, we combed records of young children's spontaneous language production (MacWhinney and Snow, 1985) for use of the word *almost*. These naturalistic data confirmed the experimental findings. All five children that we examined began to use *almost* before their third birthday, and they used it to designate outcomes that fell just short of being realized. Such remarks were mainly – but not exclusively – unprompted comments on minor mishaps that almost befell the children in the course of their activities. For example, Naomi (at 23 months) said, 'Almost fall down', Ross (at 34 months) said, 'I almost got that squirt', and Adam (at 44 months) said, 'You almost broke my arm'. In summary, whether we use children's differentiation between a near-accident and a more unlikely accident, their prompted descriptions of a near-mishap, or their spontaneous remarks about a near-mishap, there is clear evidence that 2- and 3-year-old children understand how an observed outcome might have turned out differently. Even if children of this age do not produce conditional utterances with an 'if-then' format, they can conceive of ways in which reality might have turned out differently. We may now ask whether they think through what would have happened if antecedent circumstances had been different.

Thinking About Counterfactual Antecedents

To examine children's ability to think about counterfactual antecedents, we showed 3- and 4-year-olds a simple causal sequence, and then posed a counterfactual question about what might have happened instead (Harris, German and Mills, 1996, experiment 1). To answer the counterfactual question correctly, children had to be able to set aside the actual antecedent plus the outcome that they had just observed, imagine that antecedent being replaced by a different antecedent, and then predict the outcome. This task is presumably more taxing than the identification of an outcome that just fails to materialize in that children have to consider counterfactual outcomes that showed no obvious sign of almost coming to pass. They only become feasible, granted an important change in the antecedent conditions. An example will make the procedure clearer. In one episode, children were told:

> 'One day the floor is nice and clean.' (Children's attention was drawn to a clean surface.) 'But guess what! Carol comes home and she doesn't take her shoes off.' (A doll was brought to the edge of the surface.) 'She comes inside and makes the floor all dirty with her shoes.' (The doll was walked across the surface, leaving dirty footprints.)

Children were then asked two questions to check that they understood both the current situation ('Is the floor dirty now?') and the initial situation ('Was the floor dirty before?'). Finally, the critical test question was posed. Children were asked to imagine the likely outcome of a different antecedent situation. For example, 'What if Carol had taken her shoes off, would the floor be dirty?' As might be expected, very few errors were made on the two check questions. Children could identify the current situation and the previous situation. More importantly, children were also quite accurate on the test questions, with 3-year-olds correct on 75 per cent of the episodes, and 4-year-olds correct on 87 per cent. Thus, at an age when children have not fully mastered the production of counterfactual conditional sentences, they can readily think about what might have happened but did not. More specifically, children can set aside the causal sequence they have just seen, imagine a different antecedent condition (e.g. Carol removing her shoes rather than keeping them on), and work out the consequence of that counterfactual antecedent.

In our next study, we probed children's understanding more thoroughly (Harris et al., 1996, experiment 2). Conceivably, children were making use of a simple heuristic: *if the imagined antecedent does not match the actual antecedent, assume that the outcome will be different from the outcome that you have just seen.* This heuristic would give valid results for all the test questions that we used in our first experiment because we always asked children to imagine an antecedent situation that would lead to a different outcome from the one that they had seen. For example, in the episode about Carol's dirty shoes, children were asked to imagine Carol removing her shoes, so that the floor would remain clean, contrary to what the children actually saw.

Although this heuristic would work for the questions that we posed, it can lead to invalid conclusions. Say we had asked children to imagine that Carol had worn muddy boots instead of dirty shoes, then the outcome would obviously remain the same: the floor would end up getting dirty. More generally, once a sequence of events has taken place, it is possible to imagine a variety of alternative antecedent conditions. Some of these alternatives will produce the same ultimate outcome. Some will yield a different outcome. Adults appear to be sensitive to the differential outcome of these various counterfactuals, as Wells and Gavinski (1989) demonstrated. The adults in their study weighed the role of the choice of dish differently depending on whether the alternative choice would have saved Karen's life, or led to the same eventual fate. In the case of adults, it is likely that they ruminate about a variety of alternatives, especially when an outcome is dramatic, painful or unexpected. For example, in the case of a suicide or the breakdown of a relationship, a stable judgement about the 'critical' precipitating circumstance may not emerge until this retrospective speculation about how the life or the relationship might have been saved has been run through again and again.

In our next experiment, we asked 3-year-olds to consider more than one counterfactual antecedent (Harris et al., 1996, experiment 2). In particular, we asked whether they recognize that some alternatives to the actual starting condition could have prevented the actual outcome, whereas others would produce an equivalent outcome. For example, children were presented with the following episode:

> 'One day some bricks were standing up like this.' (The experimenter points to a tower of bricks.) 'But guess what! Naughty Teddy comes along and hits them with a stick like this.' (The experimenter makes Teddy knock the bricks over.)

After two check questions about whether the bricks were standing up now and whether they were standing up before, children were asked two test questions: 'If Teddy hadn't hit the bricks with his stick, would they be standing up now?' and 'If Teddy had hit the bricks with his hand instead, would they be standing up now?'

Across four such episodes, we checked to see whether children replied differently and appropriately to the two test questions – positively in the case of the question citing the elimination of the crucial causal factor (not hitting the bricks), and negatively in the case of the question citing the substitution of an equally potent causal factor (hitting the bricks with the hand rather than a stick). Three-year-olds discriminated sharply between the test questions: they realized what alteration in the earlier circumstances would or would not have made a difference to the final outcome. They were clearly not relying on the simple heuristic of assuming that any alteration in the antecedent conditions would produce a different outcome.

So far, we have established that 3- and 4-year-olds – who rarely make well-formed counterfactual conditional remarks – can nonetheless imagine an antecedent that differs from the starting condition that they actually witnessed, and work out whether or not a different outcome will ensue. As yet, however, we have only shown that children will, when asked, entertain an antecedent and consequent that differs from the one that they actually observed; we have provided no evidence that they spontaneously make use of this ability when making a causal judgement about an actual outcome. In a third study, we sought such evidence (Harris et al., 1996, experiment 3).

Following the proposals of Mackie (1974) and Wells and Gavinski (1989), we reasoned as follows: children can imagine a variety of ways in which the antecedent conditions for an event might have been different. In some of these counterfactual scenarios, the same outcome will ensue; in others, that outcome will fail to occur. To the extent that children imagine a change in a given component of the antecedent conditions and find that the observed outcome does not ensue, they will be likely to treat that component as a critical causal factor. By contrast, to the extent that children can imagine a change in a given component but find that the observed outcome still obtains, they will be likely to ignore that component as a causal factor.

This effectively means that children should identify different causal factors as playing a role depending on the alternative antecedents that they bring to mind. Accordingly, we composed stories with an experimental version and a control version with the expectation that the two versions would differ in terms of the alternative antecedent that children would bring to mind at the end of the story. Again, it will be easier to explain the procedure with the help of an example. Three- and 4-year-olds listened to stories such as the following:

> 'One day, Sally wanted to do a drawing. Her Mum said she could draw with a pencil or with a black pen. Sally said she didn't want to draw with a pencil, she wanted to draw with a black pen. Guess what! When Sally was drawing with the black pen, she touched her drawing, and made her fingers all inky.'

After each story, children were asked two questions: one about the cause of the outcome and one about how it could have been prevented. For example, for the above story about Sally, children were asked: 'Why did Sally's fingers get all inky?' and 'What should Sally have done instead so that her fingers wouldn't get inky?' We anticipated that children listening to this story would bring to mind the alternative antecedent – the pencil – speculate about what might have happened had Sally opted for that instead, and conclude that she would not have ended up with inky fingers had she made that choice. Accordingly, we predicted that children would be likely to formulate an answer to the *why* and the *prevention* question by referring to the choice that she had rejected, for example: 'Because she didn't use a pencil' or 'She should have used a pencil'.

A control version of the story was created in order to prompt children to bring to mind a different antecedent and a different counterfactual conclusion:

> 'One day, Sally wanted to do some drawing. Her Mum said she could draw with a blue pen or a black pen. Sally said she didn't want to draw with a blue pen, she wanted to draw with a black pen. Guess what! When Sally was drawing with the black pen, she touched her drawing, and made her fingers all inky.'

In this control story, Sally chose to write with a black pen just as she did in the experimental story, but her initial options were different. We anticipated that children listening to this type of story would recognize that even had Sally chosen the other pen, she would still have ended up with inky fingers. Accordingly, her choice of black as opposed to blue ink should be less salient either as a causal factor or as a preventive factor. Instead, children were expected to focus more on the role of other links in the causal chain, for example the fact that Sally touched what she had written.

To check these predictions, we examined children's replies to the *why* question and the *prevention* question to see how often they referred to the rejected option. The frequency with which children did this across the three experimental and control stories is shown in figure 6.1. Because the pattern was very similar for both 3- and 4-year-olds, data from the two age groups have been combined. Figure 6.1 shows that children did refer to the rejected option when answering both the *why* question and the *prevention* question. Not surprisingly, references to this rejected option were especially frequent when children were asked explicitly about how the outcome could have been prevented. Nevertheless, they were also provided spontaneously by the children in answering the initial *why* question. Figure 6.1 also clearly shows that children did not invoke the rejected option indiscriminately. They referred to it much less often in the control stories where the rejected option would have led to a similar mishap in any case.

Arguably, children's references to the rejected option simply reflect the structure of the experimental stories. After all, children were ex-

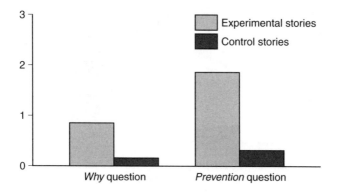

Figure 6.1 Mean number of references to the rejected option by question and story type.

plicitly told that the protagonist had two options and rejected one of them. Maybe in the context of this type of explicit reference to an alternative course of action, especially one that would have produced a different outcome, children are prompted to think about how that alternative might have led to a different outcome, but they do not ordinarily speculate in this fashion.

To assess this objection, we studied the replies that children gave when they did not refer to the rejected option. We identified a variety of replies that, despite their heterogeneity, invoked some alternative course of action that the protagonist might have taken but did not. These replies invoked counterfactual possibilities but they did not refer to the option explicitly rejected by the protagonist. For example, children might say: ''Cos she should have done it with a crayon' or 'She shouldn't have put her hand on it (i.e. her drawing)'. Figure 6.2 shows the frequency with which children produced these counterfactual replies for each question and for each type of story.

Figure 6.2 illustrates a pattern that is almost a mirror image of figure 6.1. In the experimental stories, children were likely to focus on the rejected option. In the control stories, by contrast, they were likely to focus on various other alternative courses of action. Thus, children think about what might have happened not just when some alternative choice that would have led to a different outcome is explicitly mentioned, as in the experimental stories, they can also imagine such alternatives for themselves, without prompting, and often did so in the control stories.

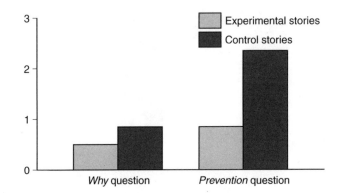

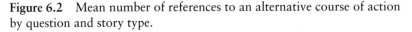

Figure 6.2   Mean number of references to an alternative course of action by question and story type.

Surveying these various references to counterfactual possibilities, be they references to the rejected choice or some other alternative, how exactly did children formulate them? What type of linguistic construction did they use, given that they have not mastered the fully fledged counterfactual conditional? We found that their replies to the initial *why* question could be allocated to one of the following eight categories, which are identified in terms of a key word that appeared in the answer:

1   *Need*, e.g.: 'Because she *needs* a coat on.'
2   *Should*, e.g.: 'She *should* have used a pencil.'
3   *Want*, e.g.: 'Because she *wanted* some sandwiches.'
4   *Didn't/Wasn't*, e.g.: ''Cos he *didn't* have (*wasn't* wearing) his boots.'
5   *Had to*, e.g.: 'Because she *had to* have her coat on.'
6   *Too*, e.g.: 'Because it (i.e., the glass) was *too* full.'
7   *Wrong*, e.g.: 'Because she had the *wrong* cardigan on.'
8   *I would*, e.g.: '*I would* wear my wellingtons.'

Figure 6.3 shows the proportion of replies made by each age group that fell into each category. It shows that children in both age groups typically thought of the mishap as the result of some departure from what might be called *standard operating procedure*. They claimed that the story character had omitted something (*Didn't*) or had failed to respect some criterion or standard (*Need, Should, Had to, Too, Wrong, I would*). The pattern was similar for both age groups save that the 4-

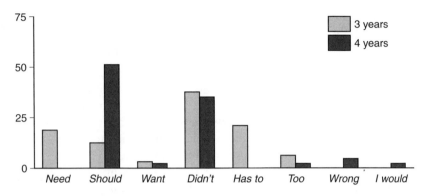

Figure 6.3 Percentage of references to an alternative course of action by age and category of answer.

year-olds mostly converged on two linguistic formulae to describe such departures (*Should* and *Didn't*). The 3-year-olds had not yet settled in such a stable fashion on these formulae and were more dispersed in the categories that they used.

Cumulatively, this series of experiments offers persuasive evidence that young children can and do engage in counterfactual thinking when they try to analyse why an event has happened or how it might be avoided. The first experiment showed that 3- and 4-year-olds can imagine a counterfactual antecedent and figure out how it would alter an observed outcome. The next experiment showed that 3-year-olds can distinguish between counterfactual antecedents that would or would not change the observed course of events. The final experiment showed that 3- and 4-year-olds use the latter distinction to explain why a mishap has occurred and also how it might be prevented. They refer in a selective fashion to those changes in the antecedent conditions that would block the observed outcome, whether it be the choice of a different option (as in the experimental stories) or an altogether different course of action (as in control stories). Scrutiny of the way that children explained the outcomes indicates that they often saw them as the consequence of some departure from standard operating procedure.

When Do Children Invoke Counterfactuals?

So far, we have seen that when children are asked to consider some untoward outcome, they are likely to mention an option or course of action that was not adopted. They do this when they are asked to explain the outcome, and when they are asked how it might have been prevented. These findings show that children are able to think about counterfactuals, and they make use of that capacity in their causal thinking. Still, there are several questions left unanswered. First, one might ask whether children only bring such thoughts to mind if they are also asked to suggest preventive measures. What would happen, for example, if children were simply asked why something had happened but not also invited to suggest how it might have been prevented? Would they still invoke counterfactual alternatives in answering the *why* question? German (1999) examined this question in a follow-up to the experiments reported above. He tested 5-year-old children on four different stories, but in each case children were simply asked why the outcome had occurred. Even in the absence of any *prevention* question, children still answered the *why* question by mentioning things that the protagonist had not done, or should have done. The implication is that counterfactual thinking comes naturally to children even when they are not explicitly prompted to think about preventive measures.

We may also ask whether the nature of the outcome disposes children to engage in counterfactual thinking. Such thinking might be especially likely to come to mind when an outcome is negative or unpleasant. Looking back over the various stories or situations that have been discussed, they all involved a negative outcome – a minor, everyday mishap in the case of Sally's inky exploits, a more exotic and serious misadventure in the case of Karen's deadly dinner. Counterfactual thinking might be less likely if the outcome is positive. Two experiments provided initial support for this conclusion. In one study, 3- and 4-year-old children listened to stories in which the protagonist chose between two options (e.g. drawing with a pen or a pencil) and ended up with either a negative outcome (e.g. inky fingers) or a positive outcome (e.g. clean fingers) (Harris, 1996a). As expected, both age groups invoked counterfactual explanations for the outcome – they said that the protagonist had *not* adopted the other option or *should* have adopted it. However, such explanations were more frequent for negative than positive story outcomes. When children explained positive outcomes, they typically referred to the option that the protagonist *had* adopted and not to the one that he or she had rejected. A similar pattern of results was obtained by German (1999).

These findings suggest that children, and indeed adults, only engage in counterfactual thinking when they are led – by virtue of the unpleasantness of the outcome – to cast their mind back to ways in which the outcome could have been avoided. However, a different interpretation is also feasible. Suppose that children engage in counterfactual thinking for both positive and negative outcomes but the way in which they formulate those thoughts differs in the two cases. In the case of a negative outcome, they effectively say: 'If only some other course of action had been adopted (e.g. *she should have used a pencil*) rather than the one that was actually pursued'. By contrast, in the case of a positive outcome, they effectively say: 'Thank goodness the actual course of action was adopted (e.g. *she used a pencil*) rather than something different'. On this account, for both positive and negative outcomes, children would mentally contrast what did take place with what might have taken place, and in each case this contrast would guide their causal conclusion, but they would refer to the actual antecedent for positive outcomes and to the alternative antecedent for negative outcomes. By implication, thoughts about what might have happened instead are pervasive whenever children engage in a causal analysis, be it positive or negative, but they are much more difficult to spot for positive outcomes because children cite the actual antecedent rather than any counterfactual alternative with which they mentally contrast that actual antecedent.

To explore this possibility, we devised a new measure of children's sensitivity to the contrast between an actual antecedent and a counterfactual alternative (Kavanaugh and Harris, 2000). Instead of telling children stories that involved a choice between objects from different categories, such as a pen versus a pencil, we devised stories with a choice between different instances of the same category. For example, the protagonist might be offered a big sandwich or a small sandwich and end up 'nice and full' after choosing the big sandwich. If children were to explain this positive outcome by explicitly referring to the distinctive feature of the particular choice made by the protagonist (e.g. 'Because he ate a *big* sandwich'), we may reasonably infer that they are mentally contrasting this actual antecedent with the counterfactual alternative that was rejected, namely the small sandwich, even if they do not refer explicitly to that rejected alternative.

Nevertheless, a more pedestrian explanation is available and needs to be ruled out: children might simply mention a defining feature of the chosen entity even if they do not mentally contrast it with the alternative choice. This explanation predicts that children would be just as likely to refer to a defining feature when the protagonist's choice played no obvious causal role in the outcome. For example, if the protagonist chooses a chicken sandwich rather than a cheese sandwich and ends up feeling nice and full, children should, on this pedestrian interpretation, also refer to a defining feature (e.g. 'Because he ate a *chicken* sandwich'). On the other hand, if children refer to such defining features only in cases where they are mentally contrasting it with an alternative that would have led to a different outcome, then children should not refer to such defining features when the protagonist's choice makes no difference to the eventual outcome. To decide between these two competing predictions, we gave 3- and 4-year-old children experimental stories in which the option chosen by the protagonist was critical to the positive or negative outcome of the story, and control stories in which the option chosen by the protagonist was irrelevant to the outcome. In both experimental and control stories, the two items were distinguished by an explicitly mentioned, defining feature. Children's explanations were analysed for the frequency with which they referred to this defining feature. Figure 6.4 shows that references to the defining feature were frequent for the experimental stories but quite rare for the control stories. Moreover, this pattern emerged for positive and negative outcomes alike.[1] These findings show that contrastive thinking – in which an actual and an alternative antecedent are mentally compared – is widespread when children are asked for the explanation of an outcome. Even when their explanation refers only to an actual antecedent in the causal sequence that they observed, they contain telltale indications that the actual antecedent is being mentally contrasted with an alternative.

Implications for Children's Causal Thinking

The main burden of this chapter has been that counterfactual thinking comes readily to very young children, and is deployed in their causal analysis of an outcome. Having established this relationship between causal explanation and counterfactual thinking, we may consider the nature of that relationship in more detail. Arguably, counterfactual

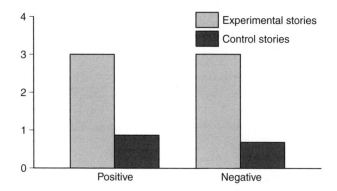

Figure 6.4 Mean number of references to the defining feature of the chosen option by outcome and story type.

thinking cannot help children to reach a novel, causal conclusion because whenever they consider what might have happened instead, they have to rely on a body of pre-existing causal knowledge. However, this argument may not be correct. Conceivably, children know whether or not a given outcome occurs following a variety of antecedent conditions without having explicitly identified any of those antecedents as a cause of the outcome in question. They have simply observed and remembered various recurrent sequences without having drawn any particular conclusion about the cause of the outcome under consideration. If this argument is valid, children could think about what would have happened if the antecedent conditions had been different without having a genuinely causal understanding of the counterfactual sequence that they contemplate. Only when children start to engage in counterfactual thinking do they start to draw causal conclusions from their knowledge of various recurrent sequences.

One implication of the claim that counterfactual thinking helps children to identify hitherto unrecognized causal agents is that children will be more sensitive to certain causal agents than others. In particular, for any given class of outcome, the strategy of mentally contrasting an actual antecedent with an alternative antecedent will alert them to those causal factors where such variation is easily detected, but it will lead them to ignore causal factors where such variation is less evident. Consider, for example, children's understanding of psychological causation, and specifically their understanding of the role played by desires and beliefs in causing action. Extensive analysis by Bartsch and Wellman (1995) has shown that from around the age of 30 months, children talk about the way that people differ from one another in their desires. Discussion of variation among people with respect to their beliefs emerges later – at around 36 months. By implication, children register variation in desire earlier than variation in belief. Accordingly, we would expect children to offer desire-based explanations for action earlier than belief-based explanations. Further analysis by Bartsch and Wellman (1995) supports this prediction. Young children offer desire-based explanations several months earlier, and more often, than belief-based explanations.

A similar point emerges from the study of children's understanding of a physical principle – the speed with which a pendulum swings back and forth. By observation and experimentation, children can work out that the rate of oscillation is governed by the length of the string, but not by other initially plausible candidates, such as the weight of the pendulum itself, the force with which it is set in motion, or the height from which it is released (Inhelder and Piaget, 1958). It is interesting to note that variation in all four of these factors can be easily observed: children can try using a short string and can replace it with a long string. Similarly, variation in the weight of the pendulum, the force of the push and the height from which it is released can all be observed. Indeed, variation in weight, force and height are plausible candidates in so far as they do affect the speed and trajectory of a freestanding object when it is thrown in the air – even though, as it happens, they have no impact on the rate of oscillation. There is, however, a fourth factor that children are not likely to consider. If we take a pendulum to the moon, its rate of oscillation is markedly reduced. Children's neglect of the role of gravity as an explanatory factor is not surprising once we acknowledge that they are not sensitized to any variation in its strength – it remains a constant.

In conclusion, the argument set out in this chapter elaborates on an earlier claim. The findings reported in chapter 2 show that young children – even at 2 years of age – can entertain an unfolding chain of events in their imagination. The findings reported in this chapter suggest that children use that capacity to analyse an actual chain of events. In their imagination, they consider what alternative sequence might have occurred had the antecedent circumstances been different. In this way, children's analysis of reality is infused by their ability to imagine what might have happened instead. Nonetheless, it can be argued that children, and indeed adults, only consider a limited set of antecedent alternatives in their imagination – guided by the type of variation that they have observed in the past. An important implication is that our causal analyses may be quite blinkered. In paying attention to variation that we have detected in the past, certain constants are likely to elude us, despite their causal power.

Note

1   Our results suggest that children mentally contrast what did happen with what might have happened irrespective of whether the outcome is positive or negative. However, if we focus not on *contrastive* thinking but rather on the tendency to ruminate about how things might have turned out differently, a different pattern emerges, at least from research on adults. The main determinant of the frequency, persistence and accessibility of such 'if only' thoughts is ultimately emotional rather than cognitive. Specifically, adults are especially prone to resort to such thoughts when they find an outcome distressing (Roese, 1997). By implication, counterfactual thinking can take the form of wishful thinking. Once set in motion, it offers a way to liquidate – at least in the imagination – the unpleasantness of reality. Ironically, as discussed in chapters 1 and 2, Piaget described such manoeuvres as characteristic of children's pretend play, and saw them as further evidence of children's tendency to assimilate and distort reality via the imagination (Piaget, 1962, p. 131). However, if the current analysis is correct, the capacity for counterfactual thinking is not just a retreat from reality; rather, it can provide an important step toward the causal analysis of reality.

7

Obligation and Violation

Ross (aged 3 years 5 months): 'We'll be good if you give us chocolate.'
Father: 'You better talk to Mommy.'
Ross: 'I want to talk to *you* about chocolate.'
Father: 'How come?'
Ross: 'Because we will be good.'
Father: 'You won't be good without it.'
Ross: 'Because we *will* be good if you give us that.'

(MacWhinney, 1991)

In chapter 6, I argued that children use their capacity for counterfactual thinking to analyse the cause of an outcome. Especially in the case of a negative outcome, they are likely to invoke an alternative course of action that would have prevented the mishap. Such explanations are often tinged with a prescriptive force. Children suggest that the person suffering the mishap ought not to have fallen short of some norm, or has not carried out a prescribed or canonical action. In this chapter, I examine children's sensitivity to rule violation more directly. To set the scene, we need to take a backward look at research on adult reasoning.

Detecting Violation of a Rule

In 1966, as part of a research programme on reasoning, Peter Wason devised a task to study the ability of adults to check for violations of a conditional rule. The rules in question were relatively simple *if-then* statements. For example, adults were shown a set of four cards and told that each card had a letter on one side and a number on the other. They were then given the following rule: 'If a card has a vowel on one side, then it has an even number on the other side'. Their task was to check the validity of the rule in relation to the four cards on the table, which showed on their visible face a vowel, a consonant, an even number and an odd number, respectively. In practice, this meant that they were asked to study the four cards and decide which of them they needed to turn over to check whether the rule was being violated. Most participants realized that it was appropriate to turn over the card displaying a vowel – to confirm that there was indeed an even number on the other side, as stated in the rule. However, only a minority realized that it was also appropriate to turn over the card displaying an odd number, in case there was a vowel on the other side. After all, a combination of a vowel and an odd number would break the rule. Wason's interpretation of this omission was that adults had difficulty in recognizing that they should actively seek out cases that falsify the rule. More generally, Wason and Johnson-Laird (1972) linked their findings to a wider theme: that adults are prone to conceptualize rules in terms of cases that conform to the rule. They do not readily seek out cases that would amount to a violation.

The difficulty that adults have with this reasoning task proved wide-ranging and mysterious. Wason found that very few adults get it right and even professional logicians are prone to get it wrong. Subsequent research has gone through various twists and turns in trying to discover the source of the difficulty. Some studies suggested that adults' performance improved if they were asked to check a less abstract rule. For example, Johnson-Laird, Legrenzi and Legrenzi (1972) reported that adults were quite accurate at checking an *if-then* rule stating that if a letter is sealed, it bears a higher-value stamp. Most people realized that they should turn over a letter without a higher-value stamp to check if it was sealed or not. Note that from a strictly logical point of view, this concrete task has the same format as the more abstract letter-number task. However, the improvement found on this less abstract rule proved elusive. Other apparently concrete rules provoked the same level of error as Wason had found.

A conceptual breakthrough was made when two partially convergent analyses were published by Cosmides (1989) and by Cheng and Holyoak (1985). Despite a fundamental disagreement – which I will discuss later – these authors agreed on one key observation. It was not the concreteness of the rule that helped adults, but rather the nature of the *if-then* relation implied by the rule. If we compare the vowel-even number rule first used by Wason (1966) with the postage rule introduced later by Johnson-Laird et al. (1972), there are two important differences. First, the postage rule is admittedly more concrete. In addition, however, it can be construed as a prescriptive rather than a descriptive rule – a rule that specifies what should be done rather than what is done. The difference between a descriptive rule and a prescriptive rule comes out clearly if we consider the implications of cases that violate each type of rule. A case that violates a descriptive rule effectively renders that rule false. For example, a card displaying a vowel on one side and an odd number on the other side falsifies any rule claiming that a vowel is always accompanied by an even number. The situation is different for the postage rule. If we come across a sealed envelope without the appropriate stamp, the rule is not false. We have simply met a case that does not conform to it. In short, the descriptive validity of a rule is automatically undermined by counter-instances. The prescriptive validity, on the other hand, is not necessarily thrown into doubt by counter-instances. Of course, there are prescriptive rules that do lose their force through sheer disuse. Gentlemen, if they still exist, need no longer raise their hat to a lady. Yet they should still keep their word, even if many do not.

Several experiments indicated that it was indeed the shift from a descriptive rule to a prescriptive rule that produced the observed improvement in performance. Cheng and Holyoak (1985) carried out an especially revealing study. They gave adults a conditional prescriptive rule couched in the following abstract format: 'If one is to take action "A", then one must first satisfy precondition "P"'. As in the original Wason task, there were four cards, but this time the cards displayed whether the action was being taken or not on one side, and whether the condition was being met or not on the other side. The majority of adults correctly understood that they should turn over the card showing the action being taken in order to see if the condition had been met. They also realized that they should turn over the card showing the condition not having been met, in case it showed the action being taken. On the other hand, when these same adults were given an abstract letter-number task similar to the one that Wason had originally used, only a small minority checked the correct cards.

Why should adults do so much better on prescriptive rules even when they are couched in abstract terms? Cheng and Holyoak (1985) and Cosmides (1989) suggest that they assimilate such rules to a schema or dedicated mode of reasoning that allows them to draw out the implications of any conditional, prescriptive rule accurately and efficiently.

A straightforward implication of this type of rule is that someone who takes the specified action without meeting the condition is violating the rule. So, a card that displays the action being taken is a candidate for breach of the rule – the other side of the card may show that the condition has not been met. Similarly, a card that displays the condition not being met is also a candidate for a breach of the rule – the other side of the card may show that the action is being taken nonetheless. More generally, the casting of the rule into a permission format draws attention to the possibility of a potential breach, and adults are accurate in seeking out such cases. In retrospect, therefore, it seems that Wason's assertion that adults have difficulty in seeking out violations of a rule is too general. They may well have difficulties if the rule is couched as an assertion about the way things are. On the other hand, adults are well aware that rules and prescriptions are constituted against a backdrop of potential violation, and they turn out to be adroit at seeking out such violations.

The main disagreement between Cheng and Holyoak (1985) and Cosmides (1989) centres on the psychological origin of this alleged advantage for reasoning about prescriptive rules. Cheng and Holyoak argue that human social life is rich in conditional prescriptive rules. Encounters with many different rules of this type mean that a schematic representation of their typical features is gradually induced. As a result, when people encounter a novel rule, they assimilate it to the schema. Cosmides, by contrast, while agreeing that our social life is abundantly regulated by conditional rules and agreements, proposes that we understand them not via abstraction and induction from experience but with the help of a specialized cognitive module. In the course of evolution, she argues, the human species has established a lifestyle that depends on cooperative bargaining. In that context, we have evolved a module that enables us rapidly to work out the implications of an agreed exchange or contract in which a benefit or permit is promised provided some stipulated condition is met. We are especially attuned to the possibility of cheating in relation to a contract that we might embark on. Selection pressures would operate against those who tolerate cheating because they would be constant losers or victims (Cosmides and Tooby, 1992).

Despite their disagreement about the ultimate basis for reasoning about rights and obligations – so-called deontic reasoning – each of these two accounts raises the possibility that very young children readily understand the implications of a conditional rule, either because they have successfully abstracted those implications from many previous encounters or because a facility for deontic reasoning is part of their native endowment. In particular, they should understand a rule specifying that some desirable action is allowed so long as a condition is met. If children do possess such rules, we may make three interrelated predictions: first, young children can identify actions that violate the rule, namely cases in which the desired action is taken without the condition being met; second, they can understand the conditional nature of the obligation – the condition needs to be met only if the target action is taken, but not otherwise; finally, and especially pertinent to the theme of this book, children should readily compare the actual and the non-actual, in this case by contrasting the violation with what ought to have been done instead.

To test these ideas, we told children stories in which the main character was allowed by his or her mother to engage in some desirable activity provided a condition was met (Harris and Núñez, 1996, experiment 2). For example, a story character might be told by his mother that he could do some painting provided he wore an apron. Children were then presented with four pictures. The pictures showed each possible combination of the protagonist engaged in the target activity or engaged in some different activity (for example, painting or doing a puzzle) while concurrently either meeting or not meeting the condition for the target activity (for example, wearing or not wearing an apron). Figure 7.1 shows the four pictures used for the painting story. Once the four pictures had been displayed and described, children were asked to point to the picture where the protagonist was being naughty, and not doing what he or she had been told. Unlike the original task used by Wason, children needed only to identify which of the four cards displayed a violation – they did not need to seek out a violation

Figure 7.1   The four pictures used for the painting-apron story.

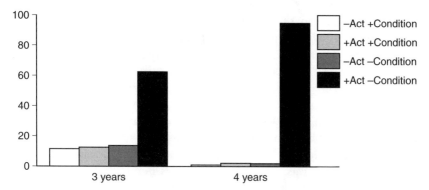

Figure 7.2   Percentage of choices for each picture by age.

by turning over any of the cards. Nonetheless, the task included a critical feature of Wason's task: the need to distinguish between cases that do and do not breach the rule.

Three- and 4-year-old children proved to be strikingly accurate in spotting the violation. They realized that a violation would occur if the target action was taken but the specified condition was not met. Figure 7.2 shows that the overwhelming majority of their choices were appropriately directed at the picture showing the action being taken without the condition having been met (+ Act − Condition) − for example, the child doing some painting without wearing an apron.

Children also appeared to understand the *conditional* nature of the obligation imposed on the story protagonist. They did not misinterpret the permission rule as a generalized imperative such as: 'Put your apron on'. Had they succumbed to this plausible error, they should have identified the story character as being naughty when carrying out any activity without meeting the specified condition, for example doing a puzzle without an apron. The rarity with which children chose this picture (− Act − Condition) shows that they realized that the condition needed to be met only if the target action was being carried out.

In detecting the violation, were children able to conceptualize what the story character had not done but ought to have done? Evidence for this type of counterfactual thinking emerged from their justifications. After they had made their choice of picture, children were asked to justify it − to say what the story character in the picture was doing that was naughty. Their justifications could be allocated to four different categories. In *irrelevant* justifications, they made no informative reference to the condition, the rule or the act (e.g. 'That one' or 'He's naughty in that picture'). In *act* justifications, they referred to the action that called for fulfilment of a condition, but they made no explicit mention of whether or not that condition had been fulfilled (e.g. 'Doing some painting'). In *rule* justifications, they echoed or reformulated the prescription made by the protagonist's mother in the story (e.g. 'She should put her apron on'). Finally, in *missing condition* justifications, children pointed out how the story protagonist had not met the specified condition (e.g. 'He hasn't got his apron on') or was doing something incompatible with meeting it (e.g. 'She's got her apron off').

Figure 7.3 shows the frequency with which children offered each type of justification. *Missing condition* justifications were the most frequent by far. It is interesting to note that such justifications typically focused on the *absence* of something. Children drew attention to what the protagonist was not doing or had failed to do. Thus, the frequency of these justifications confirms that young children readily construe an observed act in terms of some idealized template. The template is not a mental prototype into which the act is assimilated. Instead, it serves as a standard or canon with which the observed act is contrasted. Children are alert to, and can explicitly comment on, the ways in which the act departs from that template. In particular, they notice when the target action is being carried out in the absence of the specified condition. In the previous chapter, I argued that children's judgements about the causation and prevention of a given outcome are infused with counterfactual thinking. The observed sequence of

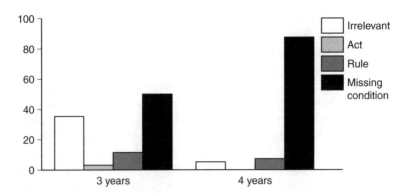

Figure 7.3   Percentage of justifications by age and category.

events is compared to some alternative sequence of events – one that did not occur, but could have. In making judgements about naughtiness, children again appear to rely on counterfactual thinking. The observed course of action is evaluated in terms of its departure from some alternative but prescribed course of action.

Thinking About Novel Rules

In the experiment just described, children were presented with rules that had two potentially helpful features. First, they were likely to be familiar. For example, children who attend a preschool get used to donning an apron for activities like painting. Second, the rules included a precautionary element in that fulfilment of the condition would be likely to reduce the chances of a mishap in carrying out the activity. For example, putting on an apron means that clothes are less likely to be splashed with paint. Indeed, when they explained why the story protagonist was being naughty, some children spontaneously mentioned this possibility (e.g. 'He hasn't got his apron on – he'll get it on his jumper', ''Cos she's painting without her apron on. It'll get on her lovely clothes'). Either of these features might have helped children to pick out violations of the conditional rule and underpinned their references to the counterfactual possibility of meeting the prescribed condition.

However, the claim that children possess a schema or module for reasoning about conditional deontic rules implies that they should recognize deviations from rules that lack both of these features: rules that are novel and rules that specify an arbitrary rather than a precautionary link between action and condition. To test this possibility, we gave 3- and 4-year-old children two types of rule (Harris and Núñez, 1996, experiment 3). Some children were given familiar, precautionary rules – for example, that one should wear a helmet while riding a bicycle or wear an apron while doing some painting. Other children were given novel rules without any plausible precautionary relation between condition and action. We created these latter rules by recombining the elements of familiar, precautionary rules. For example, recombining the rule about wearing an apron while painting with the rule about wearing a helmet while cycling yielded two novel rules with an essentially arbitrary relation between condition and action: that one should wear a helmet while painting, and that one should wear an apron while riding a bicycle.

Figure 7.4   The four pictures used for the painting-helmet story.

In other respects, the procedure in this experiment was similar to that described for the first study. Children listened to stories in which a conditional rule was announced. They were shown four pictures depicting the protagonist engaged either in the target activity or in another activity, while concurrently either meeting the condition or not. Once the pictures had been presented and described, children were asked to pick out the picture where the character was being naughty and not doing what he or she was told. Figure 7.4 illustrates the four choices for one of the novel, arbitrary rules: that a helmet should be worn while painting.

Three- and 4–year-old children performed well on both types of rule. Admittedly, performance was a bit better for the familiar, precautionary rules. Yet children also performed quite accurately on the novel, arbitrary rules.[1] Figure 7.5 shows the number of choices devoted to each of the four pictures. For both types of rule, it is clear that children overwhelmingly chose the appropriate picture – for example, the picture of the protagonist painting without an apron in the case of the familiar rule, and painting without a helmet in the case of the novel rule. Children's justifications followed a similar pattern. As in the initial study, they focused on the missing condition whether it was a familiar condition for the action in question or a novel condition. Overall, the results of this study show that although children are slightly more accurate when they are given familiar, precautionary rules to think about, they can also handle novel, arbitrary rules. These findings provide strong support for the proposal that very young children have a schema or module for processing conditional prescriptive rules. They readily work out the implications of rules that they have never before encountered.

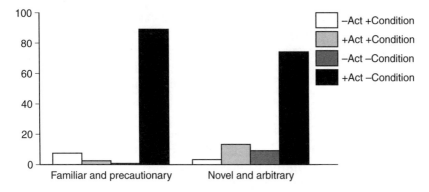

Figure 7.5   Percentage of choices for each picture by type of rule.

Children's reactions to these novel, arbitrary rules suggested that they recognized their oddity. They often smiled or looked quizzically at the experimenter. Still, they readily accepted the rules as a way of determining whether or not the story character was being naughty. Indeed, casual observation suggests that children are confronted by sundry rules that lack any precautionary element. When parents want to persuade a fractious child to do something, they often construct a bribe that is presented as a conditional, permission rule: 'I'll read you a story if you put your pyjamas on' or 'We can go to the swimming pool if you have a nap first'. Rules of politeness may also take this conditional format, and here too, the link between condition and action is essentially arbitrary: 'If you say "please" you may have some more' or 'You can get down from the table if you ask properly'. Even in cases where the rule is precautionary – for example, wearing a helmet when you wear a bicycle – the rationale may not be obvious to young children. Given that children may face a barrage of apparently arbitrary conditional rules, it is not so surprising that they understood the implications of the quaint rules that we concocted.

Prescriptive versus Descriptive Rules

To demarcate children's competence more clearly, we need to show its limits. One obvious and plausible demarcation is connected to the distinction between descriptive and prescriptive rules introduced at the beginning of the chapter. Recall that adults are much more proficient at seeking out violations of prescriptive than descriptive rules. Indeed, the distinction between these two types of rule made sense, in retrospect, of several seemingly inconsistent findings. Does the same cleavage appear in children's detection of rule violations? To explore this possibility, we gave children conditional rules embedded in two different story formats (Harris and Núñez, 1996, experiment 4). In one format, the rule was presented – as in the previous studies – in a prescriptive manner. In each story, the mother was said to impose a prescription on the main character. In the other format, the rule was presented in a descriptive manner. In each story, it was the story protagonist rather than his or her mother who announced the rule, stating it in the form of a factual generalization about his or her behaviour.

One additional feature of this study should be underlined. Suppose that children heard a story character offer a factual generalization such as: 'If I ride my bicycle, I always put a helmet on'. Children might reinterpret such a familiar conditional rule as a prescription, even though it is explicitly announced as a description. Effectively, they might construe a story character as saying: 'If I ride my bicycle, I *have to* put a helmet on'. Any such reinterpretation would obviously attenuate potential differences between the two types of rule. To reduce the likelihood of such reinterpretation, we used unfamiliar rules, comparable to the novel rules described earlier, for both the prescriptive and the descriptive format. For example, one of the rules in the prescriptive format was presented as follows: 'This is a story about David. One day David wants to do some painting. His Mum says if he does some painting he should put his helmet on'. In the descriptive format, the rule was presented as follows: 'This is a story about David. One day David wants to do some painting. David says that if he does some painting he always puts his helmet on'.

The task given to the children varied across the two formats in keeping with the different status of the rule. For the prescriptive format, children were asked, as in previous experiments, to identify a transgression: to say which picture showed the protagonist being naughty and not doing what his or her mother had said. In the descriptive format, by contrast, they were asked to identify an inconsistency: to say which picture showed the protagonist doing something different, and not doing what he or she had said.

Children's performance differed sharply across these two formats. As can be seen in figure 7.6, they were quite accurate with the pre-

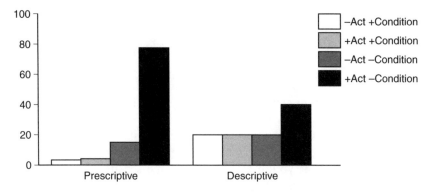

Figure 7.6 Percentage of choices for each picture by type of rule.

scriptive format. Performance was much less accurate with the descriptive format. The correct picture attracted only marginally more choices than the three incorrect pictures. A similar pattern emerged for children's justifications. As usual, children mostly referred to the missing condition in the prescriptive format. In the descriptive format, such references were much less frequent. Instead, children frequently gave irrelevant justifications. Looking at individual patterns of performance, 60 per cent of the children in the prescriptive format managed to both choose the correct picture and justify their choice of picture by referring to the missing condition for at least five of the six stories, but this high level of performance was reached by only 10 per cent of the children in the descriptive format.

Overall, this study reveals a cleavage in children's handling of conditional rules. On the one hand, they readily grasp what would constitute a deviation from a conditional rule stating what someone should do. Having identified that deviation as naughty, children point to an alternative course of action that the story protagonist might have adopted – and indeed, should have adopted. At the same time, they are quite poor at understanding what would constitute a deviation from a conditional rule stating what someone does do. Apparently, the cleavage observed among adults reaches back into early childhood.[2]

Deliberate versus Accidental Violations

To the extent that children castigate the protagonist for not adopting the prescribed course of action, they appear to imply that he or she is a free agent who could have acted differently. Making this same point differently, we might expect them not to reproach someone who is not a free agent – someone who involuntarily as opposed to deliberately fails to meet the specified condition. After all, if the breach is genuinely involuntary, the agent could not really have acted differently. The suggestion that young children might be sensitive to whether a breach is accidental or deliberate flies in the face of a long tradition of research. Ever since Piaget's pioneering investigation of the development of moral judgement, it has been claimed that young children ignore the intention behind a person's action and focus primarily on its consequences. However, recent experiments have uncovered a striking sensitivity to intention among young children. For example, Meltzoff (1995) and Carpenter, Akhtar and Tomasello (1998) report that when young infants ranging from 14 to 18 months watch an adult carry out an action that is not completely successful, for example a failed attempt to poke a stick into a hole, they copy the intended act rather than the unsuccessful action that they actually saw. If children are sensitive very early on to what an agent is aiming to do, they may take that into account in making a moral judgement.

To assess this possibility, we gave 3- and 4-year-olds stories in one of two formats (Núñez and Harris, 1998, experiment 1). In the standard format, no information about the story protagonist's intention was available. The four pictures showed the protagonist either engaged or not engaged in the target action, and either meeting or not meeting the specified condition (just as in figure 7.1, presented earlier). In the intention format, by contrast, information about the protagonist's intention was available. The four pictures showed the protagonist either engaged or not engaged in the target action, while failing to meet the condition either deliberately or accidentally. For example, in the case of the rule about wearing an apron while painting, the protagonist was shown either deliberately removing the apron or with the apron slipping off by accident. Figure 7.7 illustrates the four pictures used for this rule in the intention format. The picture on the right shows the protagonist deliberately taking off his apron even though he is painting a picture.

Figure 7.7   Four pictures used in the intention format.

As expected, 3- and 4-year-olds performed well in the standard format. However, they performed almost as accurately in the intention format. They rarely judged accidental non-compliance as naughty. Instead, they directed most of their choices at the deliberate violation. Figure 7.8 shows the frequency with which children selected the correct picture in the intention format. This figure also shows the results of a similar study carried out in Colombia among children attending a preschool in Cali. The accuracy of these children was slightly lower, but the overall pattern of results was very similar (Núñez and Harris, 1998, experiment 2). Thus, contrary to what might be expected on standard accounts of young children's moral judgement, they did take the intentions of the protagonist into account: they reproached a story character who deliberately flouted the specified condition, but they rarely condemned an accidental breach.[3]

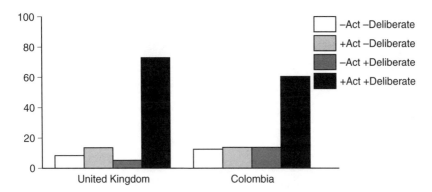

Figure 7.8   Percentage of choices for each picture by country.

The Source of Authority

So far, I have described conditional rules that are imposed on children by adults. Do children ever impose such rules on themselves? Susan Isaacs, who kept detailed records of children's social life at the Malting House School in Cambridge during the 1930s, reports some intriguing episodes. Dan aged 3 years asked Frank aged 5 years if he could play with Frank's toy airship. At first Frank refused, but he relented after the following dialogue (Isaacs, 1933, p. 97):

> DAN: 'Frank, I have a big motor bus, and you can use that.'
> FRANK: 'Have you? Can I?'
> DAN: 'Yes, and now will you let me use your airship?'

A similar bargain was struck some two months later. This time, Harold aged 5 years asked Dan to give him the large wooden motor bus 'for keeps'. Harold offered his motor bus in exchange and after a long discussion, Dan agreed (Isaacs, 1933, p. 100). In each of these two episodes, it is the children who propose the exchange, agree to it and carry it through. A plausible implication, therefore, is that children realize that such agreements have a binding quality. In particular, they understand that if one party has met their side of the bargain – for example by handing over an agreed item – the other party is obliged to uphold their side as well. To explore children's understanding of such exchange agreements, we gave 3- and 4-year-olds stories about a boy and a girl who agreed to swap items in their possession, such as col-

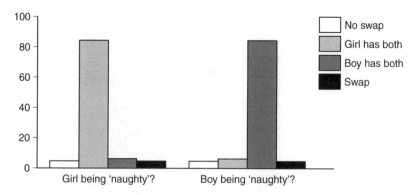

Figure 7.9 Percentage of choices for each picture by question.

oured pens (Harris, Núñez and Brett, 1999, experiment 1). Children were then shown pictures illustrating various possible outcomes: each child holding onto their original item, the girl in possession of both items, the boy in possession of both items, and the agreed swap having taken place. Children were asked to indicate the picture where: (1) the girl was being naughty or (2) the boy was being naughty. As shown in figure 7.9, children were very accurate in either case. When asked about the girl being naughty, they appropriately chose the picture of her holding onto both items, and when asked about the boy they chose the picture of him holding onto both items.

Children also offered an appropriate justification for their choices: they pointed out that the malefactor had either reneged on the exchange (e.g. 'She's not sharing them, not giving him one' – 'He didn't let her have his pen') or had ended up with both items (e.g. 'She's got two pens' – 'He's got both of the pens'). Once again then, children justified their choice of picture by reference to some counterfactual possibility that had not been realized, namely the swapping of the two items.

In a follow-up experiment, we probed children's understanding more extensively. We asked them to indicate not only where (1) the girl was being naughty and (2) the boy was being naughty, but also where (3) both children had been good and carried out the exchange as agreed. In addition, to find out whether children in a very different culture understand such exchange agreements, we questioned children in a primary school in Bhaktapur, a market town in the Kathmandu valley of Nepal. Figure 7.10 shows the pattern of choices for the three different test questions.

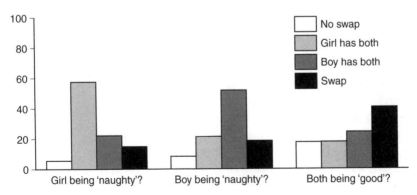

Figure 7.10   Percentage of choices for each picture by question.

A comparison of figures 7.9 and 7.10 shows – as one might expect – that performance was not as accurate when children were asked to select three different types of protagonists as opposed to just two. Nevertheless, they answered these three questions in a flexible manner. Their preferred choice among the four pictures shifted appropriately depending on whether they were asked to pick out the picture where the girl was being naughty, the boy was being naughty, or where both children were being good and abiding by their agreement.

Conclusions

Summing up the findings from this series of experiments, young children are remarkably clear about the implications of conditional, prescriptive rules: they can identify violations of novel as well as familiar rules; they understand that these rules impose a conditional rather than a general obligation to fulfil the specified condition; they condemn a violation that involves a deliberate rather than an accidental failure to meet the condition; and they acknowledge the obligations that arise from peer agreements as well as adult injunction. This pattern holds up among 3-year-olds as well as 4-year-olds, and it is found in Europe, South America and Asia.

All of this early competence might be taken to support the concept of a module for deontic reasoning, as advocated by Cosmides (1989). Certainly, the available evidence does not rule out that proposal. However, it is also important to acknowledge that young children are showered – bombarded, even – with *if-then* directives, whether in the form of bribes, warnings, threats or commands. Indeed, such directives form a substantial proportion of the conditional reasoning that parents, teachers and even older siblings employ in their conversations with preschool children (Dunn and Brown, 1993; Scholnick and Wing, 1991). Moreover, longitudinal analysis reveals that a high proportion of children's *if-then* reasoning is produced in the context of such conditional directives, and this is particularly true for children below 3 years of age. As Dunn (1988) has pointed out, children are likely to find such directives provocative – after all, they impinge directly on their options. In line with that proposal, it is interesting to note that the overwhelming proportion of children's *if-then* statements include a reference to the self (Scholnick and Wing, 1995). Hence, it is feasible to claim that children do not start off with any privileged grasp of the deontic domain. Rather, they rapidly construct schemas pertinent to that domain because on the one hand they possess a general ability to grasp *if-then* relationships, and on the other hand they are led to apply that capacity to material that is of considerable personal relevance, namely the plethora of conditional directives that other people – children as well as adults – direct at them.

Whatever the ultimate origin of children's facility at deontic reasoning, their frequent allusion to the unmet condition when justifying their judgements reinforces an important theme of this book. From an early age, children perceive and judge an action by contrasting it with a counterfactual alternative. In this respect, there is a straightforward parallel between children's causal judgements as described in the last chapter and their deontic judgements as described in this chapter. Nonetheless, there is an obvious and important difference between the two types of judgement. In making a deontic judgement, children do not simply invoke a counterfactual alternative as a mere possibility – they imply that the counterfactual possibility *ought to* have been realized. Where does the concept of obligation come from?

In considering this issue, it is helpful to distinguish between two different questions. First, we can ask how children come to grasp the notion of obligation itself. Alternatively, we can ask how they come to regard certain kinds of action as obligatory. Developmental research has focused on the second question to the neglect of the first. In particular, there has been a sustained effort to show that young children recognize that one ought to refrain from some actions because they are morally wrong, and from other actions because they violate agreed norms or conventions (Turiel, 1998). However, it is important to notice that an analysis of how children differentiate between, or justify, various types of obligation does not illuminate the question of how children acquire the concept of obligation in the first place. For example, suppose we conclude that 3- and 4-year-old children understand that one ought not to hit people – even in the absence of an external authority that condemns such actions – because they appreciate that such actions cause distress. In that case, we have analysed how children come to recognize the specific obligation of not hitting people, but we have not analysed how they acquire the notion of obligation itself. Of course, it might be objected that there is no such thing as a general concept of obligation. Rather, children slowly grasp particular types of obligations – some obligations are moral, others are conventional, and still others are prudential or precautionary. Because the basis for such obligations is so diverse, there is little point in assuming that some generalized and transferable notion of obligation crosscuts these various domains.

However, on close scrutiny, this objection is not very plausible, for three reasons. First, children tend to use the same deontic vocabulary – 'you have to', 'you should' or 'you must' in talking about a medley of obligations, whether it is the obligation to tell the truth, not to put one's elbows on the dining table, or to fasten one's seat-belt. Second, as we have seen in the series of experiments described in this chapter, children happily accept the extension of the modal *must* to an arbitrary, novel condition, and having accepted that extension, they go on to condemn the failure to meet that condition as *naughty* and to explain that judgement in terms of what *should* or *ought* to have been done instead. Thus, children have a well-organized cluster of deontic terms – the application of one modal term easily entrains other terms in that semantic cluster. Third, psycholinguistic research shows that children start to use deontic modals such as *have to* and *must* at 2 to 3 years of age (Shatz and Wilcox, 1991). They use such terms in connection with actions that are regulated by normative constraints (Gerhardt, 1991) and consistent with the analysis so far, they use those terms to refer not only to constraints that are imposed externally by adults but also in the context of self-regulatory norms that they introduce themselves, especially in the context of play (Vygotsky, 1978, p. 99).

These various considerations suggest that by the age of 2 or 3 years, children have acquired a generalized notion of an obligation – an action that has to be carried out, or carried out in a particular way. On this account, it is misleading to portray the young child as someone who thinks of each novel obligation as a new conceptual departure. Rather, any novel obligation is understood in the light of a well-organized, pre-existing concept of constraint. The constraints in question can be imposed by a variety of parties – by adult prescription, by a peer agreement, by prudential considerations and even by physical laws. In all such cases, children articulate the constraint by talking about what someone *has to* or *must* do. Children's understanding of the differences among the various types of constraint, for example their ability to differentiate between the obligations imposed by peer agreement as compared to adult authority, or between the obligations imposed by social conventions as compared to moral principles, is a refinement that can build on a pre-existing and wide-ranging notion of constraint.

So, where does the notion of constraint itself come from? The beginnings of an answer can be found if we return to the claim that has echoed across the last two chapters: children analyse a sequence of events, and more specifically human action, in terms of a contrast between what was done and what was not done. Thus, for any given action that might be carried out, children can conceive of a counterfactual alternative – a scenario in which some alternative action was carried out, different from the one that was actually undertaken. Nonetheless, in a variety of circumstances, and for a variety of reasons, they will also appreciate that the two choices have a different outcome. One of the two possibilities will lead to a reprimand, distress, danger or disorder. In short, this analysis implies that children's understanding of obligation or constraint amounts to a conjunction of two different concepts: the concept of a free agent who can either carry out or withhold a given action, and the concept of a goal-directed agent whose action leads to a particular outcome – an outcome that may be positive or negative. The sense of constraint or obligation arises insofar as the child realizes that if a given outcome is to be achieved (or avoided), then a free agent *has to* or *must* carry out one course of action rather than another.

There is, however, a potent objection to this attempt to reduce the notion of obligation to the conjunction of agency and goal-directedness. Arguably, it is perfectly sensible to talk of someone honouring an obligation whose breach would entail no positive or negative consequences for the agent in question.[4] By implication, there can be obligations that serve no purpose. However, it is possible that this objection is too sophisticated to capture the concept of obligation used by preschool children. Rightly or wrongly, they may assume that the presence of an obligation automatically entails a purpose. Indeed, if young children do make that assumption, it would offer a satisfactory explanation for the fact that they greet so many adult directives with the question: 'But, *why* do I have to?'

Notes

1 Although children performed slightly better on the familiar, precautionary format than the novel, arbitrary format, this difference was not statistically significant.

2 A possible objection to this conclusion is that the instructions given to

children in experiment 4 (Harris and Núñez, 1996) were not equally clear for the two types of rule. Recall that children were asked to identify the picture showing the protagonist doing something *naughty* for the prescriptive rule, and to identify the picture showing the protagonist doing something *different* for the descriptive rule. For young children, 'different' might be less easily understood and a less salient marker for rule deviation than 'naughty'. Indeed, O'Brien, Dias, Roazzi and Cantor (1998) have argued that in the case of conditional descriptive rules, it is more appropriate to ask children to seek out examples that constitute a falsification of the alleged rule (i.e., show it to be untrue) rather than ask them to seek out a violation. In line with that argument, they found that pre-school children are quite accurate at selecting a picture showing that a descriptive conditional is a lie – just as accurate as they are at selecting a picture showing that a prescriptive conditional has been violated. On the other hand, Cummins (1996) found that preschoolers were less accurate in selecting a picture to show that a descriptive conditional was untrue than in selecting a picture to show that a prescriptive conditional had been violated. In short, there is considerable evidence that preschool children are very alert to violations of prescriptive, conditional rules. The extent to which they can be as accurate in identifying violations – or falsifications – of descriptive, conditional rules remains to be established.

3   Fiddick (1998) argues on evolutionary grounds that as a species we are likely to be especially sensitive to the role of intention in cases where one person cheats on another (e.g. in the case of an agreement to exchange certain goods). In such cases, it is to our advantage to assess whether a party to an agreement is likely to renege in the future, and a repetition is more likely when the breach is deliberate. If the breach is in a prudential or precautionary context, assessments of intention may be less critical. After all, an accidental or an intentional breach may be equally risky. However, the findings of Núñez and Harris (1998) show that young children are quite sensitive to the role of intention even in precautionary contexts. More research is needed to sort out whether children and adults differ in their sensitivity to intention across different types of breach.

It is also worth remarking that, despite their ability to take account of intention in judging a transgression or violation, it is unlikely that children do this systematically. For example, when children, or their precious possessions, are hurt, they may fail to acknowledge that the harm was accidental, even in the face of an insistent attestation by the perpetrator.

4   I am grateful to Peter Carruthers for pointing out this objection.

Imagination Functions

1. absorbed in a make-believe or fictional world - that retains many of the causal principles of the real world

2. Make comparisons between actual outcomes and various alternatives (counterfactual thinking)

3. To explore the impossible and magical - in which causal violation can happen (but it is not real).

RWB

4. To create an alternative/parallel world in which impossible events do happen - but this is a real world.

8

Beyond Possibility

In previous chapters I have argued that children use their imagination for two major functions: first, to become absorbed in a make-believe or fictional world, albeit one that retains many of the causal principles found in the real world, and second, to make comparisons between actual outcomes and various alternatives that might have occurred instead. In this chapter, I examine a third function of the imagination: to explore the impossible and the magical. My broader aim is to show that contemporary analyses of cognitive development are too narrow.

Children, even in the preschool period, are often portrayed as small scientists who construct increasingly objective theories about the world. It is acknowledged that their understanding is incomplete, but their limitations are attributed to ignorance or naivety rather than to a fundamentally non-scientific approach. I shall argue that this portrait of early cognitive development is too rationalistic. First, I review evidence suggesting that children do indeed resemble scientists in one important respect. They recognize various constraints on what can possibly happen. Moreover, as children's causal understanding widens, it slowly encompasses events that once appeared to violate their limited causal understanding. Hence, fewer and fewer of the phenomena that children encounter can sustain their initial promise of being genuine violations of ordinary, causal constraints. Nonetheless, children's growing appreciation of those constraints does not mean that they restrict their horizon to possible outcomes. On the contrary, their increasing recognition that certain possibilities are excluded enables them to identify a set of impossible outcomes. Under normal circumstances, these impossible outcomes do not occur

Traditional portrait of early cog. dev. is too rationalistic

and they cannot be observed. Nevertheless, children can happily explore them in their imagination.

This means that the direction of cognitive development is different from that of science. In science, the recognition that a particular possibility, such as alchemy or Lamarckian inheritance, is a blind alley means that activity is eventually directed elsewhere and that branch of the science slowly withers away. Experimentation is simply deemed unproductive. In cognitive development, by contrast, the recognition of the impossible need have no such effect. After all, children are not engaged in a programme of experimental research and they are not ultimately in search of truth and objectivity. Under normal circumstances, most allegedly magical phenomena will be impossible to observe or reproduce, and that may mean that children become sceptical about their existence. However, that scepticism need not prevent children from exploring such phenomena in their imaginative excursions. Indeed, they are supported in doing so by many cultural forms, including fairy tales, rituals and religion.

Early Research on Magical Thinking Among Young Children

Early research on children's conception of the world suggested that they make no clear distinction between ordinary causation and magical processes. Instead, they assume that various mechanical or physical events can be realized through a form of personal efficacy or power. For example, in one of his earliest studies, Piaget (1928) argued that 3- and 4-year-olds frequently claim that external and independent movements of inanimate objects are brought about by their own gestures or movements. He proposed that even 8-year-olds might think that objects such as clouds or rivers move, not by virtue of independent physical laws, but according to human desires and purposes.

However, this characterization of early causal thinking soon came under fire. The Chinese psychologist Huang investigated Piaget's claims in a thorough and well-designed study (Huang, 1930). He presented children ranging from 4 to 10 years with a variety of natural phenomena in which a familiar, physical principle was violated. For example, children might be shown water in a glass tube with a piece of paper covering the mouth of the tube. When the tube was turned upside down, the water did not spill out. In the face of this unexpected outcome, children rarely mentioned the role of air pressure, but neither did they propose a magical explanation. Instead, they explained the anomaly in terms of familiar, physical principles. For example, they invoked the notion of 'stickiness': 'I think there is something sticky on the paper or on the glass' or ''Cause the paper is so thick and it sticks'. One 6-year-old even demonstrated her claim that the water made the paper sticky by putting a piece of paper to her wetted lips. Reviewing a large number of studies investigating children's causal understanding, Huang (1943) came to the conclusion that children's dominant mode of explanation is in terms of plausible, physical causes. Admittedly, their explanations may be naive or incorrect, but they do not systematically invoke magic.

Margaret Mead (1932) also questioned Piaget's characterization of young children's causal thinking. If anything, her findings are even more surprising than those of Huang because she tested Manus children growing up in a culture where a belief in sorcery was prevalent among the adults. She asked the children to explain a variety of phenomena, but found that they rarely invoked magic or sorcery. For example, children were asked about a canoe that had drifted from its moorings. Hinting at a supernatural explanation, Mead asked: 'That canoe is bad, isn't it? It's drifting'. However, the children resisted this suggestion and focused instead on a more straightforward physical explanation. Indeed, they offered explanations similar to those discussed in chapter 6. They pointed to some departure from ordinary procedure: 'It wasn't fastened right. It will float away' or 'Popoli (to whom the canoe belonged) didn't fasten it. Popoli will lose his canoe'. Mead concluded that a systematic belief in the power of magic is something that the child might eventually acquire from the surrounding adult culture but is not a mode of thought that comes early or naturally.

More recent research has reinforced the conclusions reached by Huang and Mead. In a variety of domains, notably the physical, biological and psychological domains, it has been shown that children construct increasingly accurate and objective accounts of what happens and why (Gopnik and Meltzoff, 1997; Wellman and Gelman, 1998). By implication, they have little use for magical forms of explanation, contrary to Piaget's early portrait. However, it would be a mistake to conclude that children entirely banish magical phenomena from their cognitive agenda. Even if they rarely have recourse to magic as a form of explanation, they still acknowledge magical outcomes as a special class of phenomena. A study by Phelps and Woolley (1994) is especially revealing. On one reading, their findings reinforce contemporary thinking: children mostly invoke the relevant causal principles, even when faced with puzzling phenomena. On another reading, however, the findings show that impossible or magical outcomes do occupy a place in children's conceptual landscape.

Children aged 4, 6 and 8 years were given a set of puzzling demonstrations that varied in complexity. For example, a relatively simple demonstration involved a clear jar with a magnifying glass in the lid that enlarged the appearance of pictures dropped inside the jar. A more complicated demonstration involved a special box, which (by virtue of a hidden compartment plus an arrangement of mirrors) made coins disappear when they were dropped into the box. Each of these demonstrations violated principles familiar even to the youngest children – objects do not suddenly change shape or size, and nor do they suddenly disappear. Nonetheless, the demonstrations differed in the availability of a plausible non-magical explanation. Even the youngest children had some rudimentary knowledge of magnifying lenses, so that they were in a position to figure out why the picture in the jar appeared to change size. On the other hand, even the oldest children had difficulty in figuring out the working of the hidden compartment and the arrangement of mirrors that made coins disappear. Granted that the demonstrations varied in complexity, it was possible to ask whether even the oldest children would invoke magic provided they were sufficiently baffled.

Analysis of the overall pattern of responding showed that children in all three age groups typically responded to the demonstrations in one of two ways: either they supplied an appropriate physical explanation and denied that the outcome was magical, or they could offer no relevant physical explanation and agreed that the outcome was magical. Making the same point differently, the tendency to offer a physical explanation or to invoke magic were mutually exclusive responses – children rarely offered both for a single demonstration. As might be expected given the wider physical knowledge of older children, the balance between these two responses altered with age. Whereas 4-year-olds rarely offered a physical explanation and often invoked magic, 8-year-olds showed the reverse pattern – they mainly supplied a physical explanation and rarely invoked magic.

When children agreed that an outcome was magical, what kind of magic did they have in mind? Arguably, they were thinking simply in terms of the kind of deceptive ploys that stage magicians use, rather than any 'genuine' form of magic. To examine this question, Phelps and Woolley asked children whether the demonstration was 'real magic' or 'just fooling you'. Most of the younger children claimed that 'real magic' was involved, whereas most of the older children claimed that they had been fooled.

These findings point to a limited but important niche for magic in children's understanding of the world. Admittedly, they mostly invoke ordinary, non-magical explanations and they do not use magic as a genuine form of causal explanation. In this respect, the conclusions reached by Huang and Mead are correct. However, magic is a classification that children sometimes have recourse to when they lack an ordinary causal explanation for a given phenomenon. Hence, there is no genuine competition between magic and causal explanations – or rather, the competition is at best one-sided. In the course of development, children's occasional references to magic yield to causal explanations, but the reverse does not occur. Nonetheless, even if children do not actively invoke magic as a genuine form of explanation, they do use the category of magic to identify a special class of phenomena. Children classify an outcome as magical if they (1) judge it to be a clear violation of what should happen – granted ordinary causal principles; and (2) cannot readily explain the violation by invoking any supplementary principles. Younger children think of such inexplicable violations as 'real' magic. Older children are more likely to insist they have simply been fooled.

The number of observable phenomena that will be classified as magical will presumably decline as children acquire a more wide-ranging understanding of causation. Hence, it is tempting to conclude that children ultimately have no need of the category. There are no observable phenomena that can count as genuine violations of causal principles – just a small residual set of apparent violations, the tricks that conjurors perform. However, this conclusion would be premature. It begs the important question of whether children focus primarily on outcomes that they can observe in the real world. More specifically, although it is indeed plausible to expect that children will be increasingly hard-pressed to observe outcomes that they accept as genuine instances of magic, they can easily contemplate such outcomes within the confines of their imagination. Indeed, on this account, the range of potential instances of magic is likely to wax rather than wane as children's causal understanding grows and they grasp the range and complexity of constraints on what can ordinarily happen. For any given constraint, it is always possible for them to imagine its violation. To take just one example, as children get older they increasingly understand the finite nature of the biological machine and the concomitant inevitability of death. Armed with that understanding, they are in a position to construe immortality as a miraculous defiance of ordinary causation rather than as an empirical possibility.

In sum, we have arrived at the following somewhat paradoxical conclusion: as children get older and extend their causal understanding, the number of impossible or 'magical' phenomena that they observe in their everyday life declines, and when do they do observe such a phenomenon, they are likely to regard it as a trick or illusion. At the same time, the number of impossible phenomena that they can conceive of increases. Hence, in studying the prevalence of magical thinking during childhood, we need to be very clear to distinguish between two sets of phenomena: observable phenomena that can be encountered in daily life and unobservable phenomena that can be contemplated in the imagination, or in the context of various cultural forms such as fairy tales. Observable instances of magic become less frequent in the course of development as prosaic, physical explanations for initially mysterious outcomes become increasingly available. At the same time, possible or imaginable instances of magic become more widespread as children's grasp of the constraints on what is possible becomes firmer and more wide-ranging.

This analysis departs both from Piaget's early account and from contemporary accounts of cognitive development. Contrary to Piaget's claims, and in partial agreement with Huang, Mead and a host of recent investigators, there is little indication that magical forms of explanation offer any serious competition to ordinary, non-magical, causal explanations even among young children. At the same time, contrary to contemporary theorizing, magic is not a completely empty category: it is a category that young children use to classify impossible or extraordinary outcomes. Nor does that category necessarily fall into desuetude as they get older. Magic may not be observed but it can be imagined. Below, I seek to put these conclusions on a firmer footing.

Violating Ordinary Causal Constraints

The data presented so far suggest that young children regard an outcome as magical if it violates their ordinary causal understanding and if they have no alternative explanation to account for that violation. Notice that on this account children will not invoke magic simply because an outcome is mysterious. For example, when a television is switched on and a picture appears on the screen, children will not judge the outcome to be magical even if they have no idea how the picture is generated. It is only when a mysterious outcome violates their ordinary causal principles that children classify it as magical. A further implication concerns the unfamiliarity of the outcome. The research carried out by Phelps and Woolley (1994) deliberately included various unusual phenomena that children were unlikely to be acquainted with. It is tempting to think, therefore, that children restrict the category of magic to such unfamiliar outcomes. However, the account developed above tempers that assumption. It predicts that children will also judge completely familiar outcomes to be magical provided that they are brought about in a way that violates their ordinary causal principles.

To explore this prediction, Carl Johnson and I asked 4- and 6-year-olds to think about the same, familiar outcome brought about in two different ways, one ordinary and the other extraordinary (Johnson and Harris, 1994). For example, children might be shown two boxes with a marble placed inside one of them, and asked to consider the possibility of moving the marble from one box to the other with their hand, or alternatively moving it by simply thinking very hard. For each possibility, children were asked to say whether they could bring about the outcome in that way or whether it would be magic.

In constructing test pairs, we identified four different constraints likely to be familiar to young children: (1) inertia – inanimate objects do not move spontaneously; (2) constancy – inanimate objects do not spontaneously change their shape or identity; (3) permanence – inanimate objects do not spontaneously disappear or cease to exist; and (4) non-creation – inanimate objects do not spontaneously come into existence. For any given principle, we asked children to think about an outcome brought about either in violation of the principle or in conformity with it.

Figure 8.1 shows that both the 4- and 6-year-olds were much more likely to judge that the extraordinary outcomes were magic than the ordinary outcomes. This differentiation was made with respect to each of the four principles. Admittedly, children's performance was not perfect. Both age groups sometimes judged that perfectly ordinary outcomes were magical, but we suspected that these errors occurred

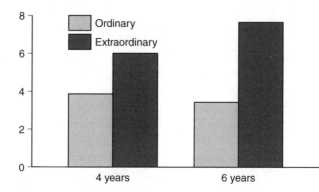

Figure 8.1 Mean number of 'magic' judgements by age and item type.

because children often 'echoed' the last-mentioned option, namely magic.

In a follow-up experiment, we simplified the task and tested 3- and 4-year-olds. Children were introduced to two different characters depicted in drawings: a child (called either Jack or Jill) and Magic Fairy. We explained that the child could do lots of ordinary things but could not do anything magical, whereas Magic Fairy always liked to do things that were magic, and never bothered doing things the ordinary way. As in the initial study, the test items included violations of the four principles of inertia, constancy, permanence and non-creation. For example, one pair involving the principle of inertia was as follows: 'One day, Jack and Magic Fairy had two toy cars. One of them made their car go across the floor all by itself without pushing it; the other pushed their car across the floor'. Children were asked to say who had produced each type of outcome by pointing either to the drawing of the child or to the drawing of Magic Fairy. The frequency with which 3- and 4-year-olds chose Magic Fairy rather than the child is shown in figure 8.2 for the two types of outcome. Both age groups made a clear distinction between ordinary and extraordinary outcomes, almost invariably choosing the child as the agent of the ordinary outcomes and Magic Fairy as the agent of the extraordinary outcomes.

These two studies support the claim that young children classify familiar outcomes as magical if they violate their causal principles. The second study is especially convincing in showing that the distinction between ordinary and magical processes is sharply made and

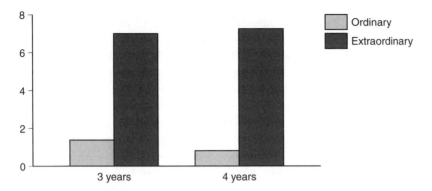

Figure 8.2 Mean number of 'Magic Fairy' judgements by age and item type.

emerges early in development. Notice also that children never observed the outcomes in question. Rather, they were asked to consider various potential outcomes in their imagination. Apparently, they are able to contemplate such imagined outcomes and appropriately classify them as either ordinary or magical. Still, we asked children to reflect on only a modest sample of anomalous outcomes – those that violate various principles of 'folk physics'. Moreover, the ones that we chose resemble the tricks that children might have seen a conjuror perform. Our results might only show that children have a narrow and relatively superficial concept of magic and magicians. They might apply the term magic to the type of tricks that they have seen in a magic show – coins that disappear, rabbits pulled out of hats, and so forth and they might think of a magician as someone capable of performing that kind of trick. On this account, they would lack a truly generative notion of 'magic'. They would not apply it to other anomalous outcomes, even if they were clear violations of causal principles that they understand and recognize.

To assess this claim, we can ask if there is any evidence that children will classify other types of anomaly as magical – notably, those that they are unlikely ever to have seen in the course of a magic show. Karl Rosengren and his colleagues studied young children's understanding of biological transformations (Rosengren, Kalish, Hickling and Gelman, 1994). Four- and 5-year-olds were shown two pictures depicting the same animal with a change of either size or shape. They were then asked whether the animal could undergo such a change. Some of the changes were biologically possible – for example, an increase in size or in complexity – whereas others were biologically impossible – for example, a decrease in size or complexity. Children distinguished sharply between the two types of change. They accepted that increases in size and complexity could occur, but they denied that decreases in size and complexity could occur. Thus, children appeared to recognize certain basic constraints on the direction of biological growth. Nevertheless, in a follow-up study, 4- and 5-year-olds accepted that a magician could bring about either type of change – a decrease as well as an increase in size or complexity.[1] Thus, children do appear to have a generative notion of magic that is rooted in their causal understanding – it is not one that is restricted to the kind of tricks that they have seen a conjuror perform. Children were asked a further question that reinforces this conclusion. They were asked to say how the magician could perform the change. Rosengren and his colleagues looked for indications that children were thinking of the change in terms of a mere conjuring trick or sleight-of-hand. Only a couple of children gave any such indication. The large majority said that the magician would use magical powers and potions.

Taken together, these experiments show that young children understand several fundamental constraints: that matter cannot be created out of nothing; that inanimate objects do not change their shape or identity; and that complicated processes such as growth and ageing are irreversible. Children use these principles to assess what is ordinarily possible, but they also use them to classify certain violations as magical. These violations need not be phenomena that they observe – they can be outcomes that they are invited to imagine. This distinction between what is ordinarily possible and what might take place under extraordinary conditions turns out to be quite widespread. There are two other significant contexts in which it enters children's thinking: fairy tales and religious teaching.

Fairy Tales

Bruno Bettelheim argued that fairy tales offer children a view of the world that helps them to cope with their anxieties and frustrations. The story protagonist usually manages to outwit an all-powerful father figure in the form of a giant, or to escape from a demanding mother figure in the form of a witch. Bettelheim also insisted that fairy tales echo children's conception of causality. Citing Piaget's early research (Piaget, 1929), he argued that children have a naive, precausal understanding of the world. For example, they believe that the kinds of transformation that take place in a fairy tale – a frog that changes into a prince or sisters that change into statues – are possible in reality (Bettelheim, 1991, pp. 46–7). However, as we have seen, Piaget's claims about young children's naive conception of the world have turned out to be too negative. For example, 6-year-olds understand that it is impossible to change one natural kind abruptly into a very different kind, or to change an animate being into an inanimate object (Keil, 1989), and 4- and 5-year-olds judge that certain within-species transformations are impossible (Rosengren et al., 1994). By implication, young children will frequently recognize the dramatic transformations that occur in fairy tales for what they are: violations of ordinary, causal constraints.

Support for this alternative view emerges from an intriguing study carried out by Eugene Subbotsky (1994). He questioned 4-, 5- and 6-year-olds about spatial and temporal transformations. Children were asked whether they could pass through a solid barrier, and also whether it could be done in a fairy tale. Similarly, they were asked whether a person or an object could travel back in time so as to become younger or newer, and again whether such a transformation was possible in a fairy tale. For each type of transformation, the children made a sharp distinction between real life and fairy tales. All children denied that it is possible to pass through a solid barrier and almost all of them denied that it is possible to travel back in time. On the other hand, they all acknowledged that such transformations could happen in a fairy tale. Thus, contrary to Bettelheim's claims, fairy tales may engage children not because they coincide with children's magical conception of the world but because various emotionally charged twists to the plot – such as the magical transformation of a central character – violate that conception. Indeed, as Subbotsky's results indicate, children come to appreciate the special conventions of fairy tales. Not only can they identify a given transformation as magical when they encounter it in a particular fairy tale, they also learn that fairy tales are a distinctive genre where such ordinarily impossible transformations may take place.[2]

Religious Beliefs

Key religious concepts build on, but also violate, our ordinary causal notions. For example, religious ontologies frequently include special beings that share many ordinary human qualities – they can see and hear, receive messages, and express desires and judgements. At the same time, these beings are credited with extraordinary powers: they may be able to pass through solid barriers, they may be able to read our innermost thoughts and they may enjoy immortality (Boyer and Walker, 2000).

Arguably, young children fail to grasp this complex package of the ordinary and the extraordinary. Certainly, stage-based accounts of children's developing conception of God have implied that they have, at best, a concrete, human-like conception of God (Goldman, 1964). However, religious concepts typically violate key ontological principles that are established relatively early. Even infants are puzzled by ordinary objects that pass through a solid barrier (Baillargeon, 1994; Spelke, 1990). Preschoolers gradually appreciate that knowledge depends critically on perceptual access (Perner, 1991, ch. 7). Young schoolchildren start to build a biologically based understanding of the processes that support life and the inevitability of death (Slaughter, Jaakkola and Carey, 1999). Accordingly, we might expect that even young children appreciate that whatever God's resemblance to ordinary mortals, he must also possess extraordinary powers.

Strong evidence for this claim has been obtained by Justin Barrett (in press). Children were asked to say what various ordinary living beings would know about the contents of a box that they could not see inside – either because the box was closed or because it was dark inside it. In addition, however, children were asked what God would know about the contents of the box. In line with a solid body of evidence (Wellman, Cross and Watson, 1999), 5- and 6-year-olds realized that ordinary beings – for example, their own mother – would not know what was inside the box. By contrast, these same children claimed that God would know. They realized that God's knowledge, unlike that of ordinary beings, would not depend on his being able to see inside the box. These findings offer a powerful demonstration that young children: (1) understand a basic constraint on the knowledge available to ordinary creatures; (2) concurrently appreciate that God is not subject to that constraint; and (3) can accurately infer what he

[handwritten margin note: children do appreciate God's extraordinary powers.]

would know in the absence of the constraint. Apparently, children do not simply regard God as a mysterious and unpredictable anomaly – they can work out the conclusions that he would draw given his extraordinary powers. It is too early to say whether this conclusion will hold up with respect to other aspects of religious ontology. For example, we do not know what children would claim about God's immortality. For the time being, however, the proposal that children are alert to the way that religious concepts combine the ordinary and the extraordinary is a provocative working hypothesis.

The Infusion of Everyday Reality

So far, I have implied that children come to understand a set of principles or constraints that apply to the ordinary world. At the same time, they are able to entertain violations of those constraints. Although they may not be able to observe such violations in the course of their everyday life, they can contemplate them in their imagination. Indeed, fairy tales and religious concepts actively invite children to consider obvious and striking violations of basic physical, biological and psychological constraints.

We might press this conclusion further by insisting that children set up a firm and impenetrable barrier between two different mental spheres: the sphere of mundane reality where ordinary causal principles hold sway, and the world of fantasy and metaphysics, where the impossible can happen. However, this dualistic account would not do justice to young children's ontological framework. It seems more plausible that children construct a semi-permeable boundary between the world of the imagination and the world of actual possibilities. In particular, there are some occasions when possibilities that they have contemplated in their imagination infuse their conception of what could happen in the real world. Captured by their imagination, they start to wonder if transformations that are normally impossible might nevertheless occur. They do not entertain the existence of magic only when confronted head-on by a mysterious, observable outcome. Rather, they adopt a more open-minded attitude, half-wondering whether – or even hoping that – magic might be on offer. Several experiments from different laboratories suggest that for some children, at any rate, this description is apt.

Consider an adult who watches a film that portrays a late-night accident: a car careers off the road and kills a pedestrian. After the film, the person goes home. The final section of that journey involves a walk along a poorly lit street. The person sees car lights rapidly approaching in the distance. It would not be surprising if, under these circumstances, the person started to imagine the possibility of an accident, and even to act as if that possibility might be realized by keeping well away from the kerb.

Notice that this hypothetical case is more complex than the imaginary episodes discussed in chapter 4. To the elements discussed in that chapter, namely emotional involvement in a purely fictional episode, we have added another element, namely a real context that serves as a potential setting for the actualization of the fantasy. It may be perfectly clear that the film is over and that the accident was a mere fiction. Nonetheless, the filmgoer's imagination, activated by the scene in the film, serves as a pointer to what might happen in an actual setting. The subjective likelihood of an accident is likely to be greater than on earlier journeys along that same street. In short, the person's imagination infuses their appraisal of what can happen in a given setting.

Are children also prone to such imaginative infusion? As discussed in chapter 4, a child who starts to think about a monster may begin to feel anxious at the mere contemplation of that fantasy. In itself, that would not amount to the imaginative infusion of reality, just described. Suppose, however, that the child is trying to go to sleep and begins to think about the possibility of a monster lying in wait under the bed. Under these circumstances, the child may begin to fret that there really is a monster lurking there. Indeed, the child's imagination may be sufficiently vivid that prosaic causal considerations, such as how the monster got there in the first place, may be ignored. Below, I describe several experiments where such infusion effects, as I shall call them, have been demonstrated.

In an initial study, we asked children aged 4 and 6 years to conjure up a pretend creature in their imagination (Harris, Brown, Marriott, Whittall and Harmer, 1991, experiment 4). However, we did not simply invite them to visualize these creatures in their mind's eye, as we had done in the experiments described in chapter 4. Children came into the experimental area, typically a room or separate space at their school, and were shown two black boxes. We deliberately made these boxes quite large – approximately 1 metre square – so that they could plausibly 'accommodate' various make-believe creatures: puppies, rabbits and more disturbing creatures such as monsters.

Children first established that both boxes were empty. They were invited to look inside each of them to satisfy themselves on this point. Next, they were asked to pretend that there was a creature inside one of them. Half the children in each age group were asked to pretend that there was a rabbit inside the box, and half to pretend that there was a monster. They were also asked to think of these creatures as having various additional characteristics – nice and friendly and wanting to be stroked in the case of the rabbit, mean and horrible and wanting to chase the child in the case of the monster.

Once this pretence had been established, the experimenter feigned to have forgotten a gift that she was going to give the child. She explained that she would leave the room to get it and asked children to wait there for her. Before leaving she checked two points. First, she asked the children whether there really was a rabbit or monster in the box, or whether they were just pretending. Irrespective of age, almost all of the children agreed that they were just pretending. Second, she asked them if it was all right for her to leave them alone to wait for her while she went to get the gift. Most of the children agreed to this plan, although a small minority asked her not to leave. All of these four children had been asked to imagine a monster – rather than a rabbit – inside the box. The experimenter responded to each of the four by opening the two boxes to show that they were empty, and then asking the child again whether she might leave. However, all of the children insisted that they did not want to be left alone because they were scared. Accordingly, the experimenter stayed and sought to reassure them.

Turning to those children who were willing to be left alone, we were especially interested in whether they would approach either of the boxes, and if so, which. A video of children's behaviour during the experimenter's absence showed that almost half of the children opened one or both of the boxes. In doing so, they typically focused more on the box containing the imaginary creature. Whether it contained a pretend monster or a pretend rabbit, children touched it more quickly than the neutral box (see figure 8.3). In addition, they were likely to touch and open it more often than the neutral box. Apparently, children were curious about the pretend box. Their reasons for being curious emerged more clearly in the next stage of the experiment.

After an absence of two minutes, the experimenter returned and talked to the children about what they had done and thought while she was away. In particular, they were asked: 'Were you sure there was nothing inside the box or did you wonder whether there was a

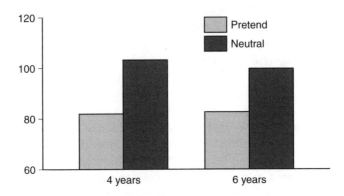

Figure 8.3   Mean number of seconds to touch each box as a function of age.

bunny (or monster) inside?' Half the children insisted that they were sure that nothing was inside, but the remainder acknowledged that they did indeed wonder if there was a creature inside the box. The pattern of replies produced by this latter group was intriguing. Recall that before she left them alone, the experimenter had asked children whether there was really a creature in the box, or whether they were just pretending. Almost all of them said that they were just pretending. Why then did a considerable proportion subsequently acknowledge that they had wondered, while the experimenter was out of the room, whether the box contained the creature in question? Why might these children claim on the one hand that an imaginary creature was 'just pretend', but also wonder if the same creature might be inside the box?

The infusion hypothesis helps to explain this shift. It suggests that the very act of imagining a creature in the box infuses children's appraisal of reality, or more precisely their assessment of what the box might contain, despite its having been visibly empty when first examined. That possibility becomes sufficiently plausible for some children that they start to wonder if there really is a creature inside the box.

In our next experiment, we looked more closely at the different patterns of responding that I have mentioned until now only in passing (Johnson and Harris, 1994, experiment 3). Why did some children investigate the pretend box while the experimenter was gone, and why did other children ignore the boxes altogether? We already have part of an answer. In line with the 'infusion' hypothesis, some children candidly admitted that they wondered whether the pretend box contained the creature that they had imagined. Our hunch was that it was precisely this possibility that lured them from their chair to investigate. But why did other children sit in their chair, ignoring the boxes?

The experiment in question was modelled on the one that I have just described, but we introduced several changes. First, we tested a wider age range: 3-, 5- and 7-year-olds. Second, instead of a monster or a rabbit, we asked children to pretend that there was either some ice-cream or a fairy in the box. The idea behind this manipulation was to check whether children would investigate the pretend box in connection with an inanimate substance as well as an animate creature. Third, and most important of all, we looked more closely at the possible link between the replies that individual children gave to the experimenter when she returned after her brief absence, and their prior behaviour while she had been away.

Our earlier finding of selective investigation of the pretend box proved to be a robust phenomenon. Children opened it more quickly and more often than the neutral box. On her return, the experimenter asked the children if they had wondered whether there was anything inside the box. On the basis of their replies, children could be split into three groups: so-called *credulous* children who admitted that they did indeed wonder if there was something inside the box, *sceptical* children who claimed that they were sure that there was nothing inside the box, and a small number of children who were *unsure* and wavered in their replies. Just over half the children gave credulous replies, somewhat less than half gave sceptical replies, and a small minority were unsure.

Having identified these three groups, we looked at what children in each group had done during the experimenter's absence. Figure 8.4 shows that most of the credulous children opened the box containing the pretend entity. Sceptical children, by contrast, were more likely to ignore the box. Thus, there was a clear link between children's behaviour toward the box containing the imaginary entity and their stance during the subsequent interview. Children who entertained the possibility that there might be something in the box were likely to look inside it. Children who were convinced that the box was empty ignored it and simply waited for the experimenter to come back.[3]

In a further interview question, children were asked to justify their credulity or their scepticism. Credulous children were asked: 'How

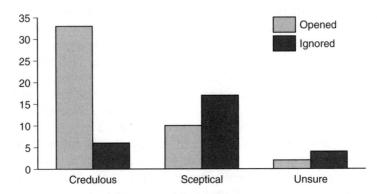

Figure 8.4   Number of credulous, sceptical and unsure children who opened or ignored the pretend box.

did you think the ice-cream (or a fairy) got inside the box?' Sceptical children were asked: 'How did you know there wasn't any ice-cream (or a fairy) in the box?' Replies were classified in terms of the kind of consideration that children mentioned. For example, they might refer to physical or spatial features of the boxes (e.g. 'It was empty before') or they might refer to magical causation (e.g. 'A witch made a spell on her (the fairy) and made her get in there').

Sceptical children mostly justified their stance by invoking the principles of non-creation and impenetrability. They pointed out that the boxes had been empty before or that there was no way for anything to get inside. Some of the credulous children also mentioned the physical or spatial layout to justify their stance, but they also embroidered on mundane reality to explain how it was possible for something to have entered the box, for example: 'She came through a window and flew in the box when I opened it but I didn't see her 'cos she's teeny'. Explicit references to magic, including the use of spells or a magic wand, were almost exclusively confined to credulous children.

In sum, we identified two broad patterns of responding: credulity and scepticism. Credulous children – who admitted to wondering if the imagined entity was actually in the box – were likely to open the pretend box and to justify their credulity by referring either to special types of displacement or to magic. By contrast, sceptical children – who insisted that the boxes were empty – were likely to ignore the pretend box and to justify their scepticism in terms of familiar physical and spatial constraints. Finally, a small group of unsure children vacillated between these two reactions, displaying a mixture of credulity and scepticism. Below, I explain in more detail how the hypothesis of reality infusion can explain these two different reactions.

The overall process may be conveniently divided into three successive phases: imagining, likelihood-appraisal and action. In the initial phase, we may assume that all the children respond in essentially the same way: following the experimenter's prompt, they imagine the appropriate entity inside the pretend box, be it animate or inanimate, prosaic or magical. The second phase takes place when the children are left to their own devices by the experimenter. Having previously imagined an entity in the pretend box, such thoughts remain readily available, in the sense that they easily spring to mind. For the neutral box, by comparison, such thoughts are less available. Mental 'availability' is known to increase the subjective likelihood of an event or situation. For example, an adult who has recently read about, and can easily bring to mind, a plane disaster is likely to rate the likelihood of a similar disaster as greater than someone who cannot readily bring to mind such a disaster (Tversky and Kahneman, 1973). By extension, if the idea of an entity in the box is readily available, this should increase its subjective likelihood. However, during this second step, we may also expect children to bring further considerations to bear before acting. As discussed earlier, young preschool children understand principles such as non-creation and impenetrability. These principles would imply that the box – which was demonstrably empty at the outset – remains empty. However, despite their grasp of such principles, children can also imagine their circumvention or violation: a creature might manage to enter the box unobserved or even mysteriously pass through its solid exterior. These latter considerations would pull children in the direction of credulity rather than scepticism.

Summing up this second step, we may suppose that when children are left alone with the pretend box, the thought that there might be a monster or a fairy in the box comes easily to mind. In assessing the feasibility of this idea, children are swayed in two opposite directions: the principles of non-creation and impenetrability lead them toward scepticism – the box was empty before, so how could anything be inside it now? Other thoughts tug them toward credulity – the box was indeed empty before, but maybe in some enigmatic fashion there is an object or creature in there right now. Depending on the outcome of this appraisal process, we should see two different courses of action in the third phase: the dismissal of any temptation to open the box and, on the other hand, the impulse to engage in 'reality-testing' – to check whether the imagined entity is indeed inside the box. These are, of course, the two impulses that we observed.

One intriguing but unanswered question raised by this analysis is why a particular child displays a sceptical or credulous reaction. Two different explanations are feasible. One possibility is that the different reactions reflect relatively stable personality differences among children. For example, certain children might find it relatively easy to construct a fantasy about the creature in the box that is vivid, lifelike and absorbing. Indeed, research with adults indicates marked individual differences in the tendency toward absorption, especially in the context of fantasy-oriented activities such as daydreaming, reading or role play (Tellegen and Atkinson, 1974). Moreover, adults prone to such imaginative absorption are likely to report that it has been a stable disposition that reaches back into childhood (Lynn and Rhue, 1986). Arguably, for children who are prone to such imaginative absorption, considerations of plausibility might exert a weak inhibitory role. In that case, such children would tend to display a consistently credulous reaction across a range of situations. However, an alternative explanation for the fact that children tend to show either a credulous or a sceptical reaction is that our experiments create a situation where the impulses toward those two reactions are in very close competition with one another. On this account, the outcome of the competition between the two impulses would depend mainly on those situational factors that serve to strengthen or undermine one impulse relative to the other, rather than on individual personalities. In the next section, I describe some experiments where the impulse toward credulity was indeed strengthened.

Probing Children's Credulity

In our experiments, we stimulated children's imagination in a relatively direct fashion by explicitly asking them to pretend that something was in the box. However, the hypothesis that I have set out predicts that less direct methods of stimulating the imagination might be just as effective, if not more so, in infusing children's appraisal of reality. In a variety of ingenious experiments, Eugene Subbotsky has examined the impact of various stories about magical transformations. In one study, children were first questioned about the possibility of changing a drawing into the object that it depicts (Subbotsky, 1985). For example, they were asked whether a drawing of an elephant could be changed into a real elephant if a magic word were pronounced. Most 4-year-olds and all 5- and 6-year-olds denied that this was ordinarily possible. Children were then told the story of 'The magic box', which described a girl called Masha who received the box as a present. The box could transform a drawing of an object into the object itself if the drawing was placed inside the box and the magic words, 'Alpha, beta, gamma' were pronounced over it. The story told how Masha did not believe this at first, but tried the box and became convinced that it really could do magic.

A few days after hearing this story, children visited the laboratory and the experimenter offered to show them 'the same magic box that was given to Masha'. Children were shown an attractive box together with drawings depicting a variety of objects – a brooch, a fountain pen, a spider, and so forth. The experimenter left children alone briefly, saying that they could use the box while he was away, and reminding them that the box wouldn't 'hear' the magic words unless they were said aloud. When left alone, most of the children tried to transform the pictures into objects. They typically selected a picture of one of the more attractive objects – for example, the brooch or the pen rather than the spider – put it into the box, and pronounced the magic words. Some elaborated on this by making a gesture over the box, as they said the words. They would then open the box, and express puzzlement or surprise at the fact that no transformation had occurred. A small minority of the children made no attempt at a magical transformation: they either fiddled with the objects or looked at them with indifference.

These findings fit readily into the three-part hypothesis described above: the fairy story serves to plant the idea of a magical transformation. That idea is brought to mind when the experimenter hands the children a box that is allegedly the same as Masha's magic box. In the absence of the experimenter, the children adopt either a credulous or sceptical stance. They accept that the box has magical powers and can transform pictures into objects, or they treat it as an ordinary box and turn their attention elsewhere. Most of the children adopt the credulous stance, but some remain sceptical.

One might argue, however, that children who tried out the box had no illusions about its magical powers. Instead, they were just engaging in a piece of play acting, repeating in a pretend fashion what Masha had done but with no expectation that it would have any effect. This alternative interpretation is unlikely given the nature of children's comments in an interview with the experimenter following his return. Most children characterized their attempt as a 'failure', implying that they had been really trying to transform the drawing and not simply play acting. Indeed, they also sought advice from the experimenter about how to make the box work.

An alternative objection is that children were not play acting but merely going along with the experimenter's suggestions as he left the room. After all, he had told the children that they could use the box if they so wished, and he had also mentioned that the magic words had to be said aloud. Arguably, children were simply acting on his suggestions but did not consider themselves to be emulating the story protagonist Masha. A related study by Subbotsky (1994) shows, however, that children's credulous stance cannot be reduced simply to compliance with the experimenter. Using a similar methodology to the drawing study, Subbotsky tested children's belief in the possibility of magical rejuvenation. After hearing a fairy story about a girl called Lena who drank some magic water and turned into a much younger child, children were introduced to some so-called magic water and shown that it could indeed rejuvenate an old, crumpled postage stamp (this was demonstrated by means of a box with a hidden contrivance permitting a switch between the old stamp and a new one). The experimenter then suggested that the magic water might have an equally rejuvenating effect on the children themselves – turning them into a little boy or girl – and invited children to try it out. Most 4- and 5-year-olds resisted this invitation, and continued to resist when the experimenter repeated the request and promised a postage stamp as a reward. Even among 6-year-olds, the majority refused initially, and less than half complied when the request was repeated. Such widespread resistance indicates that children's actions are not simply based on unthinking compliance with the experimenter's suggestions. Rather, their actions are guided by a readiness to entertain the possibility of extraordinary transformations, whether undesirable or desirable.

Finally, it could be objected that children's credulity in these experiments is only to be expected. After all, the experimenter shows them a box or some water and implies that the objects have magical properties. If an adult accepts that magic is possible, why should children remain sceptical? This argument identifies what is likely to be a contributory factor in shifting children from a sceptical to a credulous stance. At the same time, the underlying implication – that children always yield to adult suggestion – is overstated. Recall that the children interviewed by Mead (1932) contradicted her suggestion that sorcery might explain the drifting canoe. More generally, developmental research has shown that young children are often resistant to adult feedback. To take but one example, they do not always change their judgement about conservation in the light of adult correction (Field, 1987). Indeed, simply telling children that their judgement is right or wrong is much less effective in eliciting conservation judgements than encouraging them to engage in an active reconsideration of the problem. Thus, children are more likely to produce conservation responses if they are asked to *explain* an adult's conservation judgement. This shift is especially likely if children have already given indications of conceptualizing the conservation problem in more than one way (Siegler, 1995). By analogy, if children are willing to take up an adult's suggestion that various causal constraints may be violated, it is not likely that such an idea has simply been foisted on them by an authority figure. Rather, it is a possibility that children are willing to entertain and examine for themselves.

Conclusions

In this chapter, I have retreated back toward the early portrait of children's imagination as a capacity that tempts them toward 'autistic' thinking. Under certain conditions, children are lured to contemplate and explore possibilities that their objective causal analyses would lead them to reject. However, it is worth emphasizing that my retreat is only partial. In line with a long tradition of research dating back to the 1930s, I have argued that children do not regularly invoke magic as an explanatory mechanism, even if – in puzzlement at the violation of some familiar causal principle – they are willing to classify causal anomalies as 'magic'. Much of children's exploration of the magical or miraculous necessarily takes place in their imagination, nurtured by the surrounding culture. In the context of fiction and also religion, they are led to think about various transformations and capacities that would ordinarily be impossible. Occasionally, however, as the final series of experiments has shown, their imaginative exploration is translated into a half-belief that everyday reality might also violate its customary causal regularities. Children mostly live in the ordinary world and expect mundane causal principles to hold sway, but, like adults, that does not prevent them from speculating and even hoping that it might be otherwise.

Notes

1   Ideally, we should like to know if children would judge a given change to be magic if it were to occur, whereas Rosengren et al. (1994) asked children whether a magician could bring about a given change. Nonetheless, their results show that children think of certain biological transformations as impossible, unless brought about by the power of magic.

2   It is interesting to speculate that fairy stories might have a special emotional impact on children precisely because they embrace non-standard causal sequences. Recall that chapter 2 indicated that children tend to think of a make-believe world as following the same causal regularities as the real world. To the extent that such a default assumption is not brought into play when children contemplate the world of fairy tales, they may find the cruelty and power of some of the central characters less upsetting than they would in more realistic fiction.

[handwritten marginal note: fairy-tales offer a world in which causal order can happen]

3   One possible explanation for the link between behaviour toward the pretend box and children's replies is that in the interview children simply made post-hoc self-attributions to explain their otherwise 'mindless' behaviour. More specifically, some children may have ignored the boxes – perhaps because they found something else to explore or think about. They then offered a retrospective justification – they stated their belief that the boxes were empty all along. Other children wandered toward the boxes, and having had their attention called to one of them in the earlier pretend period, they looked in that box – not because they wondered if the pretend creature was inside but out of idle curiosity. Then, when asked whether they wondered if the pretend creature was inside the box, they accepted this as a plausible retrospective explanation for their behaviour. This explanation in terms of post-hoc self-attribution is not implausible, but two considerations undermine it. First, children were not asked why they did or did not look in the box but what they thought or believed as they pursued either course of action. Hence, they were not asked to explain their behaviour. Second, even if children did, in fact, assume that the interviewer was requesting an explanation for their having looked in the box, they could still reasonably insist that they thought it was empty – after all, there are reasons for opening a box even if it is known to be empty. Yet, most children who looked in the box claimed that they wondered if the pretend creature might be in the box and not that they were sure it was empty.

Nevertheless, in future research it will be important to try to elicit children's thoughts and beliefs in a way that renders such post-hoc self-attributions an unlikely interpretation. This can be achieved by gathering data on children's thoughts as they approach the boxes and not in a subsequent interview. We are currently exploring a variant in which children are tested in pairs and their spontaneous remarks to one another during the experimenter's absence are discreetly recorded. Preliminary findings show that some pairs of children voice the possibility that the creature is in the box not just during the retrospective interview but also during the experimenter's absence (Kavanaugh and Harris, 1999a).

9

Language and Imagination

In this chapter, I come back to two questions that have surfaced at various points in earlier chapters: what is the relationship between language and the imagination, and why is it that children readily depart from the actual and the veridical so early in their cognitive development? I think that the answers to these two questions are intimately connected with one another. First, however, it will be helpful to review some of the main conclusions that have emerged so far.

The Work of the Imagination

1   When they engage in pretend play, children imagine a possible situation and various transformations of that situation that might take place. In their role play, children project themselves into such imaginary situations, adopting a particular identity and perspective. Such role play is associated with later skill and precocity at reading mental states.
2   Children assume – by default – that transformations of a make-believe situation are brought about in the same way as transformations of a real situation. For example, in games of pretend play, when make-believe tea is poured into a cup, it is attributed the same physical properties and powers as real tea. An imaginary companion is attributed the same basic psychology as a real person.
3   An imagined encounter can drive the emotional system in much the same way as an actual encounter.
4   Nevertheless, young children can distinguish between an actual

and an imaginary situation. Indeed, older children – like adults – can exploit this distinction to regulate their emotional reaction to a piece of fiction.

5 When presented with false or unfamiliar premises, children, including preschoolers, can reach appropriate inferential conclusions. However, the inferences that they draw, and the justifications that they offer, vary depending on the stance that children are led to take toward those premises by their conversation partner. In particular, children may be led to accept the premises and analyse their implications, or they may instead fall back on their own empirical knowledge.

6 Children can compare an actual sequence of events with an imagined counterfactual alternative. They invoke such comparisons in making both causal and moral judgements.

7 Finally, although children assume that mundane causal constraints normally apply to an imagined situation, they can contemplate the violation of such ordinary constraints. They do not do this on a routine basis, but they are capable of doing so when prompted by special settings or genres, such as fairy tales or religious teaching.

When we examine this suite of abilities in detail, some of its design features are quite intricate. Children process an actual event and an imagined event in the same way – with no clear-cut distinction being made between them – insofar as the same causal assumptions are applied to both, and they are appraised for their emotional implications in a similar fashion. Nonetheless, children do not confuse what is real and what is imaginary. They make that distinction at an early age; they sometimes deploy it to moderate their emotional reactions; and they are willing to acknowledge that imaginary worlds need not always display the causal constraints that obtain in the real world. Exactly how children manage to orchestrate this complex suite of abilities is not yet clear. In the future, we may look forward to the development of more detailed models of the processing involved, constrained by the design features set out above.[1]

The Traditional Portrait of Children's Imagination

In the first chapter, I argued that research on the early development of the imagination has been constricted by the theoretical framework in which it was placed by Freud and Piaget. Children's imagination, and especially their involvement in pretend play, was seen as an 'autistic' mode of thought that involved: (1) a turning away from genuine social engagement; (2) the satisfaction of frustrated desires; and (3) the suspension of an objective analysis of reality. By contrast, I claim that young children's imagination is: (1) well attuned to social engagement; (2) not driven by frustrated desires; and (3) amplifies children's analysis of reality. Let us take each of these points in turn.

Almost from its earliest manifestation in the context of pretend play, children's imagination can be recruited in social contexts. Even 2-year-olds accept and respond to the stipulations of a pretend partner. Notice, moreover, that this social responsiveness is not simply a matter of children starting to produce their own independent pretend play when encouraged to do so by another person. The make-believe world in which children start to participate is a collective enterprise – it is *shared* with their partner, as shown by their appropriate rejoinders to pretend stipulations, requests and questions. This joint construction of a make-believe world becomes more sustained and elaborate as children develop increasingly rich and sustained play episodes, especially with other children.

Moreover, it is not just in the context of pretend play that children's imagination is nicely adjusted to input from other people. Recall that the deductions that children are prepared to make and the causal constraints that they apply vary depending on their assessment of the mode of discourse that they are faced with. They make different inferences in response to a dramatic, make-believe intonation as compared to a matter-of-fact delivery, and they assume different causal constraints depending on whether they are faced with mundane assertions or fairy stories. In short, children's imagination, both when it first emerges and thereafter, scarcely involves any turning away from social contact. It is well attuned to the overtures and stipulations of a play partner and it is increasingly attuned to the type of assertion made by a conversation partner.

To what extent is children's fantasy life guided by unfulfilled desire and emotional need? I conclude that this common assumption has yielded little empirical fruit. Consider the type of role play that children begin to engage in from the third year onward. Arguably, they create imaginary companions to satisfy some thwarted need for friendship. However, there is at best a very weak correlation between the dearth of actual companions and the invention of an imaginary one.

Moreover, that correlation can be attributed to opportunity rather than need. Children who lack actual companions may simply have more time to play with an imaginary companion. In addition, it requires considerable faith in a need-based analysis to insist that children's squabbles and disappointments with their imaginary companion are the product of thwarted desires. Even more resistant to a desire-based analysis is the phenomenon of imaginary monsters. What emotional satisfaction might children derive from the invention of something that frightens them and keeps them awake?

We gain a more plausible understanding of the relationship between emotion on the one hand and imagination on the other if we recognize that the causal arrow typically travels in the reverse direction. It is not the emotional needs of children that give rise to the invention of an imaginary character or scene, but rather that such inventions give rise to various emotions: depending on the nature of the imaginary actions and events, children may feel frightened, frustrated or satisfied.

In any case, it is obviously a mistake to think that children's imagination is only activated in unstructured contexts in which they are left to their own devices and desires. Spontaneous inventions – such as the creation of an imaginary companion or monster – may be striking examples of the autonomy of children's imagination, but there are innumerable contexts in which it is activated by external input in a relatively constrained fashion. For example, their encounters with fictional characters and events arouse emotion. Again, it is problematic to assume that such emotion is a response to thwarted desire and much more plausible to assume that it is triggered by their appraisal of the imaginary encounter.

Finally, in those cases where children observe an actual outcome and start to think about ways in which it might have turned out differently, it could be argued that such counterfactual thinking is desire-based. It might reflect a longing for things to be otherwise, especially in cases when some mishap or disappointment has occurred. However, children's counterfactual thinking is equally triggered by positive outcomes, even if more subtle analysis is needed to detect such thinking at work.

In sum, there is no systematic evidence to support the common assumption that the child's imaginative life provides us with a special glimpse of desires and needs that are unfulfilled in everyday life. Admittedly, the emotion that the child displays in the context of an imagined event will resemble the emotion that the child would display in the context of everyday life because equivalent appraisal processes are brought to bear on each event. But that does not mean that the emotions are at the helm, constantly steering the imagination toward various satisfactions that reality excludes. It makes more sense to conclude that it is the imagination that enables the child to contemplate particular encounters, and those imagined encounters – like actual encounters – can evoke feelings of dissatisfaction or satisfaction, disappointment or relief, fear or excitement, as the case may be.

Finally, we may consider the extent to which children's imagination allows them to retreat from an analysis of reality. At first sight, it seems paradoxical to insist that children's counterfactual thoughts enlarge their engagement with reality. To the extent that such thoughts lead them to put reality to one side, surely they must diminish the analysis of reality itself. This conclusion presupposes that the analysis of reality consists in a contemplation of only what actually happened. Yet historical, legal and scientific analyses constantly bring into focus the contrast between what did happen in the circumstances, and what would have happened had antecedent circumstances been different. Young children's capacity to do likewise should be seen as an early example of a mode of judgement that persists into maturity, and not as a primitive or 'autistic' mode of thought that increasing objectivity will suppress.

The Relationship Between Language and the Imagination

At the end of chapter 4, I discussed the paradox that an imagined situation can drive our emotional system in much the same way as a real encounter. I offered two speculative functional explanations for that alleged equivalence, but I cautioned that both speculations might be misplaced. Granted the increasing neurological evidence that perception and imagery enjoy multiple common pathways, it can be argued that the emotional equivalence of actual and imagined encounters – far from being paradoxical – is exactly what might be expected.

However, a different, and more resistant, paradox comes into view if we focus not on the link between imagination and emotion but on the development of the imagination itself. This is especially true if we concentrate on what I have regarded as the very earliest manifestation of the imagination, namely the early production and comprehension of pretend play. In a creative and influential analysis of pretence, Alan Leslie pointed out that such play is puzzling: 'After all, from an evolutionary point of view, there ought to be a high premium on the veridicality of cognitive processes. The perceiving, thinking organism ought, as far as possible, to get things right' (Leslie, 1987, p. 412). What advantage might there be in a disposition to invent imaginary creatures and episodes? To answer this question, Leslie proposed various computational rules to prevent children's grip on reality from being infected by make-believe premises. More importantly, he claimed that children's capacity for pretence marks the onset of their understanding of various mental states. In particular, he argued that their engagement in pretend play, whether alone or in concert with another person, would not be possible if they did not understand the mentalistic nature of pretence. Indeed, by virtue of parallels between the two mental states, Leslie concluded that the emergence of pretence implies not just an understanding of the mental foundations of pretence, but also marks the onset of an equivalent understanding of belief.[2] Thus, Leslie's proposal is that the functional mystery of pretend play is resolved once we recognize that it is one of the earliest manifestations of children's ability to understand how the mind works.

At first sight, this proposal is attractive and plausible. Certainly, a great deal of speculation and analysis has been devoted to the claim that a theory of mind, whatever its origin, would confer considerable advantages on a species with a complex and rapidly changing mix of competitive and cooperative interaction (Byrne and Whiten, 1988; Humphrey, 1976; Whiten and Byrne, 1991). Moreover, there is evidence that deficits in pretend play are – just as Leslie would expect – associated with difficulties in understanding belief: autistic children – whose pretend play is often limited – frequently have difficulty in making sense of people's beliefs.[3] There is also evidence – reviewed in chapter 3 – that among normal children frequent pretend play, or at least frequent role play, is linked to good performance on various assessments of mental state understanding.

However, despite these empirical findings, there is an emerging consensus that Leslie's conceptualization of pretence is wrong.[4] In particular, it has been argued that young children can engage in pretence, and indeed join in with another person's pretence, even if they do not possess any insight into the mental state of pretending. In much the same way, they can hold a belief even if they lack any insight into the mental state of believing. To the extent that engaging in pretend play, including joint pretence, does not presume a mentalistic understanding of pretence, much less a mentalistic understanding of belief, Leslie's proposed solution to the evolutionary paradox of pretence is undermined. Pretence is not an early manifestation of the child's developing understanding of mind, even if it is associated – in the longer term – with good performance on various tests of mental state comprehension. Hence, the question remains – why should the human species be disposed to invent imaginary creatures and make-believe situations? Is there a more plausible explanation for such a peculiar departure from veridicality?

My own proposal takes up, with some major changes, a suggestion made by Piaget (1962). He claimed that the emergence of pretend play and the emergence of language are closely intertwined. In particular, he argued that they should both be seen as members of a wide-ranging semiotic function that emerges in the course of the second year. However, in keeping with his negative stance toward pretend play, Piaget insisted that pretence uses a relatively restricted and inferior symbolic code. Unlike language, which makes use of genuinely arbitrary and socially agreed signs, pretend play relies on idiosyncratic and partially iconic gestures and props to convey its meaning.

My proposal, by contrast, implies a collaborative and complementary relationship between pretence and language. The key concept for linking the two functions is what has come to be known as the *situation model*. As reviewed in chapters 3 and 4, there is now a wealth of evidence showing that when adults process a connected narrative, they construct – in their imagination – a mental model of the narrative situation being described. Moreover, as the narrative unfolds, they update that situation model so as to keep track of the main developments in the plot (Zwaan and Radvansky, 1998; Zwaan, 1999). In building such a situation model, the listener (or reader) typically imagines the ongoing scene from a particular spatio-temporal locus. That deictic centre, as it is called, is usually selected in relation to the movements and actions of the main protagonist. Objects that are close to the main protagonist are mentally located in the foreground of the situation model. Similarly, events that have just befallen or are about to befall the protagonist are also foregrounded. In either case, they are 'kept in mind' by the listener, and easily accessed when later information calls for their retrieval. Finally, as they construct a situation model, adults interpolate causal connections between successive actions and episodes, even when such connections are not explicitly stated in the narrative.

Children appear to display a similar set of cognitive processes when they engage in pretend play. First, when they watch a play partner enact a pretend episode, children build in their mind's eye a representation of the ongoing changes and transformations that occur in the make-believe world. In addition, various aspects of children's early role play reveals their disposition to adopt a given spatio-temporal perspective on a make-believe situation. When they take the part of a particular character, they give voice to the perceptual experiences, sensations, needs and moods that such a character might have in the make-believe situation. Finally, children's comprehension of episodes enacted by a play partner shows that they readily interpolate causal connections between successive make-believe situations, even when those connections are not explicitly enacted by the partner.

I suggest that this coincidence between the ways in which adults process narrative discourse and the ways in which children engage with a make-believe situation is – on close examination – no coincidence.[5] We need only make the plausible assumption that children process narrative discourse in much the same way as adults – they use a situation model. Evidence consistent with that assumption was presented in chapter 3. Recall that when children reproduced a simple story, they imposed a situation model with a consistent perspective on the story events, in much the same way as adults. Granted the assumption that children deploy a situation model when listening to connected discourse, we may effectively conclude that children's capacity to construct a situation model serves a double function. On the one hand, it permits them to engage in pretend play, especially joint pretend play with an unfolding, episodic structure; on the other hand, it permits them to process narrative discourse.

There is, however, an important objection to this proposal, certainly if it is construed as a serious attempt to explain why children are disposed to depart from the veridical so early in their cognitive career. The suggestion that pretence, or rather the cognitive process that underpins pretence, enables children to make sense of narrative discourse seems to deepen rather than resolve the mystery. Why should nature have equipped children to abandon the veridical not just when engaged in pretend play but also when understanding language? After all, the content of a story – like the content of a bout of pretend play – is fictional rather than factual. Effectively, we have solved one mystery by landing ourselves with a second.

To surmount this objection, we may reformulate the proposal as follows. In the course of language development, children increasingly need to construct a situation model, not just when they listen to a prototypical narrative in the form of a story or fairy tale, but whenever they encounter connected discourse whose deictic centre is displaced from the here and now. This form of discourse includes stories and fairy tales, but it is by no means exhaustively defined by them. It also includes discourse about displaced events – events occurring at a time and place removed from the context in which the conversation itself take place. Some of these conversations will involve a joint discussion of an event that the child witnessed. Thus, even at 2 or 3 years of age, children start to engage in a collaborative recollection of the past, typically in concert with a parent (Nelson, 1993). However, some conversations will inform the child about an event that is planned but has not yet occurred, or an event in the past that he or she did not witness. In each of these contexts, the child cannot rely on the *retrieval* of an existing situation model stored in long-term memory to understand the information being provided. No such situation model exists because the child has never witnessed the event being described. By implication, the child has to construct and update a situation model on the spot, guided by the successive assertions of his or her interlocutor. This situation model may well pertain to reality – it may be a description of a highly probable event in the future or some event in the past that actually happened. Nonetheless, a child who constantly sought to understand someone's current utterance by taking it to be a reference to current and immediate reality, where what is current and immediate is defined in terms of the time and place of the conversation, would be fundamentally restricted in their comprehension of language. By implication, the understanding of connected discourse is only feasible for a creature who is capable, temporarily, of setting current reality to one side and constructing a situation model pertaining to a different spatio-temporal locus. The ability to do exactly that – to set current, objective reality to one side and to construct a revisable situation model – underpins young children's comprehension of an unfolding narrative chain in the context of pretence, as described in chapters 2 and 3.

My proposal, then, for the puzzling emergence of pretend play in young children is that the cognitive capacity that underpins pretend play – the capacity to construct a situation model – is an endowment that enables children to understand and eventually produce connected discourse about non-current episodes. This proposal is in keeping with the roughly synchronous emergence of pretend play and language in young children. It is also consistent with the evidence presented in chapter 2 showing that once those two functions have emerged, children can immediately coordinate them. Recall that even 2-year-olds are not confined to discourse about actual events – they can discuss purely imagined events. The proposal is consistent with the marked limitations in both pretend play and language comprehension among the higher primates.[6] It is consistent with the restrictions displayed by autistic children both in generating pretend play and in engaging in connected discourse.[7] It also fits the plausible hypothesis that the understanding of mental states, especially beliefs, is not available to 2-year-olds but is an emergent consequence of children's ability to engage in dialogue. Conversation is, after all, one of the most complex and transparent vehicles by which we make our thoughts known to one another.[8]

Finally, this proposal invites the tantalizing speculation that the particular evolutionary path taken by modern *Homo sapiens* was marked not just by the emergence of complex language or the ability to conjure up situations in the imagination. Rather, at some point in our evolutionary history, there was an explosive fusion of these two capacities. That fusion of language and imagination would have enabled us to pursue a new type of dialogue – to exchange and accumulate thoughts about a host of situations, none actually witnessed but all imaginable: the distant past and future, as well as the magical and the impossible.

Notes

1 See Leslie (1987) for a pioneering attempt to provide a processing model, and Nichols and Stich (2000) for criticism and elaboration. These authors do not analyse the entire suite of abilities that I have described, but they offer a good starting point for a processing account of pretence.

2 Leslie (1994) has since claimed that various processing constraints might delay children's understanding of belief, and notably false belief, as compared to their understanding of pretence. However, despite his acknowledgement of this décalage, he maintains that the representational machinery needed to understand the two mental states is fundamentally similar.

3 For further discussion of the extent to which children with autism are limited in their pretend play, see Harris and Leevers (2000b). For a sys-

tematic review of their difficulties in understanding belief, see Yirmiya, Erel, Shaked and Solomonica-Levi (1998).

4   See, for example, Harris and Kavanaugh (1993, pp. 75–6); Perner (1993); Jarrold, Carruthers, Smith and Boucher (1994); Currie (1998); and Nichols and Stich (2000).

5   An earlier version of this hypothesis was sketched in Kavanaugh and Harris (1999b).

6   Evidence for pretend play among the higher primates is restricted to observation of occasional pretend-like behaviour among home-reared chimpanzees (Tomasello and Call, 1997; Whiten and Byrne, 1991). I know of no evidence indicating a capacity for engaging in joint play with successive episodes, as described in chapter 2. With respect to language, the most sophisticated performance so far is probably that of Kanzi, a bonobo chimpanzee, whose ability to respond to multi-word requests (e.g. 'pour the Coke in the lemonade' and 'pour the lemonade in the Coke') is comparable to that of a normal 3-year-old child (Savage-Rumbaugh, Murphy, Sevcik, Brakke, Williams and Rumbaugh, 1993). Note, however, that the situation model required to deal with such requests can be constructed in relation to the time and place of the utterance. Indeed, some, if not all, of the items mentioned are fully visible even if the requested end state involves some displacement or recombination. More generally, Kanzi's productive repertoire is typically restricted to the immediate situation. The large majority of his utterances are directed at getting his human caretakers to do things – to fetch, carry and tickle (Greenfield and Savage-Rumbaugh, 1990).

7   For discussion of the difficulties displayed by children with autism in handling connected discourse, see Bruner and Feldman (1993).

8   For further discussion of the extent to which an understanding of mental states, especially beliefs, might be an emerging consequence of dialogue, see Harris (1996b, 1999).

References

Acredolo, L.P., Goodwyn, S.W. and Fulmer, A.H. (1995). Why some children create imaginary companions. Clues from infant and toddler play preferences. Paper presented at the Biennial Meeting of the Society for Research in Child Development, Indianapolis, IN.

Ames, L.B. and Learned, J. (1946). Imaginary companions and related phenomena. *Journal of Genetic Psychology*, 69, 147–67.

Astington. J.W. and Jenkins, J.M. (1995). Theory of mind development and social understanding. *Cognition and Emotion*, 9, 151–65.

Baillargeon, R. (1994). Physical reasoning in young infants: seeking explanations for impossible events. *British Journal of Developmental Psychology*, 12, 9–34.

Baron-Cohen, S. (1995). *Mindblindness: An essay on autism and theory of mind*. Cambridge, MA: MIT Bradford.

Baron-Cohen, S., Cox, A., Baird, G., Swettenham, J., Drew, A., Nightingale, N., Morgan, K. and Charman, T. (1996). Psychological markers of autism at 18 months of age in a large population. *British Journal of Psychiatry*, 168, 158–63.

Baron-Cohen, S., Leslie, A.M. and Frith, U. (1985). Does the autistic child have a theory of mind? *Cognition*, 21, 37–46.

Barrett, J.L. (in press). Do children experience God like adults? Retracing the development of god concepts. In J. Andresen (ed.), *Religion in Mind: Cognitive science perspectives on religion*. Cambridge: Cambridge University Press.

Bartsch, K. and Wellman, H.M. (1995). *Children Talk About the Mind*. New York: Oxford University Press.

Bechara, A., Damasio, A.R., Damasio, H. and Anderson, S. (1994). Insensitivity to future consequences following damage to prefrontal cortex. *Cognition*, 50, 7–12.

Bechara, A., Damasio, H., Tranel, D. and Damasio, A.R. (1997). Deciding advantageously before knowing the advantageous strategy. *Science*, 275, 1293–4.

Bettelheim, B. (1991). *The Uses of Enchantment: The meaning and importance of fairy tales*. London: Penguin Books. (Original work published 1975.)

Binford, L. (1989). Isolating the transition to cultural adaptations: an organizational approach. In E. Trinkhaus (ed.), *The Emergence of Modern Humans: Biocultural adaptations in the Later Pleistocene*. Cambridge: Cambridge University Press, pp. 18–41.

Black, J.B., Turner, T.J. and Bower, G.H. (1979). Point of view in narrative comprehension, memory, and production. *Journal of Verbal Learning and Verbal Behavior*, 18, 187–98.

Bleuler, E. (1951). Autistic thinking. In D. Rapaport, *Organization and Pathology of Thought*. New York: Columbia University Press, pp. 199–437. (Originally published in 1912 as Das autistische Denken, *Jahrbuch für Psychoanalytische und Psychpathologische Forschungen*, 4, 1–39.)

Bower, G.H. and Morrow, D.G. (1990). Mental models in narrative comprehension. *Science*, 247, 44–8.

Boyer, P. and Walker, S. (2000). Intuitive ontology and cultural input in the acquisition of religious concepts. In K.S. Rosengren, C.N. Johnson and P.L. Harris (eds), *Imagining the Impossible: The development of magical, scientific and religious thinking in contemporary society*. New York: Cambridge University Press, pp. 130–56.

Braine, M.D.S. (1990). The 'natural logic' approach to reasoning. In W.F. Overton (ed.), *Reasoning, Necessity and Logic: Developmental perspectives*. Hillsdale, NJ: Lawrence Erlbaum Associates, pp. 135–57.

Bruell, M.J. and Woolley, J.D. (1998). Young children's understanding of diversity in pretense. *Cognitive Development*, 13, 257–77.

Bruner, J.S. and Feldman, C. (1993). Theories of mind and the problems of autism. In S. Baron-Cohen, H. Tager-Flusberg and D.J. Cohen (eds), *Understanding Other Minds: Perspectives from autism*. Oxford: Oxford University Press, pp. 267–91.

Bullock, M., Gelman, R. and Baillargeon, R. (1982). The development of causal reasoning. In W.J. Friedman (ed.), *The Developmental Psychology of Time*. New York: Academic Press, pp. 209–54.

Byrne, R. and Whiten, A. (1988). *Machiavellian Intelligence: Social intelligence and the evolution of intellect in monkeys, apes and humans*. New York: Oxford University Press.

Carpenter, M., Akhtar, N. and Tomasello, M. (1998). Fourteen- through 18-month-old infants differentially imitate intentional and accidental actions. *Infant Behavior and Development*, 21, 315–30.

Chandler, M., Lalonde, C., Fritz, A. and Hala, S. (1991). Children's theories of mental life and social practices. Paper presented at the Biennial Meeting of the Society for Research in Child Development, Seattle, WA.

Cheng, P.W. and Holyoak, K.J. (1985). Pragmatic reasoning schemas. *Cognitive Psychology*, 17, 391–416.

Christie, J.F. (1985). Training of symbolic play. *Early Child Development and Care*, 19, 43–52.

Clottes, J. (1996). Recent studies on Palaeolithic art. *Cambridge Archaeological Journal*, 6, 179–89.

Cohen, L.B. and Oakes, L.M. (1993). How infants perceive a simple causal event. *Developmental Psychology*, 29, 421–33.

Cole, M. (1977). Foreword. In A.R. Luria, *Cognitive Development*. Cambridge, MA: Harvard University Press.

Cole, M. (1990). Alexandr Romanovich Luria: cultural psychologist. In E. Goldberg (ed.), *Contemporary Neuropsychology and the Legacy of Luria*. Hillsdale, NJ: Lawrence Erlbaum Associates, pp. 11–28.

Cole, M., Gay, J., Glick, J.A. and Sharp, D.W. (1971). *The Cultural Context of Learning and Thinking*. New York: Basic Books.

Connolly, J.A. and Doyle, A.-B. (1984). Relation of social fantasy play to social competence in preschoolers. *Developmental Psychology*, 20, 797–806.

Cosmides, L. (1989). The logic of social exchange: has natural selection shaped how humans reason? Studies with the Wason selection task. *Cognition*, 31, 187–276.

Cosmides, L. and Tooby, J. (1992). Cognitive adaptations for social exchange. In J.H. Barkow, L. Cosmides and J. Tooby (eds), *The Adapted Mind: Evolutionary psychology and the generation of culture*. Oxford: Oxford University Press, pp. 163–228.

Cummins, D.D. (1996). Evidence of deontic reasoning in 3- and 4-year-old children. *Memory and Cognition*, 24, 823–9.

Currie, G. (1998). Pretence, pretending and metarepresenting. *Mind and Language*, 13, 35–55.

Custer, W.L. (1996). A comparison of young children's understanding of contradictory representations in pretense, memory and belief. *Child Development*, 67, 678–88.

Dadds, M.R., Bovbjerg, D.H., Redd, W.H. and Cutmore, T.R.H. (1997). Imagery in human classical conditioning. *Psychological Bulletin*, 122, 89–103.

Damasio, A.R. (1994). *Descartes' Error: Emotion, reason and the human brain*. New York: G.P. Putnam's Sons.

Damasio, A.R., Tranel, D. and Damasio, H. (1991). Somatic markers and the guidance of behavior. Theory and preliminary testing. In H. Levin, H.M. Eisenberg and A.L. Benton (eds), *Frontal Lobe Function and Dysfunction*. New York: Oxford University Press, pp. 217–29.

Dandoy, A.C. and Goldstein, A.G. (1990). The use of cognitive appraisal to reduce stress: a replication. *Journal of Social Behavior and Personality*, 5, 275–85.

D'Errico, F., Zilhão, J., Julien, M., Baffier, D. and Pelegrain, J. (1998). Neanderthal acculturation in western Europe? A critical review of the evidence and its interpretation. *Current Anthropology*, 39, S1–S44.

De Vega, M., León, I. and Díaz, J.M. (1996). The representation of changing emotions in reading comprehension. *Cognition and Emotion*, 10, 303–21.

Dias, M. (1988). Logical reasoning. Unpublished doctoral thesis. University of Oxford.

Dias, M. and Harris, P.L. (1988). The effect of make-believe play on deductive reasoning. *British Journal of Developmental Psychology*, 6, 207–21.

Dias, M. and Harris, P.L. (1990). The influence of the imagination on reasoning by young children. *British Journal of Developmental Psychology*, 8, 305–18.

Dockett, S. and Smith, I. (1995). Children's theories of mind and their involvement in complex shared pretense. Poster presented at the Biennial Meeting of the Society for Research in Child Development, Indianapolis, IN.

Dodd, M. and Bucci, W. (1987). The relationship of cognition and affect in the orientation process. *Cognition*, 27, 53–71.

Dowson, T.A. (1998). Rock art: handmaiden to studies of cognitive evolution. In C. Renfrew and C. Scarre (eds), *Cognition and Material Culture: The archaeology of symbolic storage*. Cambridge: MacDonald Institute for Archaeological Research, pp. 67–76.

Dunn, J. (1988). *The Beginnings of Social Understanding*. Oxford: Blackwell.

Dunn, J. and Brown, J.R. (1993). Early conversations about causality. *British Journal of Developmental Psychology*, 11, 107–23.

Dunn, J. and Dale, N. (1984). 'I a Daddy': 2-year-olds' collaboration in joint pretend with sibling and with mother. In I. Bretherton (ed.), *Symbolic Play: The development of social understanding*. Orlando: Academic Press, pp. 131–58.

Estes, D., Wellman, H.M. and Woolley, J.D. (1989). Children's understanding of mental phenomena. In H.W. Reese (ed.), *Advances in Child Development and Behavior*, Vol. 22. San Diego: Academic Press pp. 41–87.

Farah, M.J. (1988). Is visual imagery really visual? Overlooked evidence from neuropsychology. *Psychological Review*, 95, 307–17.

Fiddick, L.W. (1998). The deal and the danger: an evolutionary analysis of deontic reasoning. Unpublished doctoral dissertation. University of California, Santa Barbara.

Field, D. (1987). A review of preschool conservation training: an analysis of analyses. *Developmental Review*, 7, 210–51.

Flavell, J.H. (1978). The development of knowledge about visual perception. In C.B. Keasey (ed.), *Nebraska Symposium on Motivation*, Vol. 25. Lincoln: University of Nebraska Press, pp. 43–76.

Flavell, J.H. (1993). Discussant's comments. In J. Woolley (Chair), *Pretense,*

Imagination and the Child's Theory of Mind. Symposium presented at the Biennial Meeting of the Society for Research in Child Development, New Orleans, LA.

Flavell, J.H., Everett, B.A., Croft, K. and Flavell, E.R. (1981). Young children's knowledge about visual perception: further evidence for the Level 1– Level 2 distinction. *Developmental Psychology*, 17, 99–103.

Fletcher, K.E. and Averill, J.R. (1984). A scale for the measurement of role-taking ability. *Journal of Research in Personality*, 18, 131–49.

Freud, S. (1961a). The interpretation of dreams. In J. Strachey (ed. and trans.), *The Standard Edition of the Complete Psychological Works of Sigmund Freud*, Vols 4–5. London: Hogarth Press. (Original work published 1900.)

Freud, S. (1961b). *Formulations of the Two Principles of Mental Functioning*. In J. Strachey (ed. and trans.), *The Standard Edition of the Complete Psychological Works of Sigmund Freud*, Vol. 12. London: Hogarth Press, pp. 215–26. (Original work published 1911.)

Frijda, N.H. (1988). The laws of emotion. *American Psychologist*, 43, 349–58.

Frijda, N.H. (1989). Aesthetic emotions and reality. *American Psychologist*, 44, 1546–7.

Gerhardt, J. (1991). The meaning and use of the modals *hafta, needta* and *wanna* in children's speech. *Journal of Pragmatics*, 16, 531–90.

German, T.P. (1999). Children's causal reasoning: counterfactual thinking occurs for 'negative' outcomes only. *Developmental Science*, 2, 442–7.

Gernsbacher, M.A., Goldsmith, H.H. and Robertson, R.R.W. (1992). Do readers mentally represent characters' emotional states? *Cognition and Emotion*, 6, 89–111.

Glenberg, A., Meyer, M. and Lindem, K. (1987). Mental models contribute to foregrounding during text comprehension. *Journal of Memory and Language*, 26, 69–83.

Goldman, A.I. (1992). In defense of the simulation theory. *Mind and Language*, 7, 104–19.

Goldman, R. (1964). *Religious Thinking from Childhood to Adolescence*. London: Routledge and Kegan Paul.

Goldstein, K. (1948). *Language and Language Disorders*. New York: Grune and Stratton.

Gollnisch, G. and Averill, J.R. (1993). Emotional imagery: strategies and correlates. *Cognition and Emotion*, 7, 407–29.

Goody, J. and Watt, I. (1968). The consequences of literacy. In J. Goody (ed.), *Literacy in Traditional Societies*. New York: Cambridge University Press, pp. 27–68.

Gopnik, A. and Meltzoff, A.N. (1997). *Words, Thoughts and Theories*. Cambridge, MA: MIT Press.

Gordon, R.M. (1992). The simulation theory: objections and misconceptions.

Mind and Language, 7, 11–34.

Goy, C. and Harris, P.L. (1990). The status of children's imaginary companions. Unpublished manuscript. Department of Experimental Psychology, University of Oxford.

Greenfield, P.M. and Savage-Rumbaugh, S. (1990). Grammatical combination in *Pan paniscus*: processes of learning and invention in the evolution and development of language. In S.T. Parker and K.R. Gibson (eds), '*Language' and Intelligence in Monkeys and Apes: Comparative developmental perspectives*. Cambridge: Cambridge University Press, pp. 540–78.

Gross, J.J. (1998). Antecedent- and response-focused emotion regulation: divergent consequences for experience, expression and physiology. *Journal of Personality and Social Psychology*, 74, 224–37.

Gross, J.J. (1999). The emerging field of emotion regulation: an integrative review. *Review of General Psychology*, 2, 271–99.

Harris, P.L. (1992). From simulation to folk psychology: the case for development. *Mind and Language*, 7, 120–44.

Harris, P.L. (1993). Pretending and planning. In S. Baron-Cohen, H. Tager-Flusberg and D.J. Cohen (eds), *Understanding Other Minds: Perspectives from autism*. Oxford: Oxford University Press, pp. 283–304.

Harris, P.L. (1996a). Counterfactual thinking about positive and negative outcomes. Unpublished manuscript. Department of Experimental Psychology, University of Oxford.

Harris, P.L. (1996b). Desires, beliefs, and language. In P. Carruthers and P.K. Smith (eds), *Theories of Theories of Mind*. Cambridge: Cambridge University Press, pp. 200–20.

Harris, P.L. (1997a). Piaget in Paris: from 'autism' to logic. *Human Development*, 40, 109–23.

Harris, P.L. (1997b). On realizing what might have happened instead. *Polish Quarterly of Developmental Psychology*, 3, 161–76.

Harris, P.L. (1999). Acquiring the art of conversation: children's developing conception of their conversation partner. In M. Bennett, (ed.), *Developmental Psychology: Achievements and prospects*. London: Psychology Press, pp. 89–105.

Harris, P.L., Brown, E., Marriott, C., Whittall, S. and Harmer, S. (1991). Monsters, ghosts and witches: testing the limits of the fantasy–reality distinction in young children. *British Journal of Developmental Psychology*, 9, 105–23.

Harris, P.L., German, T. and Mills, P. (1996). Children's use of counterfactual thinking in causal reasoning. *Cognition*, 6, 233–59.

Harris, P.L., Johnson, C.N., Hutton, D., Andrews, G. and Cooke, T. (1989). Young children's theory of mind and emotion. *Cognition and Emotion*, 3, 379–400.

Harris, P.L. and Kavanaugh, R.D. (1993). Young children's understanding of pretense. *Monographs of the Society for Research in Child Development*, 58, 1, Serial No. 231.

Harris, P.L., Kavanaugh, R.D. and Dowson, L. (1997). The depiction of imaginary transformations: early comprehension of a symbolic function. *Cognitive Development*, 12, 1–19.

Harris, P.L., Kavanaugh, R.D. and Meredith, M. (1994). Young children's comprehension of pretend episodes: the integration of successive actions. *Child Development*, 65, 16–30.

Harris, P.L. and Leevers, H.J. (2000a). Reasoning from false premises. In P. Mitchell and K. Riggs (eds), *Children's Reasoning and the Mind*. Hove: Psychology Press, pp. 67–86.

Harris, P.L. and Leevers, H. (2000b). Pretending, imagery and self-awareness in autism. In S. Baron-Cohen, H. Tager-Flusberg and D. Cohen (eds), *Understanding Other Minds: Perspectives from autism and developmental cognitive neuroscience*, 2nd edition. Oxford: Oxford University Press, pp. 182–202.

Harris, P.L. and Martin, L. (1999). From Little Red Riding Hood to Othello:empathizing with a naive protagonist. Unpublished manuscript. Department of Experimental Psychology, University of Oxford.

Harris, P.L. and Núñez, M. (1996). Understanding of permission rules by pre-school children. *Child Development*, 67, 1572–91.

Harris, P.L., Núñez, M. and Brett, C. (1999). Let's swap: early understanding of social exchange by British and Nepali children. Paper submitted for publication.

Hart, H.L. and Honoré, A.M. (1985). *Causation in the Law*, 2nd edition. Oxford: Oxford University Press.

Hickling, A.K., Wellman, H.M. and Gottfried, G.M. (1997). Preschoolers' understanding of others' mental attitudes towards pretend happenings. *British Journal of Developmental Psychology*, 15, 339–54.

Hirschfeld, L.A. and Gelman, S.A. (1994). *Mapping the Mind: Domain specificity in cognition and culture*. Cambridge: Cambridge University Press.

Howes, C. (1985). Sharing fantasy: social pretend play in toddlers. *Child Development*, 56, 1253–8.

Howes, C. (1988). Peer interaction of young children. *Monographs of the Society for Research in Child Development*, 53, 1, Serial No. 217.

Howes, C. and Matheson, C.C. (1992). Sequences in the development of competent play with peers: social and social pretend play. *Developmental Psychology*, 28, 961–74.

Huang, I. (1930). Children's explanations of strange phenomena. *Psychologische Forschung*, 14, 63–183.

Huang, I. (1943). Children's conception of physical causality: a critical summary. *Journal of Genetic Psychology*, 63, 71–121.

Hughes, M. and Donaldson, M. (1979). The use of hiding games for studying the coordination of viewpoints. *Educational Review*, 31, 133–40.

Hughes, C. and Dunn, J. (1997). 'Pretend you didn't know': preschoolers' talk about mental states in pretend play. *Cognitive Development*, 12, 381–403.

Hume, D. (1978). *A Treatise of Human Nature*. Oxford: Oxford University Press. (Original work published 1739.)

Humphrey, N. (1976). The social function of intellect. In P. Bateson and R.A. Hinde (eds), *Growing Points in Ethology*. Cambridge: Cambridge University Press, pp. 303–21.

Inhelder, B. and Piaget, J. (1958). *The Growth of Logical Thinking from Childhood to Adolescence*. New York: Basic Books.

Isaacs, S. (1933). *Social Development in Young Children*. London: Routledge.

Jarrold, C.R., Carruthers, P., Smith, P.K. and Boucher, J. (1994). Pretend play: is it metarepresentational? *Mind and Language*, 9, 445–68.

Jersild, A.T. (1943). Studies of children's fears. In R.G. Barker, J.S. Kounin and H.F. Wright (eds), *Child Behavior and Development*. New York: McGraw Hill, pp. 329–44.

Jersild, A.T. and Holmes, F.B. (1935). Methods of overcoming children's fears. *Journal of Psychology*, 1, 75–104.

Johnson, C.N. and Harris, P.L. (1994). Magic: special but not excluded. *British Journal of Developmental Psychology*, 12, 35–51.

Johnson-Laird, P.N., Legrenzi, P. and Legrenzi, M.S. (1972). Reasoning and a sense of reality. *British Journal of Psychology*, 63, 395–400.

Joseph, R.M. (1998). Intention and knowledge in preschoolers' conception of pretend. *Child Development*, 69, 966–80.

Kahneman, D. and Varey, C.A. (1990). Propensities and counterfactuals: the loser that almost won. *Journal of Personality and Social Psychology*, 59, 1101–10.

Kanner, L. (1943). Affective disturbance of affective contact. *Nervous Child*, 2, 217–50.

Kavanaugh, R.D. and Harris, P.L. (1994). Imagining the outcome of pretend transformations: assessing the competence of normal children and children with autism. *Developmental Psychology*, 30, 847–54.

Kavanaugh, R.D. and Harris, P.L. (1999a). Is there going to be a real fox in here? The exploration of a shared fantasy by young children. Paper presented at the Biennial Meeting of the Society for Research in Child Development, Albuquerque, NM.

Kavanaugh, R.D. and Harris, P.L. (1999b). Pretense and counterfactual thought in young children. In L. Balter and C.S. Tamis-Lemonda (eds), *Child Psychology: A handbook of contemporary issues*. Philadelphia, PA: Psychology Press, pp. 158–76.

Kavanaugh, R.D. and Harris, P.L. (2000). Contrasting what did and did not happen: children's sensitivity to casually relevant contrasts. Paper submitted for publication.

Keil, F. (1989). *Concepts, Word Meanings and Cognitive Development*. Cambridge, MA: MIT Press.

Kerr, J. (1994). *A Most Dangerous Method: The story of Jung, Freud and Sabina Spielrein*. London: Sinclair-Stevenson.

King, N., Cranstoun, F. and Josephs, A. (1989). Emotive imagery and children's night-time fears: a multiple baseline design evaluation. *Journal of Behavior Therapy and Experimental Psychiatry*, 20, 125–35.

Koriat, A., Melkman, R., Averill, J.R. and Lazarus, R.S. (1972). The self-control of emotional reactions to a stressful film. *Journal of Personality*, 40, 601–19.

Kosslyn, S.M. (1988). Aspects of a cognitive neuroscience of mental imagery. *Science*, 240, 1621–6.

Kuczaj, S.A., II and Daly, M.J. (1979). The development of hypothetical reference in the speech of young children. *Journal of Child Language*, 6, 563–79.

Kuhn, S.L. and Stiner, M.C. (1998). Middle Palaeolithic 'creativity'. Reflections on an oxymoron. In S. Mithen (ed.), *Creativity in Human Evolution and Prehistory*. London: Routledge, pp. 165–91.

Lalonde, C.E. and Chandler, M.J. (1995). False belief understanding goes to school: on the social–emotional consequences of coming early or late to a first theory of mind. *Cognition and Emotion*, 9, 167–85.

Lang, P.J. (1984). Cognition and emotion: concept and action. In C.E. Izard, J. Kagan and R.B. Zajonc (eds), *Emotions, Cognition and Behavior*. Cambridge: Cambridge University Press, pp. 192–226.

Lang, P.J., Bradley, M.M. and Cuthbert, B.N. (1992). A motivational analysis of emotion: reflex–cortex connections. *Psychological Science*, 3, 44–9.

Lang, P.J., Kozak, M.J., Miller, G.A., Levin, D.N. and McLean, A. Jr (1980). Emotional imagery: conceptual structure and pattern of somato-visceral response. *Psychophysiology*, 17, 179–92.

Lang, P.J., Levin, D.N., Miller, G.A. and Kozak, M.J. (1983). Fear behavior, fear imagery, and the psychophysiology of emotion: the problem of affective response integration. *Journal of Abnormal Psychology*, 92, 276–306.

Lang, P.J., Melamed, B.G. and Hart, J.D. (1970). A psychophysiological analysis of fear modification using an automated desensitization procedure. *Journal of Abnormal Psychology*, 76, 220–34.

Leevers, H.J. (1997). Children's logical reasoning. Unpublished doctoral thesis. University of Oxford.

Leevers, H.J. and Harris, P.L. (1999). Persisting effects of instruction on young children's syllogistic reasoning with incongruent and abstract premises. *Thinking and Reasoning*, 5, 145–73.

Leevers, H.J. and Harris, P.L. (2000). Counterfactual syllogistic reasoning in normal 4-year-olds, children with learning disabilities, and children with autism. *Journal of Experimental Child Psychology*, 76, 64–87.

Leslie, A.M. (1982). The perception of causality in infants. *Perception*, 11, 173–86.

Leslie, A.M. (1987). Pretense and representation: the origins of 'theory of mind'. *Psychological Review*, 94, 412–26.

Leslie, A.M. (1994). Pretending and believing. *Cognition*, 50, 211–38.

Leslie, A.M. and Keeble, S. (1987). Do six-month-olds infants perceive causality? *Cognition*, 25, 265–88.

Lillard, A. (1993). Young children's conceptualization of pretend: action or mental representational state? *Child Development*, 64, 372–86.

Luria, A.R. (1934). The second psychological expedition to central Asia. *Journal of Genetic Psychology*, 41, 255–9.

Luria, A.R. (1971). Towards the problem of the historical nature of psychological processes. *International Journal of Psychology*, 6, 259–72.

Luria, A.R. (1976). *Cognitive Development: Its cultural and social foundations*. Cambridge, MA: Harvard University Press.

Lynn, S.J. and Rhue, J.W. (1986). The fantasy-prone person: hypnosis, imagination, and creativity. *Journal of Personality and Social Psychology*, 51, 404–8.

Mackie, J.L. (1974). *The Cement of the Universe: A study of causation*. Oxford: Oxford University Press.

MacWhinney, B. (1991). *The CHILDES Project: Tools for analyzing talk*. Hillsdale, NJ: Erlbaum.

MacWhinney, B. and Snow, C. (1985). The child language data exchange system. *Journal of Child Language*, 12, 271–96.

Marzillier, J.S., Carroll, D. and Newland, J.R. (1979). Self-report and physiological changes accompanying repeated imagining of a phobic scene. *Behaviour Research and Therapy*, 17, 71–7.

Mead, M. (1932). An investigation of the thought of primitive children, with special reference to animism. *Journal of the Royal Anthropological Institute*, 62, 173–90.

Meerum Terwogt, M., Schene, J. and Harris, P.L. (1986). Self-control of emotional reactions by young children. *Journal of Child Psychology and Psychiatry*, 27, 357–66.

Mellars, P. (1996). *The Neanderthal Legacy: An archaeological perspective from Western Europe*. Princeton: Princeton University Press.

Mellars, P. (1999). The Neanderthal problem continued. *Current Anthropology*, 40, 341–64.

Mellars, P. and Stringer, C.B. (1989). *The Human Revolution: Behavioural and biological perspectives on the origins of modern human*. Edinburgh: Edinburgh University Press.

Meltzoff, A.N. (1995). Understanding the intentions of others. Re-enactment of intended acts by 18-month-old children. *Developmental Psychology*, 31, 838–50.

Michotte, A. (1963). *The Perception of Causality.* New York: Basic Books. (Original work published 1946.)

Millar, W.S. (1972). A study of operant conditioning under delayed reinforcement in early infancy. *Monographs of the Society for Research in Child Development*, 37, 2, Serial No. 147.

Millar, W.S. and Schaffer, H.R. (1972). The influence of spatially displaced feedback on infant operant conditioning. *Journal of Experimental Child Psychology*, 14, 442–53.

Miller, M.A. (1998). *Freud and the Bolsheviks: Psychoanalysis in imperial Russia and the Soviet Union.* New Haven, CT: Yale University Press.

Miller, P. and Garvey, G. (1984). Mother–baby role play: its origins in social support. In I. Bretherton (ed.), *Symbolic Play: The development of social understanding.* Orlando: Academic Press, pp. 101–30.

Mithen, S. (1996). *The Prehistory of the Mind: A search for the origins of art, science and religion.* London: Thames and Hudson.

Morford, J.P. and Goldin-Meadow, S. (1997). From here and now to there and then: the development of displaced reference in Homesign and English. *Child Development*, 68, 420–35.

Neisser, U. (1967). *Cognitive Psychology.* New York: Appleton-Century-Crofts.

Nelson, K. (1993). The psychological and social origins of autobiographical memory. *Psychological Science*, 4, 1–8.

Newson, J. and Newson, E. (1968). *Four-years-old in an Urban Community.* London: George Allen and Unwin.

Nichols, S. and Stich, S. (2000). A cognitive theory of pretense. *Cognition*, 74, 115–47.

Nielsen, M. and Dissanayake, C. (in press). An investigation of pretend play, mental state terms, and false belief understanding: in search of a metarepresentational link. *British Journal of Developmental Psychology.*

Núñez, M. and Harris, P.L. (1998). Psychological and deontic concepts: separate domains or intimate connection? *Mind and Language*, 13, 153–70.

O'Brien, D., Dias, M.G., Roazzi, A. and Cantor, J.B. (1998). Pinocchio's nose knows: preschool children recognize that a pragmatic rule can be violated, an indicative conditional can be broken and that a broken promise is a false promise. In M.D.S. Braine and D.P. O'Brien (eds), *Mental Logic.* Mahwah, NJ: Lawrence Erlbaum Associates, pp. 447–72.

Patrick, C.J., Cuthbert, B.N. and Lang, P.J. (1994). Emotion in the criminal psychopath: fear image processing. *Journal of Abnormal Psychology*, 103, 523–34.

Perner, J. (1991). *Understanding the Representational Mind.* Cambridge, MA: MIT Press.

Perner, J. (1993). The theory of mind deficit in autism: rethinking the metarepresentation theory. In S. Baron-Cohen, H. Tager-Flusberg and D.J. Cohen (eds), *Understanding Other Minds: Perspectives from autism*. Oxford: Oxford University Press, pp. 112–37.

Phelps, K.E. and Woolley, J.D. (1994). The form and function of young children's magical beliefs. *Developmental Psychology*, 30, 385–94.

Piaget, J. (1923). La pensée symbolique et la pensée de l'enfant. *Archives de Psychologie*, 18, 275–304.

Piaget, J. (1928). La causalité chez l'enfant. *British Journal of Psychology*, 18, 276–301.

Piaget, J. (1929). *The Child's Concept of the World*. New York: Harcourt Brace.

Piaget, J. (1952). Autobiography. In C. Murchison (ed.), *A History of Psychology in Autobiography*. Worcester, MA: Clark University Press, pp. 237–56.

Piaget, J. (1959). *The Language and Thought of the Child*. London: Routledge and Kegan Paul. (Original work published 1923.)

Piaget, J. (1962). *Play, Dreams and Imitation*. London: Routledge and Kegan Paul. (Original work published 1945.)

Rall, J. and Harris, P.L. (2000). In Cinderella's slippers? Story comprehension from the protagonist's point-of-view. *Developmental Psychology*, 36, 202–8.

Reilly, J.S. (1986). The acquisition of temporals and conditionals. In E.C. Traugott, A. ter Meulen, J.S. Reilly and C.A. Ferguson (eds), *On Conditionals*. Cambridge: Cambridge University Press, pp. 309–31.

Richards, C.A. and Sanderson, J.A. (1999). The role of imagination in facilitating deductive reasoning in 2-, 3-, and 4-year-olds. *Cognition*, 72, B1–B9.

Rimé, B. (1995). The social sharing of emotion as a source for the social knowledge of emotion. In J.J. Russell, J.-M. Fernández-Dols, A.S.R. Manstead and J.C. Wellenkamp (eds), *Everyday Conceptions of Emotion*. Dordrecht: Kluwer, pp. 475–504.

Rinck, M. and Bower, G.H. (1995). Anaphora resolution and the focus of attention in situation models. *Journal of Memory and Language*, 34, 110–31.

Roese, N. (1997). Counterfactual thinking. *Psychological Bulletin*, 121, 133–48.

Roese, N.J. and Olson, J.M. (1997). Counterfactual thinking: the intersection of affect and function. In M.P. Zanna (ed.), *Advances in Experimental Social Psychology*, Vol. 29. San Diego: Academic Press, pp. 1–59.

Rosen, C.S., Schwebel, D.C. and Singer, J.L. (1997). Preschoolers' attributions of mental states in pretense. *Child Development*, 68, 1133–42.

Rosengren, K.S., Kalish, C.W., Hickling, A.K. and Gelman, S.A. (1994). Exploring the relation between preschool children's magical beliefs and causal thinking. *British Journal of Developmental Psychology*, 12, 69–82.

Ruffman, T., Perner, J., Naito, M., Parkin, L. and Clements, W. (1998). Older (but not younger) siblings facilitate false belief understanding. *Child Development*, 34, 161–74.

Savage-Rumbaugh, E.S., Murphy, J., Sevcik, R.S., Brakke, K., Williams, S.L. and Rumbaugh, D.M. (1993). Language comprehension in ape and child. *Monographs of the Society for Research in Child Development*, 58, 3–4, Serial No. 233.

Scholnick, E.F. and Wing, C.S. (1991). Speaking deductively: preschoolers' use of *if* in conversation and in conditional inference. *Developmental Psychology*, 27, 249–58.

Scholnick, E.F. and Wing, C.S. (1995). Logic in conversation: comparative studies of deduction in children and adults. *Cognitive Development*, 10, 319–45.

Schwebel, D.C., Rosen, C.S. and Singer, J.L. (1999). Preschoolers' pretend play and theory of mind: the role of jointly constructed pretence. *British Journal of Developmental Psychology*, 17, 333–48.

Scribner, S. (1977). Modes of thinking and ways of speaking: culture and logic reconsidered. In P.N. Johnson-Laird and P.C. Wason (eds), *Thinking: Readings in cognitive science*. New York: Cambridge University Press, pp. 483–500.

Scribner, S. and Cole, M. (1981). *The Psychology of Literacy*. Cambridge, MA: Harvard University Press.

Shatz, M. and Wilcox, S.A. (1991). Constraints on the acquisition of English modals. In S.A. Gelman and J. Byrnes (eds), *Perspectives on Thought and Language: Interrelations in development*. New York: Cambridge University Press, pp. 319–53.

Siegler, R.S. (1995). How does number change occur? A microgenetic study of number conservation. *Cognitive Psychology*, 28, 225–73.

Slaughter, V., Jaakkola, R. and Carey, S. (1999). Constructing a coherent theory: children's biological understanding of life and death. In M. Siegal and C.C. Peterson (eds), *Children's Understanding of Biology and Health*. Cambridge: Cambridge University Press, pp. 71–96.

Speisman, J.C., Lazarus, R.S., Mordkoff, A. and Davison, L. (1964). Experimental reduction of stress based on ego-defense theory. *Journal of Abnormal Psychology*, 68, 367–80.

Spelke, E. (1990). Principles of object perception. *Cognitive Science*, 14, 29–56.

Spielrein, S. (1923). Quelques analogies entre la pensée de l'enfant, celle de l'aphasique et la pensée subconsciente. *Archives de Psychologie*, 18, 306–22.

Steptoe, A. and Vögele, C. (1986). Are stress responses influenced by cognitive appraisal? An experimental comparison of coping strategies. *British*

210   References

Journal of Psychology, 77, 243–55.

Stringer, C.B. (1990). A comparative study of cranial and dental development within a recent British sample and among Neanderthals. In C. J. DeRousseau (ed.), *Primate Life History and Evolution*. New York: Wiley Liss, pp. 115–52.

Stringer, C.B. and Gamble, C. (1993). *In Search of the Neanderthals: Solving the puzzle of human origins*. London: Thames and Hudson.

Subbotsky, E.V. (1985). Pre-school children's perception of unusual phenomena. *Soviet Psychology*, 23, 91–114.

Subbotsky, E.V. (1994). Early rationality and magical thinking in preschoolers: space and time. *British Journal of Developmental Psychology*, 12, 97–108.

Sully, J. (1896). *Studies of Childhood*. New York: D. Appleton and Company.

Svendsen, M. (1934). Children's imaginary companions. *Archives of Neurology and Psychiatry*, 2, 985–99.

Tattersall, I. (1998). *Becoming Human. Evolution and human uniqueness*. Oxford: Oxford University Press.

Taylor, M. (1997). The role of creative control and culture in children's fantasy/reality judgements. *Child Development*, 68, 1015–17.

Taylor, M. (1998). *Imaginary Companions and the Children Who Create Them*. New York: Oxford.

Taylor, M. and Carlson, S.M. (1997). The relation between individual differences in fantasy and theory of mind. *Child Development*, 68, 436–55.

Taylor, M., Cartwright, B.S. and Carlson, S.M. (1993a). A developmental investigation of children's imaginary companions. *Developmental Psychology*, 29, 276–85.

Taylor, M., Gerow, L.E. and Carlson, S.M. (1993b). The relation between individual differences in fantasy and theory of mind. In J. Woolley (Chair), *Pretense, Imagination and the Child's Theory of Mind*. Symposium presented at the Biennial Meeting of the Society for Research in Child Development, New Orleans, LA.

Tellegen, A. and Atkinson, G. (1974). Openness to absorbing and self-altering experiences ('absorption'), a trait related to hypnotic susceptibility. *Journal of Abnormal Psychology*, 83, 268–77.

Tizard, B. and Hughes, M. (1984). *Young Children Learning*. London: Fontana.

Tomasello, M. and Call, J. (1997). *Primate Cognition*. New York: Oxford University Press.

Turiel, E. (1998). The development of morality. In N. Eisenberg (ed.), *Handbook of Child Psychology. Vol. 3: Social, Emotional and Personality Development*, 4th edition. New York: John Wiley, pp. 863–932.

Tversky, A. and Kahneman, D. (1973). Availability: a heuristic for judging frequency and probability. *Cognitive Psychology*, 5, 207–32.

Velasco, C. and Bond, A. (1998). Personal relevance is an important dimension for visceral reactivity in emotional imagery. *Cognition and Emotion*, 12, 231–42.

Vrana, S.R., Cuthbert, B.N. and Lang, P.J. (1989). Processing fearful and neutral sentences: memory and heart rate change. *Cognition and Emotion*, 3, 179–95.

Vrana, S.R. and Lang, P.J. (1990). Fear imagery and the startle-probe reflex. *Journal of Abnormal Psychology*, 99, 189–97.

Vygotsky, L. (1978). *Mind in Society: The development of higher psychological processes*. Cambridge, MA: Harvard University Press.

Vygotsky, L. (1986). *Thought and Language*. Cambridge, MA: MIT Press. (Original work published 1934.)

Walters, K.S. (1989). The law of apparent reality and aesthetic emotions. *American Psychologist*, 44, 1545–6.

Walton, K. (1990). *Mimesis as Make-believe*. Cambridge, MA: Harvard University Press.

Wason, P.C. (1966). Reasoning. In B.M. Foss (ed.), *New Horizons In Psychology 1*. Harmondsworth: Penguin, pp. 135–51.

Wason, P.C. and Johnson-Laird, P.N. (1972). *Psychology of Reasoning: Structure and content*. London: Batsford.

Wellman, H.M., Cross, D. and Watson, J.K. (1999). A meta-analysis of theory of mind development: false belief understanding. Poster presented at the Biennial Meeting of the Society for Research in Child Development, Albuquerque, NM.

Wellman, H.M. and Estes, D. (1986). Early understanding of mental entities: a reexamination of childhood realism. *Child Development*, 57, 910–23.

Wellman, H.M. and Gelman, S.A. (1998). Knowledge acquisition in foundational domains. In D. Kuhn and R.S. Siegler (eds), *Handbook of Child Psychology. Vol. 2: Cognition, Perception and Language*, 4th edition. New York: John Wiley, pp. 523–74.

Wells, G.L. and Gavinski, I. (1989). Mental simulation and causality. *Journal of Personality and Social Psychology*, 56, 161–9.

White, R. (1992). Beyond art: toward an understanding of the origins of material representation in Europe. *Annual Review of Anthropology*, 21, 537–64.

White, R. (1993). Technological and social dimensions of 'Aurignacian-Age' body ornaments across Europe. In H. Knecht, A. Pike-Tay and R. White (eds), *Before Lascaux: The complex record of the early Upper Paleolithic*. Boca Raton: CRC Press, pp. 247–99.

Whiten, A. and Byrne, R.W. (1991). The emergence of metarepresentation in human ontogeny and primate phylogeny. In A. Whiten (ed.), *Natural Theories of Mind: Evolution, development and simulation of everyday mindreading*. Oxford: Blackwell, pp. 267–81.

Wimmer, H. and Perner, J. (1983). Beliefs about beliefs: representations and constraining function of wrong beliefs in young children's understanding of deception. *Cognition*, 13, 103–28.

Wolf, D.P. (1982). Understanding others: a longitudinal case study of the concept of independent agency. In G. Forman (ed.), *Action and Thought*. New York: Academic Press, pp. 297–327.

Wolf, D.P., Rygh, J. and Altshuler, J. (1984). Agency and experience: actions and states in play narratives. In I. Bretherton (ed.), *Symbolic Play: The development of social understanding*. Orlando: Academic Press, pp. 195–217.

Yirmiya, N., Erel, O., Shaked, M. and Solomonica-Levi, D. (1998). Meta-analyses comparing theory of mind abilities of individuals with autism, individuals with mental retardation and normally developing individuals. *Psychological Bulletin*, 124, 283–307.

Youngblade, L.M. and Dunn, J. (1995). Individual differences in young children's pretend play with mother and sibling: links to relationships and understanding of other people's feelings and beliefs. *Child Development*, 66, 1472–92.

Zollikofer, C.P.E., Ponce de Leon, M.S., Martin, R.D. and Stucki, P. (1995). Neanderthal computer skulls. *Nature*, 375, 283–4.

Zwaan, R.A. (1999). Situation models: the mental leap into imagined worlds. *Current Directions in Psychological Science*, 8, 15–18.

Zwaan, R.A. and Radvansky, G.A. (1998). Situation models in language comprehension and memory. *Psychological Bulletin*, 123, 162–85.

Name Index

Subject Index